GREAT GOLF STORIES

Gordon Jarvie lives in Edinburgh. He did much of his growing up in Troon which boasts six fine seaside golf courses. His father was a keen golfer but he admits only to playing at golf.

GREAT GOLF STORIES

Edited by Gordon Jarvie

PAN BOOKS
IN ASSOCIATION WITH MICHAEL O'MARA BOOKS

First published 1993 by Michael O'Mara Books Limited

This edition published 1994 by Pan Books
an imprint of Macmillan General Books
Cavaye Place London SW10 9PG
and Basingstoke

Associated companies throughout the world

ISBN 0 330 32966 9

1 3 5 7 9 8 6 4 2

A CIP catalogue record for this book is available from
the British Library

Typeset by Florencetype Ltd, Kewstoke, Avon
Printed and bound in Great Britain by
Cox & Wyman Ltd, Reading, Berkshire

For Paul and Jason Cripps – two keen golfers

And to the memory of my father Alexander Jarvie
2 May 1906–5 July 1991
for many years a member of Royal Troon Golf Club,
and to the generation of sterling partners with whom he
enjoyed pitting his skills into frequent Atlantic gales –
George Menzies, Sandy Paton, David Cuthbertson, Jim
Sanson, Bill Wilson, Archie Allan, Alistair Sweet,
Tom Symington and Matthew Orr

Tam arte quam marte

Contents

Foreword

I did much of my growing up in Troon, which used to boast six fine seaside golf courses for a modest population of ten thousand souls. My father was a keen golfer, but I was so bad, I used to admit only to playing **at** golf!

I grew up in a golfing 'culture'. I used to particularly enjoy the British Open's occasional invasions of smalltown life, when all of a sudden you couldn't park your car outside your own door, when every youngster for miles around was working in the hotels, the hospitality tents, or on the course itself, and when folk were rumoured to be renting out their homes to visiting Texans or TV crews for legendary sums of money. For a week, Troon became a media-land circus and basked in the unwonted glory. And then the great and the good of the golfing world would depart, and with a municipal sigh of relief – duty done, guerdon won – Troon would drop back into the slow lane.

The stories in this collection are all from the golfing culture. In various ways, they remind me of a world which is forever young – the world in which I grew up. They remind me of magic summer mornings at six o'clock, thumping a little white ball along a dewy and deserted seaside fairway, pausing only to collect mushrooms for breakfast.

Today I still enjoy walking – or even jogging if no one is watching! – on the golf course. Nowadays it is more often a late evening than an early morning outing. And it is most often along the same Braid Hills course in Edinburgh referred to in J. M. Barrie's story from the end of the last century. In addition to straggling golfers hurrying to beat the onset of the dark, here I can watch the foxes at play above the Lang Lynn path, the herons flapping lazily down to the Braid Burn, and share the evening with an occasional rider or doggy walker. But at the far end of that same Braid Hills course, there now stands an innovation in golfing culture undreamt of by J. M. Barrie: a golfing range.

A golfing range is perhaps a symptom of our more serious and less sociable approach to sport – our no-nonsense, down-to-earth desire to acquire the relevant skills through practice. It is doubtless also a symptom of our more 'driven', more hectic pace of life. How many of us have time – or make time – for a round of golf these days? Or even time for nine holes? Judging from the number of cars in its sizeable carpark, many of us now make do with an hour on the golfing range.

There is one very nice thing about receiving your bucketful of golfballs and hitting them off into the middle distance – or perhaps failing to hit them into the middle distance – from the privacy of your own little compartment at the golfing range. Here, your idiocies go completely unseen by your fellow humans, your temper tantrums are known only to you. This is a major change. But, by the same token, your triumphs and disasters are likely to go unsung on the golfing range. So, it seems to me that somebody's going to have to soon start writing stories about a golfing range, and try to integrate this new development properly into the golfing culture. Something humorous, perhaps? Called 'Home, Home on the Range'? Just a suggestion.

Watching the myriad golfballs thwacking their way up the arc-lit range in the blue gloaming of the Braid Hills last evening, I wondered who on earth got the job of picking all those balls up – there must have been thousands of them! (J.M. Barrie's tenant at Fourteen Stubble Row would be a millionaire if he got his hands on even a quarter of that lot!) And then it struck me that the short story probably won't lend itself very well to this new aspect of the sport. Perhaps the golfing range will inspire a few haiku.

How bright the arc lights
Are they gunners or golfers
In the blue distance?

Snow scene of golfballs
Etched out by yellow arc lights
Under the night sky

I'm sure readers will be able to do a lot better than that!

* * *

It wasn't easy to decide in what order to present the stories in this collection. In the end, we plumped for a semi-chronological order. The first four stories in the book all date to the end of the nineteenth century. A batch of Edwardiana follows, this being in many ways the golden age of golfing literature – as is testified by the sheer volume and variety of golfing stories, anecdotes, cartoons and jokes, in periodicals like *Punch* and *The Strand*. More modern stories are placed towards the end of the book.

You need not be a scratch golfer in order to be able to enjoy these stories. They are not all about real matches taking place on indubitable fairways. In some, the action takes place well away from the course. Many of the stories are extremely funny, and it is perhaps notable that golf lends itself so effortlessly to humour. Although fairly recent, several of the stories in this book have already started to assume 'classic' status. In origin, they are English, American, and – of course – Scottish. I commend them all to you, and I hope they remind you of your own halcyon golfing days and games. Why – you might even find yourself writing a story about one of your own experiences!

Readers seeking more golfing stories are referred in particular to the work of P. G. Wodehouse and John Updike, both of whom have been highly prolific in the genre.

Acknowledgments

For help in putting this collection together, I should like to thank Fred Urquhart for a number of suggestions, and particularly for drawing my attention to his unpublished story; also Owen Dudley Edwards, of Edinburgh University; John Harrison, of St Andrews; and Shelley Klein and David Roberts, of Michael O'Mara Books. The staff of the National Library of Scotland provided the invariably high standard of assistance it is unwise nowadays to take for granted, and I wish to record my special thanks to that institution.

Gordon Jarvie
Edinburgh

Golf for Duffers

SIR HENRY RIDER HAGGARD

Oh! well with thee, my brother,
  Who hast not known the game,
When early gleams of gladness
Aye set in after sadness;
And still the end is other,
  Far other, than the aim.
Oh! well with thee my brother
  Who hast not known the game.

So, if memory does not deceive, runs the inspired lay of the bard of the *Saturday Review*. It is of Golf that he sings, not of Nap or Poker, or Pitch-farthing, or any other exciting, but deceitful and deleterious sport. Many have sung and written of it of late, and soon the searcher of bibliographies will find the titles of a multitude of works under the heading 'Golf.' 'What,' said a friend to this writer the other day, as he took up Mr Horace Hutchinson's contribution to the Badminton Library, 'what, all that great book about hitting a little ball with a stick!' But this and other learned works are written by 'golfers of degree,' past masters in the art of 'hitting the little ball.' It yet remains for the subject to be treated from the other side, from the point of view, and, for the comfort of the Duffer. This, the present writer considers himself qualified to do, and for the best of reasons, he wots of none who can play worse than he.

Now as all men know, or ought to know, the game of golf consists in striking a small ball of some hard material into a series of holes – generally eighteen in number – with a variety of wooden

1

and iron-headed clubs, which experience has proved to be the best adapted to the purpose. At first sight this looks easy enough. Indeed, strange as it may seem, the beginner sometimes does find it fairly easy – for the first time or two. He takes the driver with that beautiful confidence which is born of ignorance; hits at the ball somehow, and it goes – somehow; not a full drive of 180 yards or so, indeed, but still a very respectable distance. Arrived safely in the neighbourhood of the first green, he is told that he must putt the ball into a hole about the size of a jam pot. Perhaps he does it at the first attempt, and from a distance whence an experienced player would be quite content to lay his ball near the hole. Then he remarks that 'it seems pretty easy.' Probably his adversary will assent with a sardonic smile, and wait for the revenge that time will surely bring. He need not wait long; it may be today or tomorrow; but an hour will come when he will see the triumphant tyro scarcely able to hit the ball, much less to send it flying through the air, or wriggling sinuously into the putting-hole, perhaps from a dozen yards away. He will see him cutting up huge lumps of turf behind it – this diversion is called 'agriculture' – or smiting it on the head with such force as to drive it into the ground, or 'topping' it so that it rolls meekly into the nearest bush, or 'pulling' it into the dyke on the left, or 'toeing' it into the sand-bunker on the right; doing everything, in short, that he should not do, and leaving undone all those things that he should do. For days and weeks he will see him thus employed, and then, if he is a revengeful person, he will take some particularly suitable occasion, when the ball has been totally missed three or four times on the tee, say, to ask, if he, the tyro, 'really thinks golf so very easy'.

Let none be deceived – as golf is the most delightful game in the world, so it is also the most difficult. It is easier even for a person who has never handled a gun to learn to become a really good shot than for him who has not lifted cleek or driver to bloom into a golfer of the first water. To the young, indeed, all things are possible, but to few of those who begin after thirty will it ever be given to excel. By dint of hard practice and care, in the course of years they may become second or third-rate players, but for the most part their names will never appear as competitors in the great matches of the world of golf. To begin with, but a small proportion will ever acquire the correct 'swing,' that is the motion of the arms and club necessary to drive the ball far and sure. We have all heard of and seen the 'St Andrews Swing,' but how many can practise it with the results common at St Andrews and elsewhere among first-class players? When success attends in the swing, then the ball is topped or heeled, and when the ball goes off well, then the less said about the swing the better. It is instructive to watch any gathering of golfers made up for the most part of players who have not been bred to the game. The majority of them are content with the half-swing, they do not lift the club over the shoulder. If asked their reasons, they will say with truth, that there is only some thirty yards difference between a drive from a half and a drive from a full swing, and that the former is far easier and more certain than the latter. Quite so, but it is not the game; and he who aspires to learn to play the game will prefer to swing full and fail gloriously rather than to attain a moderate success in this fashion. But the swing is only one of a hundred arts that have to be learned before a man can pretend to play golf. Till he has mastered these, or a goodly proportion of them, he does not play, he only knocks a ball along, a humble amusement with which alas! most of us must needs be content for the term of our natural lives. Golf, like Art, is a goddess whom we must woo from early youth if we would win her; we must even be born to her worship. No other skill will avail us here, the most brilliant cricketer does not necessarily make a first-class golfer; on the contrary, he must begin by forgetting his cricket; he must not lift himself on his toes and *hit* like a batsman making a drive. Doubtless, the eye which helps a man to excel in shooting, at tennis, or cricket, will advantage him here to some extent, but, on the other hand, he will have much to forget, much to unlearn. He must clear his mind of all superstitions, he must humble his pride in the sand, and begin with a new heart and a meek spirit, well knowing that failure is his goal. For he will never, never learn to play – it is folly to expect otherwise. Each evening he will see his mistakes and avow amendment to himself and to his partner, and yet, when the morrow is done, will come home murmuring:

> *It was last night I swore to thee*
> *That fond impossibility.*

Impossibility! For the middle-aged duffer this word sums it all.

It may be said, Then why have anything to do with such a hopeless sport? Let him who asks play golf once, and he will understand why. He will go on playing because he must. Drink, opium, gambling – from the clutches of all these it is possible to escape, but from golf, never! Has anybody ever seen a man who gave up golf? Certainly dead donkeys are more common than these. Be once beguiled to the investment of five shillings in a driver, and abandon hope. Your fate is sure. The driver will be broken in a week, but what will you be? You are doomed for life, or till limbs and eyesight fail you – doomed to strive continually to conquer an unconquerable game. Undoubtedly golf is not so innocent as it seems, it has dangerous possibilities. Can we not easily conceive a man middle-aged, happy, prosperous, regular in his attendance at business, and well satisfied with an annual outing at the seaside? And can we not picture him again after golf has laid its hold upon him? He is no longer happy for he plays not better and better, but worse and worse. Prosperity has gone, for the time that he should give to work he devotes to the pernicious sport. He has quarrelled with his wife, for has he not broken all the drawing-room china in the course of practising his 'swing' on Sundays, and estranged his friends, who can no longer endure to be bored with his eternal talk of golf? As for the annual outing, it does not satisfy him at all; cost what it will, he must be on the links five days out of every seven. There is no need to follow him further, or we might dwell on the scene, as yet far off, for this poison is slow, when battered, broken, bankrupt, his very clubs in pawn for a few shillings, he perambulates some third-rate links, no longer as a player, but in the capacity of a superannuated caddie. Here is matter of romance indeed: the motive is generously presented to any novelist weary of portraying the effects of drink and cards.

'The Golfer's End; or, The Demon Driver,' should prove an effective title.

And yet even for those who will never really master it, the game is worth the caddie. To begin with, it has this startling merit, the worse you play the more sport you get. If the fisherman slacks his line, and lets off the salmon, or the shooter misses the only woodcock clean, or the batsman is bowled first ball off a lob, there is an end of those particular delights. But when the golfer tops his ball, or trickles it into a furze-bush, or lands it in a sand-bunker, it is but the beginning of joy, for there it lies patiently awaiting a renewal of his maltreatment. His sport is only limited by the endurance of his muscle, or, perchance, of his clubs, and at the end of the round, whereas the accomplished player will have enjoyed but eighty or a hundred strokes, the duffer can proudly point to a total of twice that number. Moreover he has hurt no one, unless it be the caddie, or the feelings of his partner in a foursome. By the way, the wise duffer should make a point of playing alone, or search out an opponent of equal incapacity; he should not be led into foursomes with members of the golfing aristocracy, that is if he has a proper sense of pride, and a desire not to look ridiculous. He should even avoid the company of members of his own family on these occasions, lest it chance that they lose respect for a man and a father who repeatedly tries to hit a small ball with a stick with the most abject results, and is even betrayed by his failure into the use of language foreign to the domestic hearth. Here is advice for him who has been bitten of the mania. Let him select a little-frequented inland links, and practise on them studiously about two hundred days a year for three years or so, either alone, or in the company of others of his own kidney. By this time, unless he is even less gifted than the majority of beginners, he will probably be able to play after a modest and uncertain fashion. Then let him resort to some more fashionable green, and having invested in an entirely new set of clubs, pose before the world as a novice to the game, for thus he will escape the scorn of men. But let him not reverse the process. Thus he who, in his ignorance or pride, takes train to Wimbledon, and in the presence of forty or fifty masters of the art, solemnly misses the ball three times on the first tee, may perchance never recover from the shock.

Nor will those years of effort and of failure be without their own reward. He will have tramped his gorsey common till every bush and sod is eloquent to him of some past adventure. This is the short green, that by some marvellous accident he once did in *one*, driving his ball from the tee even into the little far-away putting-hole. Here is a spot which he can never pass without a shudder, where he nearly killed his opponent's caddie, that scornful boy who, for many days accustomed to see him topping and putting his ball along from green to green, remained unmoved by his warning shouts of 'fore,' till one unlucky hour, when by some strange chance he drove full and fair. Crack! went the ball from his brassie. Crack! it came full on the youthful head thirty yards away, and then a yell of agony, and a sickening vision of heels kicking wildly in the air, and presently a sound of clinking silver coin. There, too, is the exact place, whence for the first (and perchance the last) time he drove over the beetling cliff, and out of the great bunker, the long way too, not the ladies' way- a feat not often accomplished by the skilful. A hundred and ninety-one yards that drive measured, though it is true an envious and long-legged friend who had forced his own ball an inch deep into the sand of the cliff, stepped it at a hundred and eighty-four. He can never forget that supreme moment, it will be with him till his dying hour. Our first large salmon safely brought to bank, a boy's first rocketing pheasant, clean and coolly killed, these afford memories that draw as near to perfect happiness as anything in this imperfect world, but it may be doubted if they can compare to the sense of utter triumph, of ecstatic exhilaration with which, for the first time, we watch the ball, propelled by our unaided skill, soar swiftly over the horrid depths of an hitherto unconquered bunker. There is a tale – a true one, or it would not be produced here – that, being true, shall be told as an example of noble patience fitly crowned and celebrated.

A wanderer musing in a rugged place was, of a sudden, astonished to see and hear an old gentleman, bearing a curiously shaped stick, walking up and down and chanting the *Nunc*

Dimittis as he walked. Moved by curiosity, he came to the aged singer, and asked,

'Why do you chant the *Nunc Dimittis* on the edge of this gulf?'

'For this reason, sir,' he answered, pointing to a golf-ball that lay upon the turf. 'For seventeen years and more I have attempted almost daily, to drive a ball across that bunker, and but now I have succeeded for the first time. The object of my life is attained, and I am ready to die. That, sir, is why I sing.'

Then the wanderer took off his hat, and went away, marvelling at the infatuation of golfers.

It need scarcely be said that the foregoing remarks apply to, and are intended for, the consideration of male duffers. It would have been agreeable to extend them to the other sex, but space demands brevity. Golf is a man's game, but here, too, women assert their rights. Not that they are all fond of it; by no means. On the contrary, a young lady has been heard, and recently, to express her decided opinion that a law should be passed against its practice during the summer months. This was a lawn-tennis young lady. And another informed this writer that she held golf to be a 'horrid game, where everybody goes off like mad, glaring at a little ball, without a word for anybody'. Others, it is true, attack the question in a different spirit – they play, and play well. It is curious to observe their style; that they do everything wrong is obvious even to the male incompetent. They stand in front of the ball, they swing their club wildly in preparation, and finally bring it down with an action that suggests reminiscences of a cook jointing veal; but the ball goes, for these young ladies have a good eye and a strong arm. Perhaps no woman-player could ever attain to a really first-rate standard, for however vigorous she may be she cannot drive like a man. But with practice there seems to be no reason why she should not approach and putt as well as any man; and certainly she can talk golfing-shop with equal persistency.

And now this duffer will conclude with a word of advice to the world at large – that they should forthwith enter the noble fraternity of duffers, of those who try to play golf and cannot. They will never succeed – at least, not ten per cent of them will succeed. They will knock balls from green to green, and reverence Mr Horace Hutchinson more truly and deeply than the great ones of the earth are generally reverenced; that is all. But they will gain health and strength in the pursuit of a game which has all the advantages of sport without its expense and cruelty; they will note many a changing light on land and sea; and last, but not least, for several hours a week they will altogether forget their worries, together with Law, Art, Literature, or whatever wretched occupation the Fates have given it to them to follow in the pursuit of their daily bread. For soon – alas! too soon – the votary of golf – that great gift of Scotland to the world – will own but one ambition, an ambition but rarely to be attained. Thus, he will sing with the poet.

> *Who list may grasp at greatness,*
> *   Who list may woo and wive;*
> *Wealth, wisdom, power, position -*
> *These make not my ambition.*
> *Nay but I pray for straightness,*
> *   And do desire to drive.*
> *Who list may grasp at greatness,*
> *   Who list may woo and wive.*

A Tale of Golf

WILLIAM GRAHAM

On the morning of the 17th August 18–, two native golfers of the famous Dubbieside, in Fife, were seen resting on the brow of the links and anxiously casting their eyes in the direction of Methil, as if expecting the smoking funnel of the ever-restless 'St. George'. Their coats of business were donned, their caps were drawn resolutely over their brows, and they examined with more than common care the knitting of their clubs, the insertion of the lead, and the indentation of the bone. From their capacious pockets they turned out ball after ball with mysterious care,[1] and the names of the makers were interchanged with reverential whispers, as they peered into one or two of the most select. At their feet reclined their caddies, grasping each a complete establishment of clubs, and listening with deep respect to the conversation of their masters. At last a towering column of smoke announced that the steamer was at hand, while from the end of the bank the florry[2] boat was plying its way to receive the passengers for Leven. The sportsmen leaped to their feet as the passengers descended the side of the steamer, and an exclamation of 'He's come!' burst from them as they saw a large package of clubs lowered down into the boat. They hastened to the sands to welcome the arrival of the stranger sportsman, who had been sent to dim the glory of Dubbieside;

---

[1]The balls were then made of leather, stuffed so full of feathers as to be at once hard and elastic.

[2]The boat which conveyed passengers ashore from the steamer at places where there was no pier, or when the tide would not allow the landing at the pier.

and there in the stern of the boat, with his arm encircling his instruments of play, did they behold the doughty champion, who was backed against the rustic players by some discomfited metropolitans, and who was destined to open the eyes of Dubbieside to its ignorance and vanity in assuming an equality with the clubs south of the Forth.

He was a short, stout-made, sandy-whiskered man; his spectacles not altogether concealing his ferrety eyes; his nose short, and ever ready to curl; and his lip compressing itself, as if it were bridling up under some slight or insult. He was the ideal of small pomposity, set off with a finical attention to dress; rings clasped his little fat fingers, and a diamond pin shone in his puffy breast. He surveyed his new brothers on the shore with an air of loftiness, although he must have known them for his intended associates and opponents, and cast on the country round a vexed look, as if his friends had compromised his dignity by sending him to a place that appeared so questionable. His stateliness, however, gave way to rage and abuse, when he found that to get ashore he must mount on the back of one of the boatmen. This mode of landing is seldom resorted to now – to ladies it was a torturing thought to be obliged to submit to be carried like babies through the breakers by some staggering boatmen who resented their fidgety movements by muttered threats of committing them to the deep, or of pinching them unceremoniously. No less torture was felt by our indignant golfer, but there was no alternative. He was horsed amid the smiles of passengers and onlookers – his legs drawn up most ungracefully to save his boots from the brine, and his face, over the shoulder of his carrier, suggesting the appearance of the man of the moon in a state of excitement. Arrived at the shore, he was set down with little ceremony, when unluckily, his first contact with the county of Fife was a sudden seat on the cold wet sand. He was soon put on his legs by his brother sportsmen, whose mixed condolence and banter were ill-calculated to soothe his ruffled feelings; but with a tremendous effort the high pressure gentleman readjusted his spectacles, and did assume enough of calmness to look contempt on all around, and discharge an execration at the county of Fife and the disgraceful incommodiousness of its conveyances.

The party now moved to the hole from which they were to strike off, the stranger receiving the proposal of a short pause at the public-house of the village with a look of horror. They were here joined by a number of second-rate golf men, and old lovers of the game who could yet, in despite of rheumatism, follow the rounds – besides a whole troop of ordinary villagers, inspired, if not with a love of golf, at least with an interest in the honour of Dubbieside. The stranger having undone his clubs, round which his red coat was tightly roped – having renounced his handsome green one with gilt anchor buttons, and relinquished it with a sigh, and a shrink of composure to his fate, to a Dubbieside caddie, whom he looked on as a second Caliban, addressed himself to the business of the day. He cast on the ground a 'Gourlay', white as snow, hard as lead, and elastic as whalebone; and the trembling caddie having, amid the whizz of a shower of novel oaths, teed it at last to his satisfaction, he seized a club which like

Cutty-Sark in 'Tam o'Shanter', was a 'supple jaud and strong', and gave it a few preparatory vibrations – then assuming the honour of precedence, he addressed his body to his ball, raised his club, and came round with a determined sweep. The missile sped right into a sandy brae, which the generality of players clear with the first stroke; but such a thing will occasionally happen with the best player. So little was thought of it, though the testy stranger glowed like a red herring; and his humour was by no means restored when he saw his partners, after 'licking their looves', make their balls fly like sky-rockets over the place where he was earthed. Away, however, the crowd moved – principals, caddies, amateurs, club-makers, weavers, and hecklers – the last class of gentlemen having at this time struck for an advance of wages; and being glad of anything about which to occupy themselves. The whole formed a ring round the stranger gentleman, who was now to dig his ball out of its lodgement of sand. The occasion, the company, the awkwardness of his position, and the consciousness of the want of sympathy in all around, contributed to heighten the angry feelings of the champion; so, darting a glance of fire at one of the hecklers, who remarked with tipsy gravity, and most offensive familiarity, in allusion to the hopeless situation of the ball, that it would require spectacles to find it out, he gave it such an ill-natured and ill-directed whack, that it sank completely into the regions of night. The hurrays of the hecklers, the yells of the boys, the placid laughter of the paralytic old players, who shook upon their sticks, and the condolence of the rival players, which was given in all the offensiveness of Scotch diminutives, now nearly threw the mortified stranger into a fit of apoplexy. The ball, however, was declared not playable; and being dug out by the fingers of the caddie was thrown back on the green, at the loss of a stroke in counting to its owner. So, reconcentrating his energy, and assuming as much calmness as could be collected in a composition so formed, he aimed a well-directed stroke. Unfortunately, at the very instant, a prophetic groan or hem from one of the flax-tearing fraternity gave a wrong turn to the blow, and swept the ill-destined ball into a bunker or sand hole. Another cheer for Dubbieside was about to be raised, when the enraged stranger grappled with the obnoxious heckler, and lustily called for a constable. This produced a rush from his companions, who in an instant released him from the clutch of the indignant golfer, around whom the released heckler began dancing and sparring, with his jacket and paper cap doffed, demanding a ring and fair play. But the honour of the links being at stake, the Dubbieside players laid hands on the shoulders of the rioters, and awed them into civility; so, after a few grumblings, the Dubbieside men having taken their second strokes which sent their balls far into safe and beautiful ground, the troop once more moved on. The metropolitan champion was now to strike his fifth stroke, or three more, and the perspiration stood in beads on his brow when he came up and beheld his infatuated Gourlay sitting as if in an egg-cup of sand. The more civilized of the idlers felt something like sympathy, and a feeling of commiseration was beginning to steal over the multitude, and when the caddie, having given the *cleek* instead of the *iron*, which the gentleman swore was the proper instrument, the said caddie was unceremoniously deposed with a cuff in the neck that sent him sprawling in the sand, and the clubs were at the same time wrenched from him by his irate master, who swore he would carry them himself. This event did not make the player more cool, or the spectators more indulgent; so when the ball was jerked from its position, it went slant over the bank to the firm bed of sand on the beach, when it rolled as on an iron floor till it cooled itself in the sea. The flaxmen, swinging arm-in-arm to the top of the bank, now burst out with a chorus of -

The sea – the sea – the open sea,
I am where I would ever be, etc.

This was too much. For a moment a sort of stupor seemed to fall on the devoted stranger; but an unearthly calmness and paleness succeeded, as he moved leisurely to the sea, picked up his ball, and put it into his pocket. He had observed the steamer on its return from Largo, and walking leisurely to the florry boat which was just going out, he arrived in time to secure his passage. His exit might have been dignified – for even the hecklers remarked that there was something 'no cannie in his look' when he left the ground, and they did not even venture to cheer – but just as the boat was shoving off, a frenzied-looking woman, running along the beach, made signs for the boat to stop, and in an instant the mother of the dismissed caddie was in the boat demanding his pay, and reparation for the damage done to her bit laddie. The approach of the obnoxious hecklers to witness this new scene, operated more on the discomfited golfer than the woman's clamour – and a bonus, most disproportionate to the damage, was slipped into the horny fist of the outraged mother, who, suddenly lowering her tone, stood upon the beach his only friend. Yet could she not, as the boat moved off, prevent the flaxmen sending after him their chorus of 'The sea, the sea', until he was seen to ascend the steamboat and suddenly disappear below.

Who or what he was remains a mystery; his backers never gave his name, or a hint of his profession. Some imagined him to be a principal Edinburgh clerk; others, a half-pay resident in Musselburgh; but who or what he really was, could not be discovered by the most curious inquirer.

A Braid Hills Mystery

J. M. BARRIE

S TUBBLE row is one of the arms which Edinburgh stretches out toward the Braid Hills, but though the tenements have been finished for eighteen months or more, a number of them are still standing empty. Fourteen and Sixteen, adjoining houses, are occupied, the former by a gentleman of unknown occupation, whose recent accession to fortune has greatly puzzled his neighbour at No. Sixteen. Until lately his impecuniosity was so notorious as to be the subject of commiseration with all his neighbours, and the tradesmen with whom he deals never met him without making pointed allusions to 'that pound note', which it seems to have been his occupation to borrow here and there. His great-coat had also been seen by the curious in a High Street window, and reports said that his furniture had gone to the pawn shop, a chair at a time. There was no other such needy person in Stubble Row, and No. Fourteen admitted it himself. Suddenly, however, his fortune seemed to change, and instead of going out of his house, furniture began to go in. At the same time he became secretive, presenting, as No. Sixteen complained, the appearance of a man who had discovered a new way of making money, and meant to keep it to himself.

The change at No. Fourteen was first discovered by No. Sixteen (who is a lady) one morning when she saw a dozen bottles of beer delivered at No. Fourteen's door. She ran round to No. Nine to say that Fourteen had got the better of another grocer, and they spent (as has since been admitted) half an hour in discussing the amount of whistling the grocer would have to go through before he saw his money. Later in the day, Sixteen was extremely disgusted to see Fourteen ostentatiously drinking beer in his back-garden, which is the exact size of a billiard table, but not the same colour. Fourteen sat on a garden chair – which looked new – with his feet resting on a clothes basket; and, while Sixteen looked on, congratulating herself that she was not as her neighbour, he accidentally knocked over the beer bottle, and broke it. Had the same thing happened to her, she would have bewailed the extra expense thus entailed; but her neighbour, who was reputed without a penny to bless himself with, laughed genially, and then flung the broken bottle over the wall into her garden. His impudence staggered her, but she picked up the pieces, meaning to return them to him at once, when she had the presence of mind to stay her hand and glance at the bottle to see what grocer's label was on it. Discovering that it had been bottled by Simpson, of the neighbourhood, whose teas will well repay a trial, if what you want is fragrance combined with economy (see handbills), she thought it her duty as a Christian to look in at Simpson's the first time she passed that way, and warn him against having any further dealings with No. Fourteen. The grocer, with whom she does not deal except for American cheese, which is one of his specialities, but not so remunerative as tea, received her curtly, and said that Fourteen's beer had been paid for, money down. He also hinted that if she thought more of her own affairs, and less of her neighbour's, she would keep her doorsteps cleaner, and she left the shop, resolved never again to do a good turn for anybody.

Had Fourteen now lapsed into his former condition of impecuniosity, Sixteen (though reluctant to think ill of anyone) would have concluded that he had merely paid for the beer in order to make a good impression, and so pave the way for running up an account at Simpson's. But a few days afterwards he was seen walking down the street under a new umbrella, and even while Sixteen was wondering with Nine whether he had got a present of it, or bought it when the shopman was not looking, a rumour spread through Stubble Row that Fourteen had been in at the butcher's and paid his long-standing account for £1, 12s. 7d. Sixteen flung on her cloak and hurried to the butcher's, where the story was confirmed. The general excitement reached its height on the 12th of last month, when a piano was delivered at Sixteen's door. Inquiries were at once instituted, when it was found that the piano had been taken on the three years' hire system, and that Sixteen had paid for a month in advance.

All this time, while the neighbourhood was thinking him over, No. Fourteen was going about as usual. Sixteen was so annoyed at her failure to unravel the mystery that she invited him to tea; but though he accepted the invitation, and both ate and drank heartily, she could get nothing out of him. He admitted that his affairs had taken a turn for the better, but beyond that remained stubbornly silent. Hitherto the chief cause of his poverty had been a disinclination to work, and it was noticed that he was still as idle as ever. He spent his days smoking in the back-garden or strolling about the streets. The only conclusion to come to, therefore, was that someone had left him money. Certain of Fourteen's male neighbours disagreed with this view however, their ground being that, when in the public at the end of the street, Fourteen occasionally let drop hints of a new profession he had invented. He was very 'close' as to what it was, but they gathered that he followed it in the night time. Probably this was a mere surmise, a deduction from the fact that he obviously did nothing during the day.

Sixteen admitted that there might be something in this theory, and was finally converted to it. Her conversion dates from the afternoon when she saw Fourteen leave his house with a heavy bag on his shoulders. It was about the size, she said, of a pillow-case and she was made suspicious by his evident anxiety not to be followed. She hurriedly put on her bonnet and ran after him. At the corner of the street, however, he was lost to view. This happened on a Monday, and on the following Monday the incident was repeated, but later in the evening.

Sixteen and Nine were at the former's window by four o'clock in the afternoon on the third Monday, resolved not to quit their post until they had solved the mystery. They waited nearly four hours before Fourteen came out. He had no bag on his shoulders this time, and they feared that their watch had been in vain. He walked down the street, and they opened the window to crane their necks after him. Their surprise was considerable when he

was seen hailing a cab. Cabs are seldom hailed in Stubble Row, except by mischievous boys. Fourteen walked alongside the cab to his house, which he entered, after first directing the cabman to wait. The excitement at No. Sixteen was now such that No. Nine hit her head on the windowsill and did not know it for some time afterwards. In a minute Fourteen emerged, staggering under the weight of a heavy sack. He put this into the cab, and drove off.

Sixteen and Nine sat looking at each other, and then had a glass of sherry in a cup. They were both rather frightened, and to this day neither can say which was the first to mention Burke and Hare. Horrible though it seemed, Fourteen was behaving in a manner that quite suggested these notorious criminals. They conveyed the bodies of the murdered persons in a sack, and sometimes they had the audacity to use conveyances. It was in the night time that they pursued their horrid calling. The more sherry Sixteen and Nine drank the more certain they felt that the case should be put into the hands of the police.

Against Sixteen's advice, Nine first told her husband of the discovery, and he did not receive her plan of action favourably. He said he would black her eye if she told tales on her neighbour. Other persons saw their duty more clearly than Nine's husband, and a meeting was held, at which they agreed to catch Fourteen red-handed on the following Monday. The local policeman pooh-poohed their suspicions, but undertook to be on the spot.

Fourteen was caught in the street with a heavy bag on his shoulders. The weight of the bag is best known to No. Four, whom it caught in the small of the back. There was a fierce strug-gle, which was only ended by the intervention of the policeman. Fourteen would not deliver up his bag until told that he would otherwise be given in charge. He then consented to divulge the contents to the policeman's eyes alone. There was an outcry against this, but the policeman assented, and to the rage of Fourteen's captors the door of Fourteen's house was closed against them.

The policeman has admitted that Fourteen attempted to bribe him, but, of course, he indignantly rejected all offers. The bag was then opened, when, to the bewilderment of the officer of the law, it was found to be full of golf balls. Fourteen subsequently made the following statement:

'It is quite true that until lately I was in very impecunious circumstances. This would not have troubled me had not my creditors taken it so much to heart. Their conversation was eternally on the one subject, and I found it tedious. Had I been able to work without exerting myself, I would gladly have embraced some trade. Unfortunately there are different laws for the rich and poor.

'I think it is only two months ago since an accident made a material difference in my circumstances. I had gone for a walk on the Braid Hills. It was a fine afternoon. A great number of golfers were engaged in play. I am not a golfer. It seems to me to be hard work. I was strolling in the long grass around the course, when my foot struck against something hard. I picked it up. It was a golf ball. A hundred yards further on I found another ball, then another. I did not know what was the value of these balls; but being anxious to make an honest living, I took them to a shop. I was surprised at the handsome price I got for them.

'Early next morning, before the golfers were out, I returned to the Braid Hills, and made a search for golf balls. I found seven. From that day I saw that I had a career before me. Every morning, while most of the citizens were sleeping, I was out on the Braid Hills pursuing my vocation. My finds varied in number, and some days I was unlucky; but, on the whole, as my skill increased, the profession became more and more remunerative. I invented one implement for picking golf balls out of long grass, and another for getting at the roots of whins. My great day was Sunday, partly because it gave me longer time to search, but mainly because Saturday is the chief day of the week for golf. Many matches take place on Saturday too. Every Monday I sold my golf balls to a firm of makers.

'My reason for keeping this a secret is that, if the new calling was generally known, I would have rivals in it. It could keep some more of us, no doubt, in comfort, but there would be a rush of needy persons. If I could have bought the monopoly I would gladly have done so, for then I could have extended my business. Instead of looking for the golf balls myself, I would have paid boys a small wage to bring them to me.

'It is only now that I realise what an excellent sport golf is. Formerly, I thought it too hard work for anybody. Of late, however, I have become quite an enthusiast. I do not play myself, but I advise all others to do so. I spend great part of my days now recommending the young to play golf, because it is a fine, healthy pastime, and the old because it gives them an appetite. I am also thoroughly of opinion that ladies should play golf. My advice is that the Braid Hills should be chosen for playing on. It is a splendid course, and I am always delighted when I see the newspapers cracking it up. I don't agree, however, with the view that the whins and grass should be cut down. That would put an end to the industry I now follow, and would naturally lessen my interest in the noble and ancient game.'

The Hong Kong Medal

WILLIAM G. VAN TASSEL SUTPHEN

At the age of thirty-five but one illusion remained to Henry Alderson, rich, single, and a member in good and regular standing of the Marion County Golf Club. It is hardly necessary to add that it was only in his capacity as a golfer that he lived again in the rose-coloured atmosphere of youth, for after the third decade there is no other possible form of self-deception. And it is equally superfluous to remark that he was a very poor golfer, for it is only the duffers at the royal and ancient game who have any leisure for the exercise of the imagination; the medal winners are obliged to confine their attention to hitting the ball clean and to keeping their eye in for short putts. It was for Henry Alderson and his kind to keep trade brisk for the ball and club makers, and to win phenomenal matches against the redoubtable *Col. Bogey* – a game which may be magnificent, but which is certainly not golf. Still, the diversion was unquestionably a harmless one, and served to keep him in the open air and from an overclose application to business. Moreover, it was absolutely certain that the secret of success lay well within his grasp. A few more days of practice, the final acquisition of that peculiar turn of the wrist, and then! – Henry Alderson took a fresh grip on the familiar lofting-iron that had deceived him so often, and topped another ball along the turf. Of course the delusion was a hopeless one, but he was happy in its possession; and if we who look on have become wiser in our day and generation – why, so much the worse for us.

It was a bright autumn morning, and Henry Alderson stood at the tee looking at the little red flag that marked the location of the

23

tenth hole, two hundred and thirty yards away. He had done fairly well on the outgoing course, but this hole had always been a stumbling-block to him, and that dreadful double hazard, a scant hundred yards down the course, looked particularly savage on this particular morning. On the left lurked an enormous sand-pit, which was popularly known as the 'Devil;' and the 'Deep Sea,' in the shape of an ice pond, was only a few yards to the right. Straight between them lay the path to glory, but for a 'slice' or a 'foozle' there remained only destruction and double figures.

Henry Alderson shuddered as he looked, and incontinently forgot all about 'slow back.' Crack! and the 'gutty' had disappeared beneath the treacherous waters of the 'Deep Sea.' With painful deliberation he teed another ball and mentally added two to his score. The club-head swung back, and for one fatal instant his eye wandered from the ball. Bang! and it had gone to the 'Devil.' Without a word Mr Alderson took his expensive collection of seventeen clubs from the hands of his caddie and descended into the bunker to meet the Evil One.

It was just fifteen minutes after eleven when Henry Alderson entered upon his ghostly conflict with all the Powers of Darkness. At twenty minutes of twelve the caddie, tired of inaction, crept cautiously to the edge of the bunker and looked in. His master held in his hand a costly patented 'driver' that was alleged to be unbreakable. Placing one foot upon the head of the club, he kicked judiciously but with determination at the precise place where the 'scare' is whipped to the shaft, and then carefully added the fragments to the heap of broken putters, cleeks, and brassies that lay before him. The boy, who was wise in his generation, waited for no more, but fled to the club-house.

Henry Alderson came up out of the bunker, took half a dozen new balls from the pocket of his red coat, and deliberately flung them into the 'Deep Sea.' He then tore his score-card into bits, divested himself of cap and shoes, laid his watch and purse where they would be readily observed, and walked with a firm step to the border of the pond.

Suddenly a quickly moving shadow projected itself over his shoulder, and a cheerful, albeit an unfamiliar, voice hailed him.

He turned away and saw a stranger close beside him. The new-comer was an odd-looking personage, dressed in a semi-clerical suit of rusty black, and carrying an old cotton umbrella and a well-stuffed carpet-bag. He had a keen-looking, smooth-shaven face, with piercing black eyes and an aggressive nose. His complexion was of a curious pallor, as though untouched by wind or sun, but there was nothing in his appearance to indicate either ill-health or decrepitude.

'Possibly a salesman,' thought Henry Alderson. 'At any rate, he's no golfer.'

'How are you making out?' inquired the stranger, in a tone of polite interest.

It was on the tip of Henry Alderson's tongue to answer, 'Fifty-five for nine holes' (his actual score being sixty-three), but at this awful moment, when all the solid realities of life were crumbling away beneath his feet, the lie seemed so small, so pitiful, so mean, and he replied, 'Came out in forty-two, but then I lost a shot through having my ball lifted by a dog.'

The stranger did not seem to be visibly impressed. 'Pooh!' he said, airily; 'I should hardly call that golf.'

'Perhaps you play yourself,' returned Alderson, with what he considered to be a sarcastic inflection.

'Not as a general thing, though I do a round or so occasionally,' said the dark gentleman, placidly. Then opening his carpet-bag and taking out a golf-ball, 'It's a very pretty drive from where we stand. If you will allow me.'

He teed the ball, and, with what seemed to be an almost contemptuous disregard of all rules for correct driving, swung against it the crook handle of his old cotton umbrella. Crack! and it went away like a rifle-bullet, close to the ground for one hundred and twenty yards, and then, towering upward in the manner of a rocketing pigeon, caught the full strength of the breeze for a hundred yards of further carry, and dropped dead on the putting-green. Henry Alderson gasped.

'Shall we walk on?' said the stranger.

It was a long putt on the green, but the umbrella was again equal to the occasion. Henry Alderson's eyes sparkled. This was an umbrella worth having.

'It makes no difference what kind of a club you use,' said the gentleman in black, apparently reading his thoughts. 'But with this particular make of ball you can accomplish any shot at will, no matter how difficult.'

'I'd like to try that kind of ball,' said Alderson eagerly. 'Can you give me the maker's address?'

'If you will accept this one, it is entirely at your service.'

Henry Alderson stretched out his hand, and then as quickly withdrew it. He remembered now that when the obliging stranger had opened his bag it had appeared to be filled with what looked like legal papers – contracts perhaps – and there was a dreadful significance in the fact that all the signatures were in red. Of course it might have been carmine ink, and probably was, but it looked suspicious.

'If it's a question of signing my name to anything,' he faltered, 'I don't think that I can accept. I've made it a rule – er – never to go upon anybody's paper. It's – er – business, you know.'

The stranger smiled indulgently. 'You are quite right. Nevertheless, you need have no scruples about accepting my gift, for there is no obligation of any kind involved in the transaction.'

Henry Alderson trembled, and looked furtively at the dark gentleman's feet, which, as he now observed, were encased in a pair of arctic galoshes some four sizes too large. Clearly there was no definite information to be gained in that quarter; and as the field that they were in was used as a pasture for cattle, the presence of hoof-marks could mean nothing either way. There was nothing to do but chance it, and he was not long in making up his mind. He took the ball and stowed it away in his pocket.

The stranger nodded approvingly. 'I think that I may congratulate you in advance upon your success in winning the club handicap this afternoon.'

'But suppose that I lose the ball?' said Alderson, with a sudden accession of doubtfulness.

'Impossible. If your caddie has been negligent, you have only to whistle, and the ball will keep on answering "Here" until you come up with it. And, moreover, it is indestructible.'

'It makes no difference what club I use?'

'None whatever. If you care to, you can drive that ball two hundred yards with a feather bolster.'

'I shall endeavour to do so,' laughed Alderson. 'You won't – er – come and have a bite of luncheon with me?'

'Not to-day,' said the stranger, politely. 'But we shall probably meet again. Good luck to you, and may your success end only with the winning of the Hong Kong Medal.'

The two men bowed, and the dark gentleman walked off. He went to the edge of the 'Devil' sand-bunker, marched straight into it, and disappeared. Moved by a sudden impulse, Henry Alderson followed and looked in. There was nothing to be seen, but he thought that he could detect a slight trace of sulphur in the air. However, one may be easily deceived in such matters.

As Henry Alderson trudged back to the club-house it seemed as though the events of the last half-hour had been nothing more than the disordered fancies of a noon-day nightmare. But there was the ball in his hand, the tangible evidence of what had happened. And, after all, the bargain had been entirely in his favour. Whoever the dark gentleman may have been, and Henry Alderson shuddered as he reflected upon one unholy possibility, he was certainly no business man. The wonderful ball was in his, Henry Alderson's, possession, and his chances of eternal salvation were as good as ever.

'Somebody has been stupid,' chuckled Mr Alderson to himself as he entered the grill-room of the club, and took up the luncheon card.

The handicap match had been put down for three o'clock. It was a monthly affair, and the winner had the proud distinction of wearing a silver cross for the following period of thirty days. It was a coveted honour, but of course not to be compared with the Hong Kong Medal, which was always played for at the end of the golfing year. No one knew why it was called the Hong-Kong Medal, and it was certain that its donor had never in his life been out of the Middle States. But the appellation seemed to chime in with the somewhat fanciful phraseology that prevails in all things pertaining to golf, and it possessed a sonorous tone that was suggestive of tomtoms and barbaric victories.

It is needless to say that Henry Alderson invariably entered all

the club competitions, and as invariably came out at the bottom of the list. And yet no one had worked harder to ensure success. He was absolutely saturated with the theory and literature of golf, and could rattle off the roster of open and amateur champions with the fluency of a prize Sunday School scholar reciting the names of the kings of Judah and Israel. He neglected nothing in the way of precept or practice, and when the club champion got married he had even thought of following his example for its possible effect upon his game. But when he ventured to propose the expedient to Miss Kitty Crake he met with a decided rebuff.

'I shall never,' said Miss Crake, 'marry a man who is not on the scratch list. When you have won the Hong Kong Medal, why, then we shall see.'

Of course, such an answer could be nothing less than the absolute of refusals. Even in his wildest dreams he had never hoped to come in better than fourth in the monthly handicaps, and that too with an allowance of thirty-six strokes. It is true that there were other young ladies who might have accepted a less heroic standard of excellence than the winning of the Hong Kong, but Henry Alderson felt that the matrimonial experiment was not worth trying unless Kitty Crake could be induced to take part in it. And so there the matter rested.

When Mr Alderson stepped to the teeing-ground that afternoon for his first drive he felt unaccountably cool and collected, in spite of the fact that Miss Crake stood in the very forefront of the 'gallery.' It was one hundred and seventy-seven yards to the first hole, and he usually 'hooked' his ball into the 'Punch-bowl' hollow at the left, or else feebly topped it along the ground in the one consuming desire to get away from the spectators. But today there should be another tale to tell. For an instant he thought of directing the magic ball to land upon the putting-green dead at the hole, but he reflected that such a phenomenal stroke would undoubtedly be put down as a fluke. It was the part of wisdom to go quietly, and so he picked out a spot some twenty yards short of the green, but in good line, and affording a generous 'lie.'

As he lifted his club and swung through he was uncomfortably conscious of having transgressed at least eighteen out of the twenty-three cardinal precepts for correct driving, but already the ball was on its way, and, amidst a hearty burst of applause, led, as he could see by Kitty Crake, it fell precisely as he had determined. A skilful approach laid him dead, and the hole was his in three. A subdued buzz ran around the circle of the 'gallery,' and everybody bent forward to watch his second drive across the 'Punch-bowl.' Straight over the yawning hollow flew the ball, and the crowd clapped again; but the play was now too far away to watch, and there were others ready to drive off. Henry Alderson disappeared in the direction of the 'meadow' hole, and Miss Crake went to the club-house piazza to make tea. 'Poor fellow,' she thought, 'his foozling will be all the worse when it does come.'

It was a very successful tournament, and Henry Alderson won it by the credible score of eighty net. He blushed as the President handed him the silver cross, but the spectators clapped vigorously; for he had always been a good fellow, albeit a bad golfer, and his victory was a popular one.

'Splendid!' said Miss Kitty Crake, and Henry Alderson ascended forthwith into the seventh heaven.

During the month that followed there were some tremendous surprises in store for the record-holders. Three days after the handicap Alderson did the course in eighty-two, thereby breaking the amateur record, and that same afternoon he tied the best professional score. The Green Committee promptly reduced him to the scratch list, and there was some informal talk of sending him to represent the club at the National Amateur meeting. Montague, the holder of the Hong Kong Medal for two years running, was visibly uneasy. He began to spend more time on the links, and held surreptitious conversations with Alderson's favourite caddie.

But there was a friend as well as an enemy to keep close watch upon Henry Alderson. There was a change in him that only Kitty Crake noticed at first – a change that both annoyed and alarmed her. The becoming modesty with which he had achieved his first successes had entirely disappeared. Almost imperceptibly he had grown self-sufficient and opinionated, and his attitude towards his fellow-players was at times little short of offensive. He seemed to take an insolent delight in openly flouting the hoary traditions of the game, and in giving the lie direct to each and every venerable truism incrusted in golfing lore. He invariably used a wrong grip; he played with a full swing for all distances, including the shortest of putts, and he never under any circumstances condescended to keep his eye upon the ball. It was maddening to his fellow-golfers, but his scores were a sufficient answer to all remonstrances. Indeed, it may be said that his steadily decreasing averages were beginning to cause the Green Committee considerable uneasiness. For a player to return cards of sixty-four and then fifty-six and then forty-nine seemed to argue unfavourably for the sporting character of the links. Such kind of play was plainly injuring the reputation of the club, and at least the Honorary Secretary was emboldened to hint as much. The very next day Henry Alderson returned a total of eighteen for the full round of holes, and handed it with a mocking smile to the Honorary Secretary himself. This was too much, and Henry Alderson was promptly summoned to appear before the outraged majesty of the Green Committee. But it all ended in smoke. No one could deny that extraordinary scores of a hole in one stroke had been made on several occasions, and in this case it was simply an established phenomenon multiplied by itself eighteen times. 'And gentlemen,' concluded Henry Alderson, 'I did it all with a wooden putter.'

The Green Committee had nothing more to say, but they were plainly dissatisfied, and at once set about putting in some new hazards.

And yet – will it be believed? – Henry Alderson was not a happy man. Egotistical and arrogant as he had become, he yet could not fail to perceive that he had lost immensely in the esteem of his club-mates. Nobody cared to play a match with him; and although at first he had put it down to jealousy, he was gradually forced to admit to himself that the reason lay deeper. Worst of all, Kitty Crake was decidedly cool in her manner towards him. He could not understand it, for his golf was certainly above reproach, and he knew that nothing now could prevent him from winning the Hong Kong Medal. Once it was pinned upon his breast he would be in a position to demand an explanation and the fulfilment of her promise. But there was still another reason for his wishing that the match was over. Strange as it may appear, the very name of golf had become an abhorrence to him. And yet it was not so strange, after all, when one stops to consider. There is nothing so tiresome as perfection, and this especially applies to golf, as possessing an essentially feminine nature. It is the capriciousness, the inconstancy, of golf that makes it a folly so adorable, and Henry Alderson's game had arrived at a pitch of intolerable perfection. He had long ago discovered that the ball would not be a party to a poor shot. Goaded into fury by the monotonous consistency of his play, he had tried the experiment of ordering the ball into a bunker, or at least a bad lie. But the soulless piece of gutta-percha would have none of his foozling. It simply would not be denied, and after a few trials Henry Alderson resigned himself to his fate, comforting himself with the reflection that, having won the medal (and Kitty Crake), he would give up golf for ever.

The day of the contest for the Hong Kong Medal had come at last, and all golfdom had assembled to see the battle. A round-robin protesting against the admission of Henry Alderson as a competitor had been presented to the Green Committee, but that autocratic body had decided to ignore the protest. 'It will be better,' said a wise man, 'to let him win rather than to give him a handle for a grievance. Let him take the medal, and then we can settle upon some pretext to expel him from the club. Montague has had detectives on the case, and thinks he can prove that Alderson has been playing tennis within the last two months. That will be sufficient in the eyes of all true golfers.'

As it happened, Alderson and Montague were paired for the great event, and, of course, they had the gallery with them. Just before they started Alderson mustered up his courage and walked over to where Kitty Crake was standing. She did not raise her eyes as he approached, and he was obliged to speak twice before he could gain her attention.

'I trust that I am to have the benefit of your good wishes,' he said, meaningly.

She looked at him in frosty surprise.

'I don't think that they will help you much.' And then, with cutting deliberation, 'I devoutly wish that the Hong Kong Medal had never existed.'

'Mr Montague and Mr Alderson,' called out the referee. The two contestants came forward, and Kitty Crake ostentatiously turned her back as the play began.

In all the annals of the Marion County Golf Club a closer and more exciting match had never been played. Montague was certainly putting up the game of his life; and Alderson, while not showing any phenomenal work, was nevertheless returning a faultless score. Not a mistake had been made on eitherside, and at the end of the seventeenth hole honours were exactly even. But Montague was visibly breaking under the strain.

When Montague stepped forward to drive for the home hole, it was plain that he was very nervous. Twice he had tried to tee his ball, but his trembling fingers refused their office, and he was obliged to call upon a caddie for assistance. As he came up for the 'address' he was deathly pale, and little beads of sweat were standing upon his forehead. The club swung back, and then descended upon the ball, but with a feeble, crooked blow that 'sliced' it hopelessly into the bushes. A groan went up. Montague had 'cracked,' and the match was lost.

Up to this point Henry Alderson had played as though in a dream. At last he understood – those cold, stinging words of Kitty Crake could have but one meaning. *She did not wish him to win!* It was only too plain that she had never loved him, and that she regretted her idle words about the winning of the medal and the promise that they implied. What was he to do?

One thing was certain: he had no chance, in any event, with Kitty Crake. Of course he might go on and win the medal, and then humiliate her by contemptuously refusing to press his claim; but the revenge was an unmanly one, and he could not bring himself to adopt it. Again, he might withdraw, and so give the prize to Montague. He knew that the latter was desperately anxious to retain possession of the trophy. It was the pride, the joy, the treasure, of his otherwise empty life. The Montague infants had all cut their teeth upon the medal's firm and glittering edge. It was the family fetish; the one thing that distinguished them from the common herd of their neighbours, who lived in precisely the same pattern of suburban villa, but whose interest in life never rose above the discussion of village improvements or the election of a vestryman. Henry Alderson hesitated; his heart grew soft within him. And yet to give it up after it had cost him so much!

'Oh yes, a fair enough player, but a trifle short on his driving.'

It was Montague who spoke, and Henry Alderson felt instinctively that the remark referred to him. His cheeks burned as he heard the half-veiled insult that only a golfer can understand in its full significance, and he incontinently forgot all about his generous resolution to withdraw. He stepped up to the tee.

'I dare say I can reach the green in two,' he said, carelessly.

The hole was some four hundred yards away, and Montague smiled sarcastically. His enemy was about to be delivered into his hands.

'I've done two hundred and forty yards of straight carry,' continued Alderson.

'Hym!' coughed Montague.

'And I'd back myself to make it three hundred.'

'Why not four?' said Montague.

'Six hundred, if you say so,' returned Alderson, hotly.

'Or perhaps out of sight,' sneered Montague.

'Off the earth,' retorted Alderson.

Montague made no reply, but turned away to hide his satisfaction. Alderson was deliberately going to 'press,' and every student of the art of golf knows what that implies. But there is nothing more uncertain than a certainty – in golf.

Henry Alderson swung down upon the ball. Shades of St Rule! but was there ever such a mighty drive? Three hundred yards away, and it was still rising into the blue ether. Another instant and it had passed entirely out of sight, lost in infinite space. The spectators gasped, and Montague turned livid. But stop a bit. Where *was* the ball? The referee looked puzzled, and the caddies stared open-mouthed into the sky. And then in a flash it dawned upon Henry Alderson that his boast had been literally made good. *He had driven his ball off the earth.*

For a moment his heart stood still. With the ball was gone his golfing reputation, and gone for ever. Was there anything else for him in life? The answer came in another flash of inspiration. Yes; he was a free man; now he could play golf again – his *own* game. Forgotten was the Hong Kong Medal; forgotten for the nonce was Kitty Crake herself. The fit was upon him – the berserker rage of the true duffer. He turned to the referee.

'I acknowledge,' he said, 'the penalty for lost ball, and play a new one.'

He teed a ball, an ordinary gutta-percha, and, swinging down upon it, made the most bungling of 'tops.' A roar of laughter went up, and Henry Alderson joined in it, the heartiest of all. He caught Kitty Crake's eye, and she was smiling too. Taking a brassie, he advanced for his second shot, and 'missed the globe' twice running. But what a delightful sensation it was! – this was something like golf.

Finally, he succeeded in playing inside of Montague, who followed with a splendidly played iron shot out of the bushes. Alderson drove into a bunker, and noted, with an exquisite thrill of pleasure, that his ball had buried itself completely in the sand. It took him three to get out, and the crowd applauded. He 'foozled' a shot into a clump of evergreens, and Kitty Crake clapped her hands. Montague made a phenomenal approach, and landed his ball dead at the hole. Alderson 'hooked' one ball, 'sliced' another, and banged a third into the flag, securing a lucky 'rub.' He missed two short putts, and then managed to hit Montague's ball, holing it, and leaving his own outside. The laughter of the 'gallery' gods cleft the skies, and the referee stepped forward.

'Mr Montague eighty strokes, Mr Alderson ninety-six. Mr Montague wins the tournament, and retains possession of the Hong Kong Medal.'

Curiously enough, it seemed as though the applause that followed the announcement was intended for Alderson rather than for the victor. Men with whom he had not been on speaking terms for months crowded around him to shake his hand. From being the most unpopular man in the club he had suddenly become a hero. It was incomprehensible. Last of all came up Kitty Crake. The crowd had drifted away, and they were alone. Her eyes were wet and shining, and she held out her hand. He took it, trembling inwardly.

'Well,' said she at length, 'the match is over: have you nothing to say to me?'

'But – but I lost it,' faltered Henry Alderson.

'Exactly; and in so doing you just managed to save yourself. You have evidently no idea how simply intolerable a champion at golf may be.'

'Oh, Kitty – ' he began; but they were already at the club-house.

After they were married he told her the whole story.

'But there is one thing I never understood,' he concluded, thoughtfully. 'If it really were the enemy of mankind, he certainly acted very stupidly in not getting my signature in the good old orthodox way. What had he to show for his side of the bargain?'

'Oh that is plain enough,' answered Mrs Alderson. 'So long as pride continues to be one of the seven deadly sins – '

'Well?'

'Why, the devil is quite justified in feeling cocksure of a medal-winner at golf. Poor Mr Montague!'

Three Edwardian Glimpses

GERALD BATCHELOR

The Four-Ball

THE GOLF CLUB,
CLIQUE-ON-SEA.

O N my arrival here early this morning I found a telegram from my cousin to say that he would not be able to play until the afternoon. I failed to get a game, but thinking that there would be a better chance of wiping out my late defeat at Westward Ho! if I could gain some knowledge of Jack's favourite course, I decided to try conclusions with 'Colonel Bogey,' who is always ready to start. Four men had taken up their position on the tee before me.

'Let's have a four-ball,' said the Mathematician. (I invented names to suit them.)

'Right,' said the Pot-hunter.

'What is it?' asked the Fat Man.

'Don't you know?' said the Money-grubber. 'Why, it's much better than a foursome. More fun for your money, you know. It's quite easy to explain. We play partners, as in Bridge; you and I, say, against Pots and Maths. Whoever does the best score wins the hole for his side. Then if one is out of it, he leaves it to the other. For instance, if you – ; but you'll soon see how it works out when we start.'

In each of these players I recognized a type unhappily by no means rare in Golf Clubs at the present day.

The Mathematician seemed to regard the game merely as an agreeable excuse for working out abstruse problems. He crept

37

round the links poring over card and pencil, and relinquished them with obvious reluctance when his turn came to play.

The Pot-hunter was one.of those selfish players who think only of their own game and of the low score which they hope to accomplish – and to talk about.

The Fat Man represented those who play simply for the sake of exercise, beating a ball along without any apparent object, anxious to reduce their weight rather than their handicap.

The Money-grubber, on the other hand, was certainly interested in the result of the game, but this keenness was probably to be attributed to the fact that he had 'a ball on' with each of his opponents. While things went well for his side this man never ceased to talk in a loud and swaggering tone.

'You start off,' he said, turning to Fatty; then, as the latter was addressing the ball, 'Mind that ditch on the right there, and be sure to clear the gorse. I always play for a pull here so as to – ah! topped it badly! What did I tell you? Well, I'll see what *I* can do. . . . Lor, what a slice! Mark it, Fatty, for goodness sake mark it, man. Did you see where it landed?'

'No,' said Fatty; 'you said you were playing for a pull, so I was looking the other way.'

'Come on, partner,' said Potts, 'I think we can do a bit better than that.'

But in spite of a terrific swing, he only sent the ball hopping into the long grass.

'Putting at the wrong end,' announced the caddie, who seemed privileged to make sarcastic remarks unrebuked, in return for doing duty for all the players. 'Good mashie shot,' he added, as Maths hit his drive high in the air. Then the party moved forward, and the hunt began.

Those who found their balls went on and holed out, each man playing without any regard to the position of the others. Thus the four, during their race to the green, spread out in a formation highly dangerous to all except the man in the extreme rear.

This point of vantage was usually occupied by Maths, who constantly halted to work out the score, meanwhile forgetting where his ball had gone to.

The others, after finishing the hole, returned to look for Maths' ball, and if it were found its owner was informed what score he had to beat.

On one occasion Fatty displayed such carelessness in addressing his putt that Grubber said, 'Careful, now, partner; you have this for it.'

'Don't talk on the stroke,' said Fatty, as he missed it; 'you put me off.'

'Well, but you must be careful,' said Grubber; 'you're not playing for yourself alone, remember. I've got money on this game.'

As may be imagined, the 'Colonel' and I did not progress very fast under the circumstances, but as I wanted to finish the round I lit a pipe at the turn and sat down for twenty minutes to let the four-ball go well ahead. At the twelfth tee, however, I again overtook them.

Fatty, who was lying on his back half asleep, was asking, 'How do we stand now?'

'All I know is that I am two under fives to here,' said Pots; 'might do rather a good round, I think.'

'Let's see,' said Maths, eagerly producing his calculations once again, 'I'm two down to you, and eight up on Grubber, and all square with Pots, while Pots is three up on – '

'No, no,' said Grubber, 'you must only reckon as *sides*. How do we stand in the four-ball?'

'Oh,' said Maths, 'I'll work that out in a minute. Wait a bit – '

At last the game got moving again, only to meet with another long delay on account of Grubber's losing a ball.

The other three went on, and I played a ball which landed close to where Grubber was standing.

He picked it up; then, seeming to notice me for the first time, called out, 'Is this your ball, sir?'

'Yes,' I said.

'What are you playing with?' he asked.

'A "Colonel,"' I replied.

'That's funny, so am I,' he said, 'and I'm sure this is mine because of this mark which – '

I was saved further discussion by the arrival of Pots, who returned to announce that he had played with Grubber's ball by mistake, and had lost it, as well as his own.

'Horrid nuisance,' he went on, 'that has spoilt my round, and I was doing quite a good score, too! Well, that makes you dormy, so here's the ball we had on the game. It will make up for the one you've lost. I've had enough of this and shall walk in now. Rotten bad luck losing a ball like that. I don't suppose I shall ever do such a good round again!'

The two marched off towards the Club House, arguing about their bets, and were soon followed by Fatty, who said he had 'worked up quite a respectable thirst'.

Maths, left to finish the four-ball by himself, persevered to the end, accompanied by the caddie's oft-repeated ejaculation, 'Glorious Devon!' in reference to the chunks of that county which Maths removed (but did not replace) at almost every stroke.

When he eventually finished, some three hours after starting, he had accumulated a mass of figures sufficient to exercise his mind for several days without giving him the trouble of walking round the links.

So the four-ball fizzled out.

The 'Lonesome'

'Talking of left-handed golfers,' said the Doctor, who never scruples to adulterate fact with fiction in his effort to sustain the interest of his tales, 'I know a young fellow who was trained from infancy to play golf ambidextrously. He could wield a club equally well either right- or left-handed. This, of course, necessitated his employing two caddies, with a double set of clubs. Nor was that all. Sometimes he would play right-handed backhanded, and at other times back-handed left-handed, if you follow me.'

'That must have been very confusing to his opponents,' I remarked.

'His opponents?' the story-teller repeated thoughtfully. 'Ah, now, that's the funny part about it. He never had any! Nobody would play with him, you see, on account of his peculiarities. He

entered for all the Club competitions, however, and the Committee were compelled to rate him at three separate handicaps. Under one he was permitted to play right-handed, under another left-handed, and under the third he was at liberty to address himself to each stroke in any manner that he pleased.

'It is a noteworthy fact that, whereas he was scratch in the first place, and plus two in the second, his allowance when he had the choice of playing either way was minus eight. This caused him great vexation, for it prevented him from attaining the height of his ambition, namely, to enter for the Amateur Championship. At the same time it probably saved the Championship management from a very perplexing dilemma, for they would, of course, have been compelled to draw him against three different opponents, giving him, in consequence, three chances to one against all other competitors.

'The difference in his handicaps must, I think, be put down to the fact that he never could decide in what manner he might make use of his extraordinary talents to the best advantage. He would address the ball first with one club, then he would turn round and see how it felt the other way with another club, until by constant grounding he appreciably improved the lie. People naturally objected to this, with the result that his thoughts were distracted, and however good the resultant shot might be, he was always disturbed by the doubt whether he might not have succeeded even better had he adopted the other method.

'A sad story, is it not? It all goes to show how disadvantageous it may be to overburden oneself with the good things of our golfing world.

'Well, as I was telling you, he was reduced to playing against himself, right hand versus left, and I daresay he would have enjoyed his matches well enough, had it not been for one unfortunate failing. He was a very bad loser! He couldn't *bear* to be beaten, and for a long time he arranged matters so cleverly that he halved all his matches on the last green. Now comes the tragedy.

'I happened to be passing the eighteenth green one day last week, when I noticed my poor young friend grovelling on the ground in evident distress. I was about to offer my personal assistance when I discovered the cause of his excitement. His right-hand game had been laid a dead stymie by its opponent.

'It was quite an easy putt, but he obstinately refused to accept the expert advice that I offered him, with the inevitable result that his right hand lost the match.

'The disgrace was unbearable. Just think of it. He had been beaten by himself!'

The Doctor rose to go.

'I should very much like to meet this remarkable player,' I scoffed; 'is he a member of your club?'

'He *was*,' the Doctor gravely replied; 'but now he is gone, poor fellow, gone to his long rest.'

'Dead?' I callously inquired.

'Oh, no,' the Doctor cried in seemly horror; 'he has been admitted to the Home for Unendurables, of which I have the honour to be a visiting physician.'

The Conquering Hero

The front door banged importantly, heavy boots came clumping along the hall, the Master staggered into the drawing-room and subsided with an assertive sigh of satisfaction into the softness of the central sofa.

'The day of my life,' he beamed; 'a red-letter day! Never have I played such sterling golf. . . . I was in champion form! . . . It was a regular exhibition match!'. . . .

The Mistress sat very upright, intent on her sewing.

'You didn't – '

'Yes, yes, I did,' the Master broke in. 'I won the Grand Championship Cup presented by our President, Count Ivan Offelitch, and valued, so I heard him say, at more than two hundred guineas. I keep it for six months only, of course, but just think how fine it will look on your silver table! . . . Yes, I know you asked me not to bring home any more prizes because the servants object to cleaning any extra silver, but this trophy is fashioned out of solid gold, and – well, I don't mind giving it a rub over with emery paper myself now and then. As to the responsibility, I met a man to-day who is willing to insure it at reduced rates for golfers, for a sovereign or two a month. . . . You really should have seen my play to-day. You would have been proud of me. Poor old Howker never got a sniff in the final. I was dormy four, but I so arranged it that I only won by a long putt on the last green. Doesn't do to break a fellow's heart, you know. Only a game, after all. Everybody was talking about me afterwards. You'd have blushed to hear their flattering remarks. I'd explain all about the match, only I'm afraid you wouldn't appreciate the beauties of it. Pity you don't play golf! The best part of it all is to come, though. As it was a holiday some of the members thought the visitors might like to have a sweepstake in the afternoon. The Secretary made the groundsman cut new holes during lunch, and there was quite a fair number of starters considering that the entrance fee was a quid.'

'You didn't – '

'Oh, yes, I really *had* to go in for it. You see, it would have seemed so unsporting of me not to enter, after winning the Cup in the morning. Besides, I was at the top of my form, and I know the course so well that I could play it blindfolded. It would have been foolhardy to chuck away a chance like that. I know you don't like me to play two full rounds a day, but somehow I don't feel a bit tired to-night. I was eighty-three net, and just as I came to the last green I heard that some stranger had put in a scratch score of seventy-nine, but what do you think I did?'

'You didn't – '

'Tear up my card? Not much! I put it in, and the stranger was disqualified for breaking our local rule about dropping instead of placing his ball off a wrong green. Served him right for not knowing the rules, eh? My score was the next best, so here I am a winner of something like thirty pounds! . . . Of course I must spend the money on something to do with golf or I should become a mere pro. at once. I stood a bottle of fizz to the other competitors, but I haven't decided what to do with the rest of the money yet. Perhaps I shall buy a piece of plate as a memento, or I may join that expensive new Club at Northsea. . . or treat myself to a holiday at Le Touquet . . . or Biarritz. . . . *What* a pity you don't play golf!'

The Mistress glanced at the clock, gathered up her work, and walked to the door.

'You didn't wipe your boots when you came in,' she said; 'go and do so at once.'

And the Master went.

Fog Golf

J. R. STAGG

FOR this sport there are three essentials – a fog, a golf-course, and two enthusiastic lunatics. My uncle is neither a golf-course nor a fog, but – well, every Saturday morning he is accustomed to meet his old friend Bolter in a round of golf *à outrance*. Both are twenty handicap men, but the affair is conducted with the solemnity of a championship. The stake, half a crown, never varies, and forfeit is exacted if either combatant is absent.

One Saturday he remarked at breakfast, 'I want you to help me with my clubs to-day, my boy.' (My uncle does not care for professional caddies. He dislikes their manner of smiling, in which he traces a supercilious air. Mr Bolter's must be either a greater nature or a more callous one.)

We were breakfasting by gaslight, owing to the thick yellow fog that rolled outside the windows. I seldom argue with my uncle, because he does not like it, but I looked my amazement.

'Yes, yes, I know!' he said testily. 'There *is* a little mist. Well, it may frighten Bolter into paying forfeit. He is five shillings up!'

* * *

The fog seemed to have thickened when we reached the clubhouse. It crept into your eyes and stung. My uncle found his clubs, and we groped our way towards the first tee. As we approached it, a muffled voice came to our ears out of the clinging vapour.

'I shall wait five minutes more, my lad,' it said triumphantly, as though in answer to a protest. 'After that, I shall claim forfeit!'

Two nebulous figures, a large and a little one, became discernible. They resolved into Mr Bolter and a small, red-haired, shivering caddy. At sight of each other the faces of my uncle and Mr Bolter fell. It appeared that both had hoped for forfeit. I know that *I* had, and I fancy that the caddy had been clinging to a similar wistful aspiration.

Our principals bowed coldly to each other. Off the golf-course they are old and dear friends; upon it they assume the bearing of duellists. Mr Bolter took the honour. He is the untrammelled type of driver that rises slowly upon both toes, and then leaves the ground altogether at the moment of problematical impact with the ball. His wholehearted style tends to variety. Upon this occasion chance willed that he should hit the missile.

'I felt it straight and clean,' he remarked to his caddy with pleasant optimism. 'We should have no difficulty in finding it.'

The child answered unemotionally that Mr Bolter had achieved a high slice. He added that they might find the ball, and then again they mightn't. It struck me that there was probably Scotch blood in his puny body. Mr Bolter appeared annoyed and disappointed.

My uncle relies for his drive (with perhaps misplaced confidence) upon a short, quick, powerful jerk. The tawny, remorseless fog engulfed his ball.

'A clinker, Harry!' he cried exultantly. 'One of the very best, wasn't it?'

Silently I led my uncle away to the left. Both of us, despite his incurably sanguine nature, knew that in all human probability he had pulled. He *always* pulls – except when he clean misses, or when there is more danger in slicing. Before we had gone six paces Mr Bolter and his small victim were invisible.

My instinct had not failed me. Unerringly, like some trained and patient hound, I led my uncle along the left-hand hedge, and there in the ditch we found his ball. He did not appear over-grateful to my instinct.

That first hole is always a long one. Today it seemed somehow to have been lengthened. Sooner or later you should come to a pond across which you have to play. Everything looked altered and unreal in the fog. I will say for my uncle that we did not have much trouble in finding his ball after each stroke.

'Short, straight, steady play is needed to-day, Harry!' he kept saying. . . . But somehow we did not come to the pond.

The next thing that I remember is finding ourselves upon a green. I removed the pin, and my uncle holed out and picked up with some quiet triumph. Nothing in the least offensive, you understand. But – 'Where's Bolter?' he asked, with just a trace of superiority.

'Where's the pond?' I rejoined, for a horrid doubt had come to me.

'We must have gone right round it,' my principal answered hopefully. 'Good Lord! . . . I do believe this is the *sixth* green!'

It was, and my uncle had handled his ball and lost the hole.

We made a wide cast to the right, my uncle frankly grumpy, and I more than ever convinced that a compass and someone who understood the use of it were essential.

'We must be near the pond,' he said at last. 'Do I or do I not hear splashing and violent language? Yes, by the Lord, there's some one in the water!'

It was Mr Bolter. It appeared that he had walked straight into the pond. Fortunately, from a humane point of view, to which Mr Bolter neglected to give expression, his caddy had been warned in time by his first scream. Mr Bolter cheered up on hearing that we had lost the hole; his caddy seemed to think that even tears were vain.

'You are very wet, Bolter,' my uncle said solicitously. 'If you would rather abandon the match and pay forfeit – '

'I am one up!' Mr Bolter answered very curtly, and led the way vaguely towards the second tee. We found it quite by chance after a protracted search.

Both of them drove, apparently in the same direction, but we could not find my uncle's ball. Mr Bolter, a being in whom golf brought out the basest instincts of humanity, made but a half-hearted effort to assist us in the search. He went back to his own ball and played it three times within a space of twenty yards. As we searched on, my uncle suddenly gave a short shriek of pain. A ball had sailed out of the fog and had struck him a stinging blow. A blurred shape came running towards us. It was Mr Bolter.

'I am sorry for hitting you,' he said triumphantly, 'but I am afraid I must claim the hole! You were in front of me, and the rules are clear upon the point.'

My uncle could only gobble with excusable rage. I, too, felt that the case was hard. Then his eye fell upon the missile that had struck him, and he gave a yell of triumph.

'By heaven, Bolter, you've played with my ball, more than once!' he howled. 'It's my hole, after all.'

Mr Bolter's jaw fell. 'I'm afraid you're right,' he admitted dolefully. 'That makes us all square, and – and I fancy my caddy has run home!'

'Mine is still here,' responded my uncle, glancing at me with the complacence of a successful trainer of lions. 'However, I will accept no advantage over you, Bolter – '

'Perhaps he can carry for us both?' suggested Mr Bolter hopefully.

And it was then that I followed slavishly the example set by that intelligent, red-haired Scottish child.

The Play's the Thing

W. A. DARLINGTON

JUST outside Mrs Rope's drive gates there lies a famous and exclusive golf-course, and when she turned her house into a Convalescent Home the secretary wrote offering the hospitality of the club to all officers who might come under her care.

Nevertheless, when Haynes and I first arrived, we were both too languid and feeble for any more exacting form of athletics than spillikins and jigsaws, and it was some time before the M.O. gave us permission to go on the links.

'And remember,' he added, 'gently to begin with. Stop at the thirteenth hole.'

* * *

'Of course,' I said apologetically to Haynes as we neared the club-house, 'I was pretty putrid before the war, so I shall be simply indescribable now.'

'My dear chap, this isn't going to be a match. Keep your excuses till we play serious golf. Today's just a gentle knock round. Here we are. I'll go and borrow some clubs; you get a couple of caddies.'

Five minutes later he rejoined me, carrying two sets of clubs.

'Hallo!' he remarked in surprise. 'I didn't know you'd brought your family. Introduce me.'

'Mabel,' I said, 'and Lucy – our caddies.'

'Girls?'

'They have that appearance. Why not?'

'They'll cramp my style horribly; I like to be free.'

'Can't you be free in French for once?'

'Most unsatisfying. Why didn't you get boys?'

'The caddy-master says (*a*) girls are better; (*b*) he has no boys; (*c*) all the boys he has are booked by plutocrats with season tickets.'

'Oh, all right. Here are your clubs – the pro. gave me the only two sets he had available. You're a bit taller than I am, so I've given you the long ones.'

I looked at them critically.

'Doesn't a pair of stilts go with them?' I asked.

'Well, mine are worse. Just a bundle of toothpicks. Here, catch hold, Lucy.'

Mabel teed up for me. I selected a driver about the length of a telegraph pole and swept my ball away. It stopped just short of the first bunker.

Haynes bent himself double to address his ball, but straightened up while swinging and missed it by a foot. At the second attempt he hooked it over square-leg's head on to the fairway of the eighteenth hole.

'*Sacré bleu!*' he said with very fair freedom, 'I'm not going all that way after it. Lucy, run and fetch it, there's a dear.'

Lucy, highly scandalized at the idea of losing a hole so tamely, started off; Mabel and Haynes and I went after my ball.

I took the mashie, because I distrusted my ability to carry the bunker with another telegraph pole. That mashie would have been about the right length for me if I could have stood on a chair while making my stroke. As it was it entered the ground two feet behind the ball and emerged, with a superb divot, just in front.

'Aren't there *any* short clubs in the bag, Mabel?' I asked. She handed me a straight-faced putter . . .

Five strokes later I picked my ball up out of the bunker.

'I'm over-exerting myself,' I said. 'We'll call that hole a half.'

Neither of us was satisfied with his tee shot at the next hole. I picked my ball out of a gorse-bush, and Haynes rescued his from a drain. Then we strolled amicably towards the third tee. Our caddies, unused to such methods, followed reluctantly.

'Was that 'ole 'alved, too, sir?' piped Mabel with anxious interest.

'It's a nice point. I hardly know. Why?'

She hung her head and blushed. A sudden suspicion struck me.

'Mabel,' I said sternly, 'are you – *can* you be – *betting* on this game?'

'Yes, sir,' she answered with a touch of defiance. 'Boys always does.'

I told Haynes, who appeared profoundly shocked.

'Good G – ? I mean, *Mon dieu!*' he exclaimed. 'What are we doing?'

'Surely you can't hold us responsible? The child's parents . . .'

'I don't mean *that*, you ass. Here we have the innocent public putting its money on our play, and we're treating the whole thing as a joke. This has got to be a match, after all. A woman's fortune hangs upon the issue – doesn't it, Lucy?'

'Yes, sir,' she answered without comprehension.

From this point the game became a grim struggle. I won the third hole in seventeen, but Haynes took the fourth in nineteen to my twenty-two.

At the fifth I noticed a pond guarding the green. I carefully circumvented this with my faithful putter and holed out in my smallest score of the round so far.

'Hi!' shouted Haynes. 'How many?' He had been having a little hockey practice by himself in the rough, and was now preparing to play an approach shot across the pond.

'Twelve!'

'Then I've this for the hole,' he yelled, and topped his ball gently into the water. . . .

So it went on – what the papers call a ding-dong struggle.

Suffice it to say that at the twelfth I was dormy one and in a state of partial collapse.

The thirteenth is a short hole. You drive from a kind of pulpit, and the green is below you, protected by large stiff-backed bunkers like pews.

'Last hole, thank Heaven,' panted Haynes. 'I couldn't bear much more. I'm all of a dither as it is.'

Mabel, twittering with excitement, teed up. I looked at the green lying invitingly below and took that gigantic putter. The ball, struck with all my little remaining strength, flew straight towards the biggest bunker, scored a direct hit on the top of it, bounced high in the air – and trickled on to the green.

Haynes invoked the Deity (even at that stressful moment, to his eternal credit, in French) and took his miniature driver. His ball, hit much too hard, pitched in the same bunker, crossed it, climbed up the face of it, and joined mine on the green. Utterly unnerved, we toddled down and took out putts. Haynes, through sheer luck (as he admits), laid his ball stone dead; I had a brain-storm and overran the hole, leaving myself a thirty-foot putt for the match. I took long and careful aim, but my hands were shaking pitifully. The ball started on a grotesquely wrong line, turned on a rise in the ground, cannoned off a worm-cast and plopped into the tin. Mabel gave a shriek of joy, and Lucy – well, I regret to say that Lucy made use of a terse expression the

French equivalent of which her employer had been at great pains to remember. Haynes and I lay flat on the ground, overcome as much by emotion as by our physical weakness.

At last I struggled to a sitting posture.

'Mabel,' I croaked, 'I shall want at least ten per cent commission for that. How much have you won?'

'Please, sir,' she cooed happily, 'a 'a'p'ny, sir.'

The Sweet Shot

E. C. BENTLEY

'No; I happened to be abroad at the time,' Philip Trent said. 'I wasn't in the way of seeing the English papers, so until I came here this week I never heard anything about your mystery.'

Captain Royden, a small, spare, brown-faced man, was engaged in the delicate – and forbidden – task of taking his automatic telephone instrument to pieces. He now suspended his labours and reached for the tobacco jar. The large window of his office in the Kempshill clubhouse looked down upon the eighteenth green of that delectable golf course, and his eye roved over the whin-clad slopes beyond as he called on his recollection.

'Well, if you call it a mystery,' he said as he filled a pipe. 'Some people do, because they like mysteries, I suppose. For instance, Colin Hunt, the man you're staying with, calls it that. Others won't have it, and say there was a perfectly natural explanation. I could tell you as much as anybody could about it, I dare say.'

'As being secretary here, you mean?'

'Not only that. I was one of the two people who were in at the death, so to speak – or next door to it,' Captain Royden said. He limped to the mantelshelf and took down a silver box embossed on the lid with the crest and mottoes of the Corps of Royal Engineers. 'Try one of these cigarettes, Mr Trent. If you'd like to hear the yarn, I'll give it you. You have heard something about Arthur Freer, I suppose?'

'Hardly anything,' Trent said. 'I just gathered that he wasn't a very popular character.'

'No,' Captain Royden said with reserve. 'Did they tell you he was my brother-in-law? No? Well, now, it happened about four months ago, on a Monday – let me see – yes, the second Monday in May. Freer had a habit of playing nine holes before breakfast. Barring Sundays – he was strict about Sunday – he did it most days, even in the beastliest weather, going round all alone usually, carrying his own clubs, studying every shot as if his life depended on it. That helped to make him the very good player he was. His handicap here was two, and at Undershaw he used to be scratch, I believe.

'At a quarter to eight he'd be on the first tee, and by nine he'd be back at his house – it's only a few minutes from here. That Monday morning he started off as usual –'

'And at the usual time?'

'Just about. He had spent a few minutes in the clubhouse blowing up the steward about some trifle. And that was the last time he was seen alive by anybody – near enough to speak to, that is. No one else went off the first tee until a little after nine, when I started round with Browson – he's our local padre; I had been having breakfast with him at the Vicarage. He's got a game leg, like me, so we often play together when he can fit it in.

'We had holed out on the first green, and were walking on to the next tee, when Browson said, "Great Scot! Look there. Something's happened." He pointed down the fairway of the second hole; and there we could see a man lying sprawled on the turf, face down and motionless. Now there is this point about the second hole – the first half of it is in a dip in the land, just deep enough to be out of sight from any other point on the course, unless you're standing right above it – you'll see when you go round yourself. Well, on the tee, you *are* right above it; and we saw this man lying. We ran to the spot.

'It was Freer, as I had known it must be at that hour. He was dead, lying in a disjointed sort of way no live man could have lain in. His clothing was torn to ribbons, and it was singed too. So was his hair – he used to play bareheaded – and his face and hands. His bag of clubs was lying a few yards away, and the brassie, which he had just been using, was close by the body.

'There wasn't any wound showing, and I had seen far worse things often enough, but the padre was looking sickish, so I asked him to go back to the clubhouse and send for a doctor and the police while I mounted guard. They weren't long coming, and after they had done their job the body was taken away in an ambulance. Well, that's about all I can tell you at first hand, Mr Trent. If you are staying with Hunt, you'll have heard about the inquest and all that probably.'

Trent shook his head. 'No,' he said. 'Colin was just beginning to tell me, after breakfast this morning, about Freer having been killed on the course in some incomprehensible way, when a man came to see him about something. So, as I was going to apply for a fortnight's run of the course, I thought I would ask you about the affair.'

'All right,' Captain Royden said. 'I can tell you about the inquest anyhow – had to be there to speak my own little piece, about finding the body. As for what happened to Freer, the medical evidence was rather confusing. It was agreed that he had been killed by some tremendous shock, which had jolted his whole system to pieces and dislocated several joints, but had been not quite violent enough to cause any visible wound. Apart from that, there was a disagreement. Freer's own doctor, who saw the body first, declared he must have been struck by lightning. He said it was true there hadn't been a thunderstorm, but that there had been thunder about all that weekend, and that sometimes lightning did act in that way. But the police surgeon, Collins, said there would be no such displacement of the organs from a lightning stroke, even if it did ever happen that way in our climate, which he doubted. And he said that if it had been lightning, it would have struck the steel-headed clubs; but the clubs lay there in their bag quite undamaged. Collins thought there must have been some kind of explosion, though he couldn't suggest what kind.'

Trent shook his head. 'I don't suppose that impressed the court,' he said. 'All the same, it may have been all the honest opinion he could give.' He smoked in silence a few moments, while Captain Royden attended to the troubles of his telephone instrument with a camel-hair brush. 'But surely,' Trent said at length, 'if there had been such an explosion as that, somebody would have heard the sound of it.'

59

'Lots of people would have heard it,' Captain Royden answered. 'But there you are, you see – nobody notices the sound of explosions just about here. There's the quarry on the other side of the road there, and anytime after 7 A.M. there's liable to be a noise of blasting.'

'A dull, sickening thud?'

'Jolly sickening,' Captain Royden said, 'for all of us living nearby. And so that point wasn't raised. Well, Collins is a very sound man; but as you say, his evidence didn't really explain the thing, and the other fellow's did, whether it was right or wrong. Besides, the coroner and the jury had heard about a bolt from a clear sky, and the notion appealed to them. Anyhow, they brought it in death from misadventure.'

'Which nobody could deny, as the song says,' Trent remarked. 'And was there no other evidence?'

'Yes, some. But Hunt can tell you about it as well as I can; he was there. I shall have to ask you to excuse me now,' Captain Royden said. 'I have an appointment in the town. The steward will sign you on for a fortnight, and probably get you a game too, if you want one today.'

Colin Hunt and his wife, when Trent returned to their house for luncheon, were very willing to complete the tale. The verdict, they declared, was tripe. Dr Collins knew his job, whereas Dr Hoyle was an old footler, and Freer's death had never been reasonably explained.

As for the other evidence, it had, they agreed, been interesting, though it didn't help at all. Freer had been seen after he had played his tee shot at the second hole, when he was walking down to the bottom of the dip toward the spot where he met his death.

'But according to Royden,' Trent said, 'that was a place where he couldn't be seen, unless one was right above him.'

'Well, this witness *was* right above him,' Hunt rejoined. 'Over one thousand feet above him, so he said. He was an RAF man, piloting a bomber from Bexford Camp, not far from here. He was up doing some sort of exercise, and passed over the course just at that time. He didn't know Freer but he spotted a man walking down from the second tee, because he was the only living soul visible on the course. Gossett, the other man in the plane, is a temporary member here, and he did know Freer quite well – or as well as anybody cared to know him – but he never saw him. However, the pilot was quite clear that he saw a man just at the time in question, and they took his evidence so as to prove that Freer was absolutely alone just before his death. The only other person who saw Freer was another man who knew him well; used to be a caddy here, and then got a job at the quarry. He was at work on the hillside, and he watched Freer play the first hole and go on to the second – nobody with him, of course.'

'Well, that was pretty well-established then,' Trent remarked. 'He was about as alone as he could be, it seems. Yet something happened somehow.'

Mrs Hunt sniffed sceptically, and lighted a cigarette. 'Yes, it did,' she said. 'However, I didn't worry much about it, for one. Edith – Mrs Freer, that is: Royden's sister – must have had a terrible life of it with a man like that. Not that she ever said anything – she wouldn't. She is not that sort.'

'She is a jolly good sort, anyhow,' Hunt declared.

'Yes, she is: too good for most men. I can tell you.' Mrs Hunt added for the benefit of Trent, 'if Colin ever took to cursing me and knocking me about, my well-known loyalty wouldn't stand the strain for very long.'

'That's why I don't do it. It's the fear of exposure that makes me the perfect husband, Phil. She would tie a can to me before I knew what was happening. As for Edith, it's true she never said anything, but the change in her since it happened tells the story well enough. Since she's been living with her brother she has been looking far better and happier than she ever succeeded in doing while Freer was alive.'

'She won't be living with him for very long, I dare say,' Mrs Hunt intimated darkly.

'No. I'd marry her myself if I had the chance,' Hunt agreed cordially.

'Pooh! You wouldn't be in the first six,' his wife said. 'It will be Rennie, or Gossett, or possibly Sandy Butler – you'll see. But perhaps you've had enough of the local tittle-tattle, Phil. Did you fix up a game for this afternoon?'

'Yes – with the Jarman Professor of Chemistry in the University of Cambridge,' Trent said. 'He looked at me as if he thought a bath of vitriol would do me good, but he agreed to play me.'

'You've got a tough job,' Hunt observed. 'I believe he is almost as old as he looks, but he is a devil at the short game, and he knows the course blindfold, which you don't. And he isn't so cantankerous as he pretends to be. By the way, he was the man who saw the finish of the last shot Freer ever played – a sweet shot if ever there was one. Get him to tell you.'

'I shall try to,' Trent said. 'The steward told me about that, and that was why I asked the professor for a game.'

Colin Hunt's prediction was fulfilled that afternoon. Professor Hyde, receiving five strokes, was one up at the seventeenth, and at the last hole sent down a four-foot putt to win the match. As they left the green he remarked, as if in answer to something Trent had that moment said, 'Yes, I can tell you a curious circumstance about Freer's death.'

Trent's eye brightened; for the professor had not said a dozen words during their game, and Trent's tentative allusion to the subject after the second hole had been met merely by an intimidating grunt.

'I saw the finish of the last shot he played,' the old gentleman went on, 'without seeing the man himself at all. A lovely brassie it was, too – though lucky. Rolled to within two feet of the pin.'

Trent considered. 'I see,' he said, 'what you mean. You were near the second green, and the ball came over the ridge and ran down to the hole.'

'Just so,' Professor Hyde said. 'That's how you play it – if you can. You might have done it yourself today, if your second shot had been thirty yards longer. I've never done it; but Freer often did. After a really good drive, you play a long second, blind, over the ridge; and with a perfect shot, you may get the green. Well, my house is quite near that green. I was pottering about in the garden before breakfast, and just as I happened to be looking toward the green a ball came hopping down the slope and trickled right across to the hole. Of course, I knew whose it must be – Freer always came along about that time. If it had been anyone else, I'd have waited to see him get his three, and congratulate him. As it was, I went indoors, and didn't hear of his death until long afterward.'

'And you never saw him play the shot?' Trent said thoughtfully.

The professor turned a choleric blue eye on him. 'How the deuce could I?' he said huffily. 'I can't see through a mass of solid earth.'

'I know, I know,' Trent said. 'I was only trying to follow your mental process. Without seeing him play the shot, you knew it was his second – you say he would have been putting for a three. And you said too – didn't you? – that it was a brassie shot.'

'Simply because, my young friend' – the professor was severe – 'I happened to know the man's game. I had played that nine holes with him before breakfast often, until one day he lost his temper more than usual, and made himself impossible. I knew he practically always carried the ridge with his second – I won't say he always got the green – and his brassie was the only club that would do it. It is conceivable, I admit,' Professor Hyde added a little stiffly, 'that some mishap took place and that the shot in question was not actually Freer's second; but it did not occur to me to allow for that highly speculative contingency.'

On the next day, after those playing a morning round were started on their perambulation, Trent indulged himself with an hour's practice, mainly on the unsurveyed stretch of the second hole. Afterward he had a word with the caddy master; then visited the professional's shop, and won the regard of that expert by furnishing himself with a new midiron. Soon he brought up the subject of the last shot played by Arthur Freer. A dozen times that morning, he said, he had tried, after a satisfying drive, to reach the green with his second; but in vain. Fergus MacAdam shook his head. Not many, he said, could strike the ball with yon force. He could get there himself, whiles, but never for certainty. Mr Freer had the strength, and he kenned how to use it forbye.

What sort of clubs, Trent asked, had Freer preferred? 'Lang and heavy, like himsel'. Noo ye mention it,' MacAdam said, 'I hae them here. They were brocht here after the ahccident.' He reached up to the top of a rack. 'Ay, here they are. They shouldna be, of course; but naebody came to claim them, and it juist slippit ma mind.'

Trent, extracting the brassie, looked thoughtfully at the heavy head with the strip of hard white material inlaid in the face. 'It's a powerful weapon, sure enough,' he remarked.

'Ay, for a man that could control it,' MacAdam said. 'I dinna care for yon ivorine face mysel'. Some fowk think it gies mair reseelience, ye ken; but there's naething in it.'

'He didn't get it from you, then,' Trent suggested, still closely examining the head.

'Ay, but he did. I had a lot down from Nelsons while the fashion for them was on. Ye'll find my name,' MacAdam added, 'stampit on the wood in the usual place, if yer een are seein' richt.'

'Well, I don't – that's just it. The stamp is quite illegible.'

'Tod! Let's see,' the professional said, taking the club in hand. 'Guid reason for its being illegible,' he went on after a brief scrutiny. 'It's been obleeterated – that's easy seen. Who ever saw sic a daft-like thing! The wood has juist been crushed some gait – in a vice, I wouldna wonder. Noo, why would onybody want to dae a thing like yon?'

'Unaccountable, isn't it?' Trent said. 'Still, it doesn't matter, I suppose. And anyhow, we shall never know.'

It was twelve days later that Trent, looking in at the open door of the secretary's office, saw Captain Royden happily engaged with the separated parts of some mechanism in which coils of wire appeared to be the leading motive.

'I see you're busy,' Trent said.

'Come in! Come in!' Royden said heartily. 'I can do this any-time – another hour's work will finish it.' He laid down a pair of sharp-nosed pliers. 'The electricity people have just changed us over to A.C., and I've got to rewind the motor of our vacuum cleaner. Beastly nuisance,' he added, looking down affection-ately at the bewildering jumble of disarticulated apparatus on his table.

'You bear your sorrow like a man,' Trent remarked; and Royden laughed as he wiped his hands on a towel.

'Yes,' he said, 'I do love tinkering about with mechanical jobs, and if I do say it myself, I'd rather do a thing like this with my own hands than risk having it faultily done by a careless workman. Too many of them about. Why, about a year ago the company sent a man here to fit a new main fuse box, and he made a short-circuit with his screwdriver that knocked him right across the kitchen and might very well have killed him.' He reached down his cigarette box and offered it to Trent, who helped himself; then looked down thoughtfully at the device on the lid.

'Thanks very much. When I saw this box before, I put you down for an R.E. man. *Ubique*, and *Quo fas et gloria ducunt*. H'm! I wonder why Engineers were given that motto in particular.'

'Lord knows,' the captain said. 'In my experience, Sappers don't exactly go where right and glory lead. The dirtiest of all the jobs and precious little of the glory – that's what they get.'

'Still, they have the consolation,' Trent pointed out, 'of feeling that they are at home in a scientific age, and that all the rest of the Army are amateurs compared with them. That's what one of them once told me, anyhow. Well now, Captain, I have to be off this evening. I've looked in just to say how much I've enjoyed myself here.'

'Very glad you did,' Captain Royden said. 'You'll come again, I hope, now you know that the golf here is not so bad.'

'I like it immensely. Also the members. And the secretary.' Trent paused to light his cigarette. 'I found the mystery rather interesting, too.'

Captain Royden's eyebrows lifted slightly. 'You mean about Freer's death? So you made up your mind it *was* a mystery.'

'Why yes,' Trent said. 'Because I made up my mind he had been killed by somebody, and probably killed intentionally. Then, when I had looked into the thing a little, I washed out the "probably".

Captain Royden took up a penknife from his desk and began mechanically to sharpen a pencil. 'So you don't agree with the coroner's jury?'

'No, as the verdict seems to have been meant to rule out murder or any sort of human agency, I don't. The lightning idea, which apparently satisfied them, or some of them, was not a very bright one, I thought. I was told what Dr Collins had said against it at the inquest; and it seemed to me he had disposed of it completely when he said that Freer's clubs, most of them steel ones, were quite undamaged. A man carrying his clubs puts them down, when he plays a shot, a few feet away at most; yet Freer was supposed to have been electrocuted without any notice having been taken of them, so to speak.'

'H'm! No, it doesn't seem likely. I don't know that that quite decides the point, though,' the captain said. 'Lightning plays funny tricks, you know. I've seen a small tree struck when it was surrounded by trees twice the size. All the same, I quite agree there didn't seem to be any sense in the lightning notion. It was thundery weather, but there wasn't any storm that morning in this neighbourhood.'

'Just so. But when I considered what had been said about Freer's clubs, it suddenly occurred to me that nobody had said anything about *the* club, so far as my information about the inquest went. It seemed clear, from what you and the parson saw, that he had just played a shot with his brassie when he was struck down; it was lying near him, not in the bag. Besides, old Hyde actually saw the ball he had hit roll down the slope onto the green. Now, it's a good rule to study every little detail when you are on a problem of this kind. There weren't many left to study, of course, since the thing had happened four months before; but I knew Freer's clubs must be somewhere, and I thought of one or two places where they were likely to have been taken, in the circumstances, so I tried them. First, I reconnoitered the caddy master's shed, asking if I could leave my bag there for a day or two; but I was told that the regular place to leave them was the pro's shop. So I went and had a chat with MacAdam, and sure enough it soon came out that Freer's bag was still in his rack. I had a look at the clubs, too.'

'And did you notice anything peculiar about them?' Captain Royden asked.

'Just one little thing. But it was enough to set me thinking, and next day I drove up to London, where I paid a visit to Nelsons, the sporting outfitters. You know the firm, of course.'

Captain Royden, carefully fining down the point of his pencil, nodded. 'Everybody knows Nelsons.'

'Yes, and MacAdam, I knew, had an account there for his stocks. I wanted to look over some clubs of a particular make – a brassie, with a slip of ivorine let into the face, such as they had supplied to MacAdam. Freer had had one of them from him.'

Again Royden nodded.

'I saw the man who shows clubs at Nelsons. We had a talk, and then – you know how little things come out in the course of conversation –'

'Especially,' put in the captain with a cheerful grin, 'when the conversation is being steered by an expert.'

'You flatter me,' Trent said. 'Anyhow, it did transpire that a club of that particular make had been bought some months before by a customer whom the man was able to remember. Why he remembered him was because, in the first place, he insisted on a club of rather unusual length and weight – much too long and heavy for himself to use, as he was neither a tall man nor of powerful build. The salesman had suggested as much in a delicate way; but the customer said no, he knew exactly what suited him, and he bought the club and took it away with him.'

'Rather an ass, I should say,' Royden observed thoughtfully.

'I don't think he was an ass, really. He was capable of making a mistake, though, like the rest of us. There were some other things, by the way, that the salesman recalled about him. He had a slight limp, and he was, or had been, an Army officer. The salesman was an ex-Service man, and he couldn't be mistaken, he said, about that.'

Captain Royden had drawn a sheet of paper toward him, and was slowly drawing little geometrical figures as he listened. 'Go on, Mr Trent,' he said quietly.

'Well, to come back to the subject of Freer's death. I think he was killed by someone who knew Freer never played on Sunday, so that his clubs would be – or ought to be, shall we say? – in his locker all that day. All the following night, too, of course – in case the job took a long time. And I think this man was in a position to have access to the lockers in this clubhouse at any time he chose, and to possess a master key to those lockers. I think he was a skilful amateur craftsman. I think he had a good practical knowledge of high explosives. There is a branch of the Army' – Trent paused a moment and looked at the cigarette box on the table – 'in which that sort of knowledge is specially necessary, I believe.'

Hastily, as if just reminded of the duty of hospitality, Royden lifted the lid of the box and pushed it toward Trent. 'Do have another,' he urged.

Trent did so with thanks. 'They have to have it in the Royal Engineers,' he went on, 'because – so I'm told – demolition work is an important part of their job.'

'Quite right,' Captain Royden observed, delicately shading one side of a cube.

'*Ubique!*' Trent mused, staring at the box lid. 'If you are "everywhere," I take it you can be in two places at the same time. You could kill a man in one place, and at the same time be having breakfast with a friend a mile away. Well, to return to our subject yet once more; you can see the kind of idea I was led to form about what happened to Freer. I believe that his brassie was taken from his locker on the Sunday before his death. I believe the ivorine face of it was taken off and a cavity hollowed out behind it; and in that cavity a charge of explosive was placed. Where it came from I don't know, for it isn't the sort of thing that is easy to come by, I imagine.'

'Oh, there would be no difficulty about that,' the captain remarked. 'If this man you're speaking of knew all about H.E., as you say, he could have compounded the stuff himself from materials anybody can buy. For instance, he could easily make tetranitroaniline – that would be just the thing for him, I should say.'

'I see. Then perhaps there would be a tiny detonator attached to the inner side of the ivorine face, so that a good smack with the brassie would set it off. Then the face would be fixed on again. It would be a delicate job, because the weight of the club head would have to be exactly right. The feel and balance of the club would have to be just the same as before the operation.'

'A delicate job, yes,' the captain agreed. 'But not an impossible one. There would be rather more to it than you say, as a matter of fact; the face would have to be shaved down thin, for instance. Still, it could be done.'

'Well, I imagine it done. Now, this man I have in mind knew there was no work for a brassie at the short first hole, and that the first time it would come out of the bag was at the second hole, down at the bottom of the dip, where no one could see what happened. What certainly did happen was that Freer played a sweet shot, slap on to the green. What else happened at the same moment we don't know for certain, but we can make a reasonable guess. And then, of course, there's the question of what happened to the club – or what was left of it; the handle, say. But it isn't a difficult question, I think, if we remember how the body was found.'

'How do you mean?' Royden asked.

'I mean, by whom it was found. One of the two players who found it was too much upset to notice very much. He hurried back to the clubhouse; and the other was left alone with the body for, as I estimate it, at least fifteen minutes. When the police came on the scene, they found lying near the body a perfectly good brassie, an unusually long and heavy club, exactly like Freer's brassie in every respect except one. The name stamped on the wood of the club head had been obliterated by crushing. That name, I think, was not F MacAdam, but W J Nelson; and the club had been taken out of a bag that was not Freer's – a bag which had the remains, if any, of Freer's brassie at the bottom of it. And I believe that's all.' Trent got to his feet and stretched his arms. 'You can see what I meant when I said I found the mystery interesting.'

For some moments Captain Royden gazed thoughtfully out of the window; then he met Trent's inquiring eye. 'If there was such a fellow as you imagine,' he said coolly, 'he seems to have been careful enough – lucky enough too, if you like – to leave nothing at all of what you could call proof against him. And probably he had personal and private reasons for what he did. Suppose that somebody whom he was much attached to was in the power of a foul-tempered, bullying brute; and suppose he found that the bullying had gone to the length of physical violence; and suppose that the situation was hell by day and by night to this man of yours; and suppose there was no way on earth of putting an end to it except the way he took. Yes, Mr Trent, suppose all that!'

'I will – I do!' Trent said. 'That man – if he exists at all – must have been driven pretty hard, and what he did is no business of mine anyway. And now – still in the conditional mood – suppose I take myself off.'

The Golfomaniac

STEPHEN LEACOCK

WE ride in and out pretty often together, he and I, on a suburban train.

That's how I came to talk to him. 'Fine morning,' I said as I sat down beside him yesterday and opened a newspaper.

'Great!' he answered. 'The grass is drying out fast now and the greens will soon be all right to play.'

'Yes,' I said, 'the sun is getting higher and the days are decidedly lengthening.'

'For the matter of that,' said my friend, 'a man could begin to play at six in the morning easily. In fact, I've often wondered that there is little golf played before breakfast. We happened to be talking about golf, a few of us last night – I don't know how it came up – and we were saying that it seems a pity that some of the best part of the day, say, from five o'clock to seven-thirty, is never used.'

'That's true,' I answered, and then, to shift the subject, I said, looking out of the window:

'It's a pretty bit of country just here, isn't it?'

'It is,' he replied, 'but it seems a shame they make no use of it – just a few market gardens and things like that. Why, I noticed along here acres and acres of just glass – some kind of houses for plants or something – and whole fields of lettuce and things like that. It's a pity they don't make something of it. I was remarking only the other day as I came along in the train with a friend of mine, that you could easily lay out an eighteen-hole course anywhere here.'

'Could you?' I said.

'Oh, yes. This ground, you know, is an excellent light soil to shovel up into bunkers. You could drive some ditches through it and make one or two deep holes – the kind they have on some of the French links. In fact, improve it to any extent.'

I glanced at my morning paper. 'I see,' I said, 'that it is again rumoured that Lloyd George is at least definitely to retire.'

'Funny thing about Lloyd George,' answered my friend. 'He never played, you know; most extraordinary thing – don't you think? – for a man in his position. Balfour, of course, was very different: I remember when I was over in Scotland last summer I had the honour of going around the course at Dumfries just after Lord Balfour. Pretty interesting experience, don't you think?'

'Were you over on business?' I asked.

'No, not exactly. I went to get a golf ball, a particular golf ball. Of course, I didn't go merely for that. I wanted to get a mashie as well. The only way, you know, to get just what you want is to go to Scotland for it.'

'Did you see much of Scotland?'

'I saw it all. I was on the links at St Andrews and I visited the Loch Lomond course and the course at Inverness. In fact, I saw everything.'

'It's an interesting country, isn't it, historically?'

'It certainly is. Do you know they have played there for over five hundred years! Think of it! They showed me at Loch Lomond the place where they said Robert the Bruce played the Red Douglas (I think that was the other party – at any rate, Bruce was one of them), and I saw where Bonnie Prince Charlie disguised himself as a caddie when the Duke of Cumberland's soldiers were looking for him. Oh, it's a wonderful country historically.'

After that I let a silence intervene so as to get a new start. Then I looked up again from my newspaper.

'Look at this,' I said pointing to a headline, *United States Navy Ordered Again to Nicaragua*. 'Looks like more trouble, doesn't it?'

'Did you see in the paper a while back,' said my companion, 'that the United States Navy Department is now making golf compulsory at the training school at Annapolis? That's progressive, isn't it? I suppose it will have to mean shorter cruises at sea; in fact, probably lessen the use of the Navy for sea purposes. But it will raise the standard.'

'I suppose so,' I answered. 'Did you read about this extraordinary murder case in Long Island?'

'No,' he said. 'I never read murder cases. They don't interest me. In fact, I think this whole continent is getting over-preoccupied with them – '

'Yes, but this case had such odd features – '

'Oh, they all have,' he replied, with an air of weariness. 'Each one is just boomed by the papers to make a sensation – '

'I know, but in this case it seems that the man was killed with a blow from a golf club.'

'What's that? Eh, what's that? Killed with a blow from a golf club!'

'Yes, some kind of club – '

'I wonder if it was an iron – let me see the paper – though, for the matter of that, I imagine that a blow from even a wooden driver, let alone one of the steel-handled drivers – where does it say it? – pshaw, it only just says "a blow with a golf club". It's a pity the papers don't write these things up with more detail, isn't it? But perhaps it will be better in the afternoon paper – '

'Have you played golf much?' I inquired. I saw it was no use to talk of anything else.

'No,' answered my companion, 'I am sorry to say I haven't. You see, I began late. I've only played twenty years, twenty-one if you count the year that's beginning in May. I don't know what I was doing. I wasted about half my life. In fact, it wasn't till I was well over thirty that I caught on to the game. I suppose a lot of us look back over our lives that way and realize what we have lost.

'And even as it is,' he continued, 'I don't get much chance to play. At the best I can only manage about four afternoons a week, though of course I get most of Saturday and all Sunday. I get my holiday in the summer, but it's only a month, and that's nothing. In the winter I manage to take a run south for a game once or twice and perhaps a little swack at it around Easter, but only a week at a time. I'm too busy – that's the plain truth of it.' He sighed. 'It's hard to leave the office before two,' he said. 'Something always turns up.'

And after that he went on to tell me something of the technique of the game, illustrate it with a golf ball on the seat of the car, and the peculiar mental poise needed for driving, and the neat, quick action of the wrist (he showed me how it worked) that is needed to undercut a ball so that it flies straight up in the air. He explained to me how you can do practically anything with a golf ball, provided that you keep you mind absolutely poised and your eye in shape, and your body a trained machine. It appears that even Bobby Jones of Atlanta and people like that fall short very often from the high standard set by my golfing friend in the suburban car.

So, later in the day, meeting someone in my club who was a person of authority on such things, I made inquiry about my friend. 'I rode into town with Llewellyn Smith,' I said. 'I think he belongs to your golf club. He's a great player, isn't he?'

'A great player!' laughed the expert. 'Llewellyn Smith? Why, he can hardly hit a ball! And anyway, he's only played about twenty years!'

Scratch Man

P. G. WODEHOUSE

A devout expression had come into the face of the young man in plus fours who sat with the Oldest Member on the terrace overlooking the ninth green. With something of the abruptness of a conjurer taking a rabbit out of a hat he drew a photograph from his left breast pocket and handed it to his companion. The Sage inspected it thoughtfully.

'This is the girl you were speaking of?'

'Yes.'

'You love her?'

'Madly.'

'And how do you find it affects your game?'

'I've started shaking a bit.'

The Oldest Member nodded.

'I am sorry,' he said, 'but not surprised. Either that or missing short putts is what generally happens on these occasions. I doubt if golfers ought to fall in love. I have known it to cost men ten shots in a medal round. They think of the girl and forget to keep their eyes on the ball. On the other hand, there was the case of Harold Pickering.'

'I don't think I've met him.'

'He was before your time. He took a cottage here a few years ago. His handicap was fourteen. Yet within a month of his arrival love had brought him down to scratch.'

'Quick service.'

'Very. He went back eventually to a shaky ten, but the fact remains. But for his great love, he would not have become even temporarily a scratch man.'

I had seen Harold Pickering in and about the clubhouse (said the Oldest Member) for some time before I made his acquaintance, and there was something in his manner which suggested that sooner or later he would be seeking me out and telling me the story of his life. For some reason, possibly because I have white whiskers, I seem to act on men with stories of their lives to tell like catnip on cats. And sure enough, I was sitting on this terrace one evening, enjoying a quiet gin and ginger, when he sidled up, coughed once or twice like a sheep with bronchitis and gave me the works.

His was a curious and romantic tale. He was by profession a partner in a publishing house, and shortly before his arrival here he had gone to negotiate with John Rockett for the purchase of his Reminiscences.

The name John Rockett will, of course, be familiar to you. If you are a student of history, you will recall that he was twice British Amateur Champion and three times runner-up in the Open. He had long retired from competition golf and settled down to a life of leisured ease, and when Harold Pickering presented himself he found the great veteran celebrating his silver wedding. All the family were there – his grandmother, now ageing a little but in her day a demon with the gutty ball; his wife, at one time British Ladies Champion; his three sons, Sandwich, Hoylake and St Andrew; and his two daughters, Troon and Prestwick. He called his children after the courses on which he had won renown, and they did not disgrace the honoured names. They were all scratch.

In a gathering so august, you might have supposed that a sense of what was fitting would have kept a fourteen-handicap man from getting above himself. But passion knows no class distinctions. Ten minutes after his arrival, Harold Pickering had fallen in love with Troon Rockett, with a fervour which could not have been more whole-hearted if he had been playing to plus two. And a week later he put his fortune to the test, to win or lose it all.

'Of course, I was mad . . . mad,' he said, moodily chewing the ham sandwich he had ordered, for he had only a light lunch. 'How could I suppose that a girl who was scratch – the sister of scratch men – the daughter of an amateur champion – would stoop to a fellow like me? Even as I started to speak, I saw the horror and amazement on her face. Well, when I say speak, I didn't exactly speak, I sort of gargled. But it was enough. She rose quickly and left the room. And I came here – '

'To forget her?'

'Talk sense,' said Harold Pickering shortly. 'I came to try to make myself worthy of her. I intended to get myself down to scratch, if it choked me. I heard that your pro here was the best instructor in the country, so I signed the lease for a cottage, seized my clubs and raced round to his shop . . . only to discover what?'

'That he has broken his leg?'

'Exactly. What a sensible, level-headed pro wants to break his leg for is more than I can imagine. But there it was. No chance of any lessons from him.'

'It must have been a shock for you.'

'I was stunned. It seemed to me that this was the end. But now things have brightened considerably. Do you know a Miss Flack?'

I did indeed. Agnes Flack was one of the recognized sights of the place. One pointed her out to visitors together with the Lover's Leap, the waterfall and the curious rock formation near the twelfth tee. Built rather on the lines of the village blacksmith, she had for many seasons been the undisputed female champion of the club. She had the shoulders of an all-in wrestler, the breezy self-confidence of a sergeant-major and a voice like a toast-master's. I had often seen the Wrecking Crew, that quartette of spavined septuagenarians whose pride it was that they never let anyone through, scatter like leaves in an autumn gale at the sound of her stentorian 'Fore!' A dynamic and interesting personality.

'She is going to coach me,' said Harold Pickering. 'I saw her practising chip shots my first morning here, and I was amazed at her virtuosity. She seemed just to give a flick of the wrist and the ball fell a foot from the pin and flopped there like a poached egg. It struck me immediately that here was someone whose methods I could study to my great advantage. The chip is my weak spot. For the last ten days or so, accordingly, I have been following her about the course, watching her every movement, and yesterday we happened to fall into conversation and I confided my ambition to her. With a hearty laugh, she told me that if I wanted to become scratch I had come to the right shop. She said that she could make a scratch player out of a cheese mite, provided it had not lost the use of its limbs, and gave as evidence of her tuitionary skill the fact that she had turned a man named Sidney McMurdo from a mere blot on the local scene into something which in a dim light might be mistaken for a golfer. I haven't met McMurdo.'

'He is away at the moment. He has gone to attend the sickbed of an uncle. He will be back to play for the club championship.'

'As hot as that, is he?'

'Yes, I suppose he would be about the best man we have.'

'Scratch?'

'Plus one, I believe, actually.'

'And what was he before Miss Flack took him in hand?'

'His handicap, if I remember rightly, was fifteen.'

'You don't say?' said Harold Pickering, his face lighting up. 'Was it, by Jove? Then this begins to look like something. If she could turn him into such a tiger, there's a chance for me. We start the lessons tomorrow.'

I did not see Harold Pickering for some little time after this, an attack of lumbago confining me to my bed, but stories of his prowess filtered through to my sick-room, and from these it was abundantly evident that his confidence in Agnes Flack's skill as an instructress had not been misplaced. He won a minor competition with such ease that his handicap was instantly reduced to eight. Then he turned in a series of cards which brought him down to four. And the first thing I saw on entering the clubhouse on my restoration to health was his name on the list of entrants for the club championship. Against it was the word 'scratch'.

I can remember few things that have pleased me more. We are all sentimentalists at heart, and the boy's story had touched me deeply. I hastened to seek him out and congratulate him. I found him practising approach putts on the ninth green, but when I gripped his hand it was like squeezing a wet fish. His whole manner was that of one who has not quite shaken off the effects of being struck on the back of the head by a thunderbolt. It surprised me for a moment, but then I remembered that the achievement of a great ambition often causes a man to feel for a while somewhat filleted. The historian Gibbon, if you recall, had that experience on finishing his *Decline and Fall of the Roman Empire*, and I saw the same thing once in a friend of mine who had just won a Littlewood's pool.

'Well,' I said cheerily, 'I suppose you will now be leaving us? You will want to hurry off to Miss Rockett with the great news.'

He winced and topped a putt.

'No,' he said, 'I'm staying on here. My *fiancée* seems to wish it.'

'Your *fiancée*?'

'I am engaged to Agnes Flack.'

I was astounded. I had always understood that Agnes Flack was betrothed to Sidney McMurdo. I was also more than a little shocked. It was only a few weeks since he had poured out his soul to me on the subject of Troon Rockett, and this abrupt switching of his affections to another seemed to argue a sad lack of character and stability. When young fellows are enamoured of a member of the other sex, I like them to stay enamoured.

'Well, I hope you will be very happy,' I said.

'You needn't try to be funny,' he rejoined bitterly.

There was a sombre light in his eyes, and he foozled another putt.

'The whole thing,' he said, 'is due to one of those unfortunate misunderstandings. When they made me scratch, my first move was to thank Miss Flack warmly for all she had done for me.'

'Naturally.'

'I let myself go rather.'

'You would, of course.'

'Then, feeling that after all the trouble she had taken to raise me to the heights she was entitled to be let in on the inside story, I told her my reason for being so anxious to get down to scratch was that I loved a scratch girl and wanted to be worthy of her. Upon which, chuckling like a train going through a tunnel, she gave me a slap on the back which nearly drove my spine through the front of my pullover and said that she had guessed it from the very start, from the moment when she first saw me dogging her footsteps with that look of dumb devotion in my eyes. You could have knocked me down with a putter.'

'She then said she would marry you?'

'Yes. And what could I do? A girl,' said Harold Pickering fretfully, 'who can't distinguish between the way a man looks when he's admiring a chip shot thirty feet from the green and the way he looks when he's in love ought not to be allowed at large.'

There seemed nothing to say. The idea of suggesting that he should break off the engagement presented itself to me, but I dismissed it. Women are divided broadly into two classes – those who, when jilted, merely drop a silent tear and those who take a niblick from their bag and chase the faithless swain across country with it. It was to this latter section that Agnes Flack belonged. Attila the Hun might have broken off his engagement to her, but nobody except Attila the Hun, and he only on one of his best mornings.

So I said nothing, and presently Harold Pickering resumed his moody putting and I left him.

The contest for the club championship opened unsensationally. There are never very many entrants for this of course non-handicap event, and this year there were only four. Harold Pickering won his match against Rupert Watchett comfortably, and Sidney McMurdo, who had returned on the previous night, had no difficulty in disposing of George Bunting. The final, Pickering versus McMurdo, was to be played in the afternoon.

Agnes Flack had walked round with Harold Pickering in the morning, and they lunched together after the game. But an appointment with her lawyer in the metropolis made it impossible for her to stay and watch the final, and she had to be content with giving him some parting words of advice.

'The great thing,' she said, as he accompanied her to her car, 'is not to lose your nerve. Forget that it's the final and play your ordinary game, and you can trim the pants off him. This statement carries my personal guarantee.'

'You know his game pretty well?'

'Backwards. We used to do our three rounds a day together, when we were engaged.'

'Engaged?'

'Yes. Didn't I tell you? We were heading straight for the altar, apparently with no bunkers in sight, when one afternoon he took a Number Three iron when I had told him to take a Number Four. I scratched the fixture immediately. "No man," I said to him, "is going to walk up the aisle with me who takes a Number Three iron for a Number Four iron shot. Pop off, Sidney McMurdo," I said, and he gnashed his teeth and popped. I shall get the laugh of a lifetime, seeing his face when I tell him I'm engaged to you. The big lummox.'

Harold Pickering started.

'Did you say *big* lummox?'

'That was the expression I used.'

'He is robust then?'

'Oh, he's robust enough. He could fell an ox with a single blow, if he wasn't fond of oxen.'

'And is he – er – at all inclined to be jealous?'

'Othello took his correspondence course.'

'I see,' said Harold Pickering. 'I see.'

He fell into a reverie, from which he was aroused a moment later by a deafening bellow from his companion.

'Hey, Sidney!'

The person she addressed was in Harold Pickering's rear. He turned, and perceived a vast man who gazed yearningly at Agnes Flack from beneath beetling eyebrows.

'Sidney,' said Agnes Flack, 'I want you to meet Mr Pickering, who is playing you in the final this afternoon, Mr McMurdo, Mr Pickering, my *fiancé*. Well, goodbye, Harold darling, I've got to rush.'

She folded him in a long lingering embrace, the car bowled off, and Harold Pickering found himself alone with this oversized plug-ugly in what seemed to his fevered fancy a great empty space, like one of those ones in the movies where two strong men stand face to face and Might is the only law.

Sidney McMurdo was staring at him with a peculiar intensity. There was a disturbing gleam in his eyes, and his hands, each the size of a largish ham, were clenching and unclenching as if flexing themselves for some grim work in the not too distant future.

'Did she,' he asked in an odd, hoarse voice, 'say – *fiancé*?'

'Why yes,' said Harold Pickering, with a nonchalance which it cost him a strong effort to assume. 'Yes, that's right, I believe she did.'

'You are going to marry Agnes Flack?'

'There is some idea of it, I understand.'

'Ah!' said Sidney McMurdo, and the intensity of his stare was now more marked than ever.

Harold Pickering quailed beneath it. His heart, as he gazed at this patently steamed-up colossus, missed not one beat but several. Nor, I think, can we blame him. All publishers are sensitive, highly strung men. Gollancz is. So is Hamish Hamilton. So are Chapman and Hall, Heinemann and Herbert Jenkins, Ltd. And even when in sunny mood, Sidney McMurdo was always a rather intimidating spectacle. Tall, broad, deep-chested and superbly muscled, he looked like the worthy descendant of a long line of heavyweight gorillas, and nervous people and invalids were generally warned if there was any likelihood of their meeting him unexpectedly. Harold Pickering could not but feel that an uncle who would want anything like that at his sickbed must be eccentric to the last degree.

However, he did his best to keep the conversation on a note of easy cordiality.

'Nice weather,' he said.

'Bah!' said Sidney McMurdo.

'How's your uncle?'

'Never mind my uncle. Are you busy at the moment, Mr Pickering?'

'No.'

'Good,' said Sidney McMurdo. 'Because I want to break your neck.'

There was a pause. Harold Pickering backed a step. Sidney McMurdo advanced a step. Harold Pickering backed another step. Sidney McMurdo advanced again. Harold Pickering sprang sideways. Sidney McMurdo also sprang sideways. If it had not been for the fact that the latter was gnashing his teeth and filling the air with a sound similar to that produced by an inexperienced Spanish dancer learning to play the castanets, one

might have supposed them to be practising the opening movements of some graceful, old-world gavotte.

'Or, rather,' said Sidney McMurdo, correcting his previous
statement, 'tear you limb from limb.'

'Why?' asked Harold Pickering who liked to go into things.

'You know why,' said Sidney McMurdo, moving eastwards as
his *vis-à-vis* moved westwards. 'Because you steal girls' hearts
behind people's backs, like a snake.'

Harold Pickering, who happened to know something about
snakes, might have challenged this description of their habits,
but he was afforded no opportunity of doing so. His companion
had suddenly reached out a clutching hand, and only by coyly
drawing it back was he enabled to preserve his neck intact.

'Here, just a moment,' he said.

I have mentioned that publishers are sensitive and highly strung. They are also quickwitted. They think on their feet. Harold Pickering had done so now. Hodder and Stoughton could not have reacted more nimbly.

'You are proposing to tear me limb from limb, are you?'

'And also to dance on the fragments.'

It was not easy for Harold Pickering to sneer, for his lower jaw kept dropping, but he contrived to do so.

'I see,' he said, just managing to curl his lip before the jaw got away from him again. 'Thus ensuring that you shall be this year's club champion. Ingenious, McMurdo. It's one way of winning, of course. But I should not call it very sporting.'

He had struck the right note. The blush of shame mantled Sidney McMurdo's cheek. His hands fell to his sides, and he stood chewing his lip, plainly disconcerted.

'I hadn't looked at it like that,' he confessed.

'Posterity will,' said Harold Pickering.

'Yes, I see what you mean. Postpone it, then, you think, eh?'

'Indefinitely.'

'Oh, not indefinitely. We'll get together after the match. After all,' said Sidney McMurdo, looking on the bright side, 'it isn't long to wait.'

It was at this point that I joined them. As generally happened in those days, I had been given the honour of refereeing the final. I asked if they were ready to start.

'Not only ready,' said Sidney McMurdo. 'Impatient.'

Harold Pickering said nothing. He merely moistened the lips with the tip of the tongue.

My friends (proceeded the Oldest Member) have sometimes been kind enough to say that if there is one thing at which I excel, it is at describing in meticulous detail a desperately closely fought golf match – taking my audience stroke by stroke from tee one to hole eighteen and showing fortune fluctuating now to one side, now to the other, before finally placing the laurel wreath on the perspiring brow of the ultimate winner. And it is this treat that I should like to be able to give you now.

Unfortunately, the contest for that particular club championship final does not lend itself to such a description. From the very outset it was hopelessly one-sided.

Even as we walked to the first tee, it seemed to me that Harold Pickering was not looking his best and brightest. But I put this down to a nervous man's natural anxiety before an important match, and even when he lost the first two holes by the weakest type of play, I assumed that he would soon pull himself together and give of his best.

At that time, of course, I was not aware of the emotions surging in his bosom. It was only some years later that I ran into him and he told me his story and its sequel. That afternoon, what struck me most was the charming spirit of courtesy in which he played the match. He was losing every hole with monotonous regularity, and in such circumstances even the most amiable are apt to be gloomy and sullen, but he never lost his affability. He seemed to be straining every nerve to ingratiate himself with Sidney McMurdo and win the latter's affection.

Oddly, as it appeared to me then, it was McMurdo who was sullen and gloomy. On three occasions he declined the offer of a cigarette from his opponent, and was short in his manner – one might almost say surly – when Harold Pickering, nine down at the ninth, said that it was well worth anyone's while being beaten by Sidney McMurdo because, apart from the fresh air and exercise, it was such an artistic treat to watch his putting.

It was as he paid this graceful tribute that the crowd, which had been melting away pretty steadily for the last quarter of an hour, finally disappeared. By the time Sidney McMurdo had holed out at the tenth for a four that gave him the match, we were alone except for the caddies. These having been paid off, we started to walk back.

To lose a championship match by ten and eight is an experience calculated to induce in a man an introspective silence, and I had not expected Harold Pickering to contribute much to any feast of reason and flow of soul which might enliven the homeward journey. To my surprise, however, as we started to cross the bridge which spans the water at the eleventh, he burst into animated speech, complimenting his conqueror in a graceful way which I thought very sporting.

'I wonder if you will allow me to say, Mr McMurdo,' he began, 'how greatly impressed I have been by your performance this afternoon. It has been a genuine revelation to me. It is so seldom that one meets a man who, while long off the tee, also plays an impeccable short game. I don't want to appear fulsome, but it seems to me that you have everything.'

Words like these should have been music to Sidney McMurdo's ears, but he merely scowled darkly and uttered a short grunt like a bulldog choking on a piece of steak.

'In fact, I don't mind telling you, McMurdo,' proceeded Harold Pickering, still in that genial and ingratiating manner, 'that I shall watch your future career with considerable interest. It is a sad pity that this year's Walker Cup matches are over, for our team might have been greatly strengthened. Well, I venture to assert that next season the selection of at least one member will give the authorities little trouble.'

Sidney McMurdo uttered another grunt, and I saw what seemed like a look of discouragement come into Harold Pickering's face. But after gulping a couple of times he continued brightly.

'Tell me, Sidney,' he said, 'have you ever thought of writing a golf book? You know the sort of thing, old man. Something light and chatty, describing your methods and giving advice to the novice. If so, I should be delighted to publish it, and we should not quarrel about the terms. If I were you, I'd go straight home and start on it now.'

Sidney McMurdo spoke for the first time. His voice was deep and rumbling.

'I have something to do before I go home.'

'Oh, yes?'

'I am going to pound the stuffing out of a snake.'

'Ah, then in that case you will doubtless want to be alone, to concentrate. I will leave you.'

'No, you won't. Let us step behind those bushes for a moment, Mr Pickering,' said Sidney McMurdo.

I have always been good at putting two and two together, and listening to these exchanges I now sensed how matters stood. In a word, I saw all, and my heart bled for Harold Pickering. Unnecessarily, as it turned out, for even as my heart started to bleed, Harold Pickering acted.

I have said that we were crossing the bridge over the water at the eleventh, and no doubt you have been picturing that bridge as it is today – a stout steel structure. At the time of which I am speaking it was a mere plank with a rickety wooden rail along it, a rail ill adapted to withstand the impact of a heavy body.

Sidney McMurdo's was about as heavy a body as there was in the neighbourhood, and when Harold Pickering, with a resource and ingenuity which it would be difficult to overpraise, suddenly butted him in the stomach with his head and sent him reeling against it, it gave way without a moment's hesitation. There was a splintering crash, followed by a splash and a scurry of feet, and the next thing I saw was Harold Pickering disappearing over the horizon while Sidney McMurdo, up to his waist in water, petulantly detaching an eel from his hair. It was a striking proof of the old saying that a publisher is never so dangerous as when apparently beaten. You may drive a publisher into a corner, but you do so at your own peril.

Presently, Sidney McMurdo waded ashore and started to slosh sullenly up the hillside towards the club-house. From the irritable manner in which he was striking himself between the shoulder blades I received the impression that he had got some sort of a water beetle down his back.

As I think I mentioned earlier, I did not see Harold Pickering again for some years, and it was only then that I was enabled to fill in the gaps, in what has always seemed to me a singularly poignant human drama.

At first, he told me, he was actuated by the desire, which one can understand and sympathize with, to put as great a distance as possible between Sidney McMurdo and himself in the shortest possible time. With this end in view, he hastened to his car, which he had left standing outside the clubhouse, and placing a firm foot on the accelerator drove about seventy miles in the general direction of Scotland. Only when he paused for a sandwich at a wayside tavern after completing this preliminary burst did he discover that all the money he had on his person was five shillings and a little bronze.

Now, a less agitated man would, of course, have seen that the policy to pursue was to take a room at a hotel, explain to the management that his luggage would be following shortly, and write to his bank to telegraph him such funds as he might require. But this obvious solution did not even occur to Harold Pickering. The only way out of the difficulty that suggested itself to him was to drive back to his cottage, secure the few pounds which he knew to be on the premises, throw into a suitcase some articles of clothing and his cheque book and then drive off again into the sunset.

As it happened, however, he would not have been able to drive off into the sunset, for it was quite dark when he arrived at his destination. He alighted from his car, and was about to enter the house, when he suddenly observed that there was a light in the sitting-room. And creeping to the window and peering cautiously through a chink in the curtains, he saw that it was precisely as he had feared. There on a settee, scowling up at the ceiling, was Sidney McMurdo. He had the air of a man who was waiting for somebody.

And scarcely had Harold Pickering, appalled by this spectacle, withdrawn into a near-by bush to think the situation over in all of its aspects and try to find a formula, when heavy footsteps sounded on the gravel path and, dark though it was, he had no difficulty in identifying the newcomer as Agnes Flack. Only she could have clumped like that.

The next moment, she had delivered a resounding buffet on the front door, and Sidney McMurdo was opening it to her.

There was a silence as they gazed at one another. Except for that brief instant when she had introduced Harold Pickering to Sidney McMurdo outside the clubhouse, these sundered hearts had not met since the severance of their relations, and even a fifteen-stone man and an eleven-stone girl are not immune from embarrassment.

Agnes was the first to speak.

'Hullo,' she said. 'You here?'

'Yes,' said Sidney McMurdo, 'I'm here all right. I am waiting for the snake Pickering.'

'I've come to see him myself.'

'Oh? Well, nothing that you can do will save him from my wrath.'

'Who wants to save him from your wrath?'

'Don't you?'

'Certainly not. All I looked in for was to break our engagement.'

Sidney McMurdo staggered.

'Break your engagement?'

'That's right.'

'But I thought you loved him.'

'No more. The scales have fallen from my eyes. I don't marry men who are as hot as pistols in a friendly round with nothing depending on it, but blow up like geysers in competition golf. Why are you wrathful with him, Sidney?'

Sidney McMurdo gnashed his teeth.

'He stole you from me.' he said hoarsely.

If Agnes Flack had been about a foot shorter and had weighed about thirty pounds less, the sound which proceeded from her might have been described as a giggle. She stretched out the toe of her substantial shoe and made a squiggle with it on the gravel.

'And did you mind that so much?' she said softly – or as softly as it was in her power to speak.

'Yes, I jolly well did,' said Sidney McMurdo. 'I love you, old girl, and I shall continue to love you till the cows come home. When I was demolishing the reptile Pickering this afternoon, your face seemed to float before me all the way round, even when I was putting. And I'll tell you something. I've been thinking it over, and I see now that I was all wrong that time and should unquestionably have used a Number Four iron. Too late, of course,' said Sidney McMurdo moodily, thinking of what might have been.

Agnes Flack drew a second arabesque on the gravel, using the toe of the other shoe this time.

'How do you mean, too late?' she asked reasonably softly.

'Well, isn't it too late?'

'Certainly not.'

'You can't mean you love me still?'

'Yes, I jolly well can mean I love you still.'

'Well, I'll be blowed! And here was I, thinking that all was over and life empty and all that sort of thing. My mate!' cried Sidney McMurdo.

They fell into an embrace like a couple of mastodons clashing in a primaeval swamp, and the earth had scarcely ceased to shake when a voice spoke.

'Excuse me.'

In his hiding-place in the bush Harold Pickering leaped as if somebody had touched off a land mine under his feet and came to rest quivering in every limb. He had recognized that voice.

'Excuse me,' said Troon Rockett. 'Does Mr Pickering live here?'

'Yes,' said Sidney McMurdo.

'If,' added Agnes Flack, 'you can call it living when a man enters for an important competition and gets beaten ten and eight. He's out at the moment. Better go in and stick around.'

'Thank you,' said the girl. 'I will.'

She vanished into the cottage. Sidney McMurdo took advantage of her departure to embrace Agnes Flack again.

'Old blighter,' he said tenderly, 'let's get married right away, before there can be any more misunderstandings and rifts and what not. How about Tuesday?'

'Can't Tuesday. Mixed foursomes.'

'Wednesday?'

'Can't Wednesday. Bogey competition.'

'And Thursday I'm playing in the invitation tournament at Squashy Heath,' said Sidney McMurdo. 'Oh, well, I daresay we shall manage to find a day when we're both free. Let's stroll along and talk it over.'

They crashed off, and as the echoes of their clumping feet died away in the distance Harold Pickering left the form in which he had been crouched and walked dizzily to the cottage. And the first thing he saw as he entered the sitting-room was Troon Rockett kissing a cabinet photograph of himself which she had taken from its place on the mantelpiece. The spectacle drew from him a sharp, staccato bark of amazement, and she turned, her eyes wide.

'Harold!' she cried, and flung herself into his arms.

To say that Harold Pickering was surprised, bewildered, startled and astounded would be merely to state the facts. He could not remember having been so genuinely taken aback since the evening when, sauntering in his garden in the dusk, he had trodden on the teeth of a rake and had the handle jump up and hit him on the nose.

But, as I have had occasion to observe before, he was a publisher, and I doubt if there is a publisher on the list who would not know what to do if a charming girl flung herself into his arms. I have told this story to one or two publishers of my acquaintance, and they all assured me that the correct procedure would come instinctively to them. Harold Pickering kissed Troon Rockett sixteen times in quick succession and Macmillan and Faber and Faber say they would have done just the same.

At length, he paused. He was, as I have said, a man who liked to go into things.

'But I don't understand.'

'What don't you understand?'

'Well, don't think for a moment that I'm complaining, but this flinging-into-arms sequence strikes me as odd.'

'I can't imagine why. I love you.'

'But when I asked you to be my wife, you rose and walked haughtily from the room.'

'I didn't.'

'You did. I was there.'

'I mean, I didn't walk haughtily. I hurried out because I was alarmed and agitated. You sat there gasping and gurgling, and I thought you were having a fit of some kind. So I rushed off to phone the doctor, and when I got back you had gone. And then a day or two later another man proposed to me, and he, too, started gasping and gurgling and I realized the truth. They told me at your office that you were living here, so I came along to let you know that I loved you.'

'You really do?'

'Of course I do. I loved you the first moment I saw you. You remember? You were explaining to father that thirteen copies count as twelve, and I came in and our eyes met. In that instant I knew that you were the only man in the world for me.'

For a moment Harold Pickering was conscious only of a wild exhilaration. He felt as if his firm had brought out *Gone With the Wind*. Then a dull, hopeless look came into his sensitive face.

'It can never be,' he said.

'Why not?'

'You heard what that large girl was saying outside there, but probably you did not take it in. It was the truth. I was beaten this afternoon ten and eight.'

'Everybody has an off day.'

He shook his head.

'It was not an off day. That was my true form. I haven't the nerve to be a scratch man. When the acid test comes, I blow up. I suppose I'm about ten, really. You can't marry a ten-handicap man.'

'Why not?'

'You! The daughter of John Rockett and his British Ladies Champion wife. The great-grand-daughter of old Ma Rockett. The sister of Prestwick, Sandwich, Hoylake and St Andrew Rockett.'

'But that's just why. It has always been my dream to marry a man with a handicap of about ten, so that we could go through life together side by side, twin souls. I should be ten, if the family didn't make me practise five hours a day all the year round. I'm not a natural scratch. I have made myself scratch by ceaseless, unremitting toil, and if there's one thing in the world I loathe it is ceaseless, unremitting toil. The relief of being able to let myself slip back to ten is indescribable. Oh, Harold, we shall be so happy. Just to think of taking three putts on a green! It will be heaven!'

Harold Pickering had been reeling a good deal during these remarks. He now ceased to do so. There is a time for reeling and a time for not reeling.

'You mean that?'

'I certainly do.'

'You will really marry me?'

'How long does it take to get a licence?'

For an instant Harold Pickering sought for words, but found none. Then a rather neat thing that Sidney McMurdo had said came back to him. Sidney McMurdo was a man he could never really like, but his dialogue was excellent.

'My mate!' he said.

Uncle James's Golf Match

'SAPPER'

'UNCLE James should be here soon,' said Molly thought-fully from the other end of the tea-table. 'For heaven's sake be nice to him, Peter.'

'When have I ever not been nice to Uncle James?' I demanded. 'But I tell you candidly, Molly, that it can't last much longer. He's only fifty-five: he will almost certainly live another forty years. And I can't stand another forty years of Uncle James.'

'I'm sure he'll leave us all his money, old boy,' she said pleadingly.

'I can't help that,' I retorted firmly – at least as firmly as I ever can retort to Molly. 'A man can buy money at too great a price. And if he brings another of his abominable inventions with him this time, I shall tell him what I think. He ought to know better at his age.'

'I know, Peter,' she answered gently. 'But it's only for the week-end . . .'

'Only!' I echoed bitterly. 'Thank God for it.'

'I must say I do hope he hasn't invented anything else for sav-ing work in the house,' she conceded. 'Servants are so difficult to find these days, and the parlour-maid seems to be settling down at last.'

'He should confine his atrocities to his own home,' I said. 'A man who tries to emulate Heath Robinson in real life ought to be locked up.'

Molly sighed. 'I know, darling,' she murmured. 'But think of the money.'

And they say that women are idealists . . .

'Take that last week-end he spent here,' I began wrathfully, and then Molly stopped me.

'Don't, dear, don't,' she begged. 'And that reminds me, they've never sent up yet to repair the kitchen ceiling.'

Mind you, if the diabolical contrivances conceived in Uncle James's perverted mind were harmless little things like patent match-boxes, or unbreakable sock-suspenders, I wouldn't mind. He is an excellent judge of wine, and has an excellent cellar – two assets which enable one to slur over small idiosyncrasies in their possessor. But – well, take that last week-end.

I feared the worst when he arrived: he was so infernally

pleased with himself. He came on Friday, and on Saturday I had to go up to Town, so my knowledge of what happened is only second-hand. I was met at the station by Molly – a rather wild-eyed Molly – who poured out the whole hideous story on the way up to the house. Uncle James had waited till I was well away before he sprang it on her – and even she had tried to be firm when she heard what it was.

'It was a patent labour-saving device for me in the kitchen, Peter,' she exclaimed weakly. 'Little pulleys and things – and bits of string. I explained everything to Martha – told her he was eccentric, and that we could take it down the instant he went – and she seemed to understand.'

She faltered a little and my heart sank.

'It took him two hours to put it up with stepladders, while Martha sat sardonically in a corner. Then he explained to us how it worked. Oh! it was awful.'

I took her arm: she was rapidly becoming hysterical.

'Of course, something went wrong. Uncle James says it was the hook coming out of the ceiling – I know the plaster is all over the floor. But whatever it was, the big saucepan of potatoes shot into the corner – Martha's corner – and she couldn't get out of the way in time.'

Molly gulped. 'She got up with potatoes all over her, and threw them one by one at Uncle James.'

'Did she hit him?' I asked eagerly.

'Twice,' answered Molly. 'Then she left the house.'

Well, now that was the last time he stayed with us. Do you wonder that at times I felt I couldn't stand it much longer? Of course, Molly's account of it was a trifle incoherent – possibly even a trifle exaggerated. But the one salient fact remains that his last visit cost us Martha.

A series of loud explosions outside the door recalled me from the bitter past, and Molly got up, looking alarmed.

'Good gracious, what's that?' she cried.

'Probably he has invented a motor-car,' I answered grimly, 'which goes sideways with the passengers underneath.'

'Do you think it's Uncle James?' she asked uneasily, and at that moment the front-door bell rang.

It was Uncle James right enough, and we went out into the hall to greet him.

'Ah! my dear children,' he cried as he saw us, 'I've arrived.'

'Anything wrong with the car?' asked Molly as she kissed him.

'Not going very well,' he answered, shaking hands with me. 'And now it's stopped altogether. I wish you'd just give me a hand, Peter.'

'Certainly.' I'm afraid my smile was a trifle strained. With an ordinary car I can compete: not with Uncle James's. 'What's the trouble?'

'Well – I'll just show you the idea,' he said cheerfully as he led the way. 'I've got a few notions of my own incorporated into the general design – little gadgets, you know. Now, first of all' – he gazed pensively at the dashboard – 'we'll try that a little farther open. And, Peter – if you just pull that wire by the steering-pillar she ought to start.'

I pulled the wire, and Uncle James tackled the starting-handle. There was an alarming report, and a cloud of white smoke which seemed to please him.

'Ah! spark's all right, anyway,' he murmured. 'Once more.'

This time she back-fired so violently that only the greatest agility on his part saved him from a broken wrist. In view of what was to come, I found myself wishing later that he hadn't been quite so agile.

'Pull harder, Peter,' he cried, returning to the assault.

I did: I pulled the whole wire out, and the car promptly started.

'I knew she'd go,' he announced complacently. 'Just a little patience wanted.'

I preserved a discreet silence as we went round to the garage: there are moments when speech is both unwise and tactless. And it was not until we were strolling back to the house, my sin still undiscovered, that I breathed again.

'You must let me run you up to the clubhouse in mine to-morrow morning, Uncle James,' I said lightly. 'Course in splendid condition.'

'Aren't you going to London to-morrow?' he demanded.

'No. I'm taking a holiday in honour of your visit.'

I forbore to tell him that Molly had threatened divorce unless I did.

'What sort of time will suit you?' I went on. 'Then I can ring up and let them know about caddies.'

Uncle James did not immediately reply, and I noticed he looked a little thoughtful.

'To tell you the truth, Peter,' he began slowly, 'I wasn't particularly anxious to play golf with you to-morrow morning. The fact is, I wanted – ' he hesitated for a moment – 'I wanted to practise a bit before I played you again.'

'Well – we won't play a serious round, Uncle James,' I said mildly. 'We might get up there and knock about a bit: have some lunch, don't you know – and play in the afternoon.'

Anything to keep him out of the house; those were Molly's instructions.

'Yes,' he agreed. 'We might do that. And in the afternoon I shall beat you.'

'Why, of course. Beat my head off.'

'I have cured my slice, Peter,' he announced.

'Good,' I cried. 'You'd have beaten me last time but for that.'

'No – not last time. But I shall this.'

There was an air of such complete conviction about his tone that I glanced at him in mild surprise. Uncle James may be and is an excellent judge of wine; Uncle James may be and is a public pest with his inventions; but Uncle James cannot be and is not and never will be a golfer. He is not like anything on this earth that I have ever seen when he gets a golf-club in his hands. He is, and I say it advisedly with due regard to the solemnity of making such a claim for any man, the worst golfer in the world.

'I have – er – turned what little ingenuity I possess, Peter, upon a lengthy and scientific consideration of the game of golf.' He spoke as a man does who weighs his words with care, and involuntarily we both paused.

'I have read many books on the game – by Vardon and Taylor and others – men doubtless well qualified to write on the subject.'

I bowed silently: speech was beyond me.

'And it seems to me,' he went on, 'that they evade the real issue. For instance now, they unite in saying that the essence of golf lies in the swing. But how am I to know that my swing is like theirs?'

'How indeed?' I murmured chokingly.

'Again they reiterate the statement, "slow back". But ideas of slowness differ.'

'True,' I agreed – 'very true.'

To see Uncle James take his club back reminds one of a man lunging furiously at a wasp.

'Two points of many, you perceive, Peter,' he continued, 'on which I came to the conclusion that a little ingenuity might be of great assistance. And so, I have – er – perfected, or am in the process of perfecting, a small device, by which the – er – comparative novice like myself can obtain mechanical assistance in carrying out these maxims.'

Thank God! Molly joined us at that moment: I was beginning to turn pale. Uncle James encased in pulleys on a Saturday morning on the links was a prospect that made me feel faint. Better a thousand times that the entire domestic staff should resign.

'Is it a very complicated device, Uncle James?' I asked feebly, and I heard Molly catch her breath.

'It takes a little adjustment,' he answered. 'And I shall require Molly's assistance.'

'Uncle James has invented something,' I explained, studiously avoiding her eye, 'which he thinks will improve his golf.'

'What sort of thing?' inquired Molly.

'It's not so much an original invention,' he explained, 'as a common-sense application of a well-known principle – the principle of elasticity.'

I suppose I looked mystified – I certainly felt it – and he beamed at us contentedly. Then he fumbled in his pocket and produced a small parcel.

'It is my firm belief,' he continued, as he undid the string, 'that with this I shall be able to reduce my handicap to single figures, or even' – he paused for a moment, and his voice shook a little at the thought – 'or even to scratch.'

At first sight the invention looked like a cross between a young octopus and the tram-lines at the Elephant and Castle. On closer inspection it looked like a nightmare. Streamers of india-rubber flowed in all directions from metal rings, terminating in little clips and loops. Some were short and some were long; some were thick and some were thin – and to each was affixed a label.

'There it is, you see,' he remarked proudly, 'neat and simple. Merely following first principles, Peter.'

'But,' I stammered, 'how does it work, Uncle James?'

'You must surely follow the main idea,' he exclaimed, with the genial toleration of the great brain. 'Each of these lengths of rubber fulfils a purpose of its own, and the thickness and length have been calculated to enable them to fulfil that purpose scientifically. For instance – this one.'

He indicated a short, stocky little fellow, with a loop at the end.

'Now, Duncan lays great stress on the action of the right elbow during the upward swing. He insists that it should be kept close to the body. By the simple process of attaching this loop round the right elbow – the result is obtained.'

'I'm afraid I'm still rather dense,' I said dazedly.

'The ring – this metal ring,' he explained a little wearily, 'is attached to the inside of my coat. From it the rubber goes to my right elbow. These others go elsewhere. Similarly with the remaining rings. Each is securely fastened inside my coat, and from them the rubber cords go to their respective places where they are secured.'

'What is the long, thin one, Uncle James?' asked Molly wildly.

'That one?' He examined the label. 'To left wrist for follow through. You see it fulfils a dual purpose. It restrains one in the upward swing – and assists one in the downward.'

And then, thank heavens! the dressing-bell rang, and we went indoors. My brain was reeling: it was incredible to think that any man could have such a mind. And what made it worse was that Molly seemed to be in a splendid temper. I even heard her congratulate her abominable relative on his cleverness.

'Could anything be better, old boy?' she said, coming into

my dressing-room. 'He'll be perfectly happy on the links, with you and his india-rubber.' She choked slightly.

'Understand me, Molly,' I answered coldly. 'I go to London to-morrow, and I do not return until Uncle James has left. I shall have a telephone message in the morning. I utterly and absolutely refuse to take your confounded relative up to the links on a Saturday morning, swathed from head to foot in rubber bands.'

'But, Peter darling,' she began soothingly.

'Go away,' I said firmly – 'go away. I hate your family.'

'But, Peter darling,' she continued, 'he won't do any harm. He can't play any worse with it on than he does with it off.'

'That,' I agreed, 'is an indubitable fact. But – why, confound it, Molly – it's against the rules. It must be against the rules. It's absolutely immoral.'

'I know, dearest,' she answered. 'But no one will find out – and it keeps him happy. After all, it's better than letting him loose in the house . . .'

Of course, I gave in finally; I knew I should, I always do with Molly. And after all she was quite right. The infernal machine would be hidden underneath his coat, and no one need know. And he *has* got a lot of money.

We got off about ten on Saturday morning – Uncle James and I. Molly had sewn the rings into his coat after dinner the night before under his expert eye; she had then superintended the connecting up in the morning after breakfast. And that completed her share of the performance. She flatly refused to accompany us to the links, on the plea of household duties. She equally flatly refused to speak to me alone, or even to meet my eye. So I placed Uncle James's bag of nineteen clubs in the car and we started.

It was a beautiful day for golf – soft, balmy, and without a breath of wind. Moreover, Uncle James was in a splendid temper.

'I shall do a good round this afternoon, Peter,' he affirmed confidently. 'Splendid device, this of mine. Tried one or two practice swings while you were getting the car.'

'Good,' I cried. With the new day had come a certain cheerful optimism, and I let the car out a bit more. 'But if I was you, Uncle James, I'd lie low about it. Don't tell anyone, and you might make a bit of money to-morrow.'

I could see the pride of the inventor struggling with the wonderful idea I had suggested. To actually beat somebody at golf! It opened a vista of possibility almost too marvellous for imagination.

'You see,' I continued craftily, 'people might belittle your game if they knew.'

I left it at that, and hoped for the best. There were quite a number of men about when we arrived at the clubhouse, and as Uncle James wanted to try his device, I fixed up a game for the morning. Then I showed him a hole where he could practise approach shots, and left him. It was a fatal move on my part: I ought to have known better. To leave Uncle James alone on a links – especially on Saturday morning – is asking for trouble. I got it.

The first man I saw as I came in after my round was Colonel Thresher. He was talking to the secretary, who was trying to soothe him.

'I'll look into it, Colonel,' he said mildly. 'Leave it to me.'

'But I tell you there's a madman on the links,' roared the irate officer. 'He's dug a hole on the seventeenth fairway big enough to bury a cow in.'

My heart sank; it was the seventeenth where I had left Uncle James.

'The damned man is a menace to public safety,' fumed the Colonel. 'He hits the ball backwards and through his legs. And he's using the most appalling language. Here he is, sir – here he is.'

I choked and turned round as Uncle James entered. I could see at a glance that he was no longer in a splendid temper. Far from it.

'The lies on this course are atrocious, Peter,' he cried as soon as he saw me – 'positively atrocious.'

I attempted to intervene – but it was too late.

'And they won't be improved, sir,' roared the Colonel, 'by

your exhibition of trench digging. Damn it – a man falling into some of those holes you've made would break his neck.'

'Confound your impertinence, sir,' began Uncle James, shaking his fist in his rage. And then he paused suddenly: in mid-air, so to speak. A spasm of pain passed over his face, and a loud twanging noise came from the region of his back. The Colonel started violently, and retreated, while the secretary took two rapid paces to the rear.

'I told you he was mad,' muttered the Colonel nervously. 'He's got a musical-box in his shirt.'

It was that remark that finished it, and removed the last vestige of Uncle James's self-control. To have his latest invention alluded to as a musical-box turned him temporarily into a raving lunatic. And as other members drew near in awestruck silence a torrent of words in a strange tongue poured from his lips. It turned out to be some Indian dialect, of which my relative knew a smattering. Unfortunately, so did the Colonel, and he answered in the same language. I gathered later from an onlooker, who also understood the lingo, that honours were about easy, with the betting slightly on Uncle James. He'd got in first with some of the choicer terms of endearment. And then Uncle still further lost his head. He challenged the Colonel to a game that afternoon for a tenner – a challenge which that warrior immediately accepted with a sardonic laugh.

To everyone else it seemed a most happy termination of the incident: to me it was the last straw. Uncle James had no more chance of beating the Colonel than I should have of beating Abe Mitchell. Not that the Colonel was a good golfer; he wasn't. But he was one of those steady players who can be relied on to go round in two or three over sevens. Which, for Uncle as his opponent, meant a victory for the Colonel by ten and eight.

However, the challenge had been given and accepted: there was nothing for it but to hope for the best. Uncle James had disappeared to wash his hands; the Colonel had been led away, breathing hard, when I suddenly thought of Molly. After all, he was *her* relative.

'Is that you, Molly?' I said over the 'phone. 'Well, the worst has occurred. Your uncle has challenged old Colonel Thresher to a game this afternoon – after the combined efforts of most of the members just prevented a free fight in the smoking-room.'

I heard her choke gently. Then – 'Well, that's all right, Peter.'

'It isn't,' I fumed. 'He's got no more chance of winning than – than – Don't you understand: Thresher called his invention a musical-box. It came into action as they were abusing one another, and twanged. It's an affair of honour with Uncle James. And if he loses, he'll never forgive us.'

'He mustn't lose, Peter.' I thought her voice was thoughtful.

'Then I wish to heaven you'd come up and prevent it,' I said peevishly.

'I will,' she said, and I gasped. 'What ball is he using?'

'Silver Kings. Red dots. But look here, Molly, you mustn't . . . It's for a tenner . . . Are you there?'

She wasn't: she'd rung off. And somewhat pensively I joined Uncle James at the bar. I never quite know with Molly: she is capable of doing most peculiar things.

'I'll teach him, Peter.' He greeted me with a scowl. 'What did he say – musical-box? The infernal scoundrel.'

'What was it that made the noise, Uncle James?' I asked soothingly.

'One of the longer rubbers got caught up in my braces,' he said. 'Incidentally it nipped a bit of my back . . . Bah! Musical-box. The villain.'

'Is it acting all right?' I led him towards the dining-room.

'I shall adjust it finally after lunch,' he stated.

'You don't think,' I hazarded, 'that as you haven't actually perfected it yet, it would perhaps be better to play without it.'

'Certainly not.' He glared sombrely at the back of his rival, and once again I heard him whisper: 'Musical-box.'

Then we sat down to lunch. It was a silent meal and I was glad when it was over. Uncle James – that genial if eccentric individual – had departed: an infuriated and revengeful man had taken his place. And what would be the result of his disposition when he forked up ten Bradburys to the Colonel was beyond my mental scope. He was never at his best on the golf-links: but this time . . .

He disappeared for a considerable time, after consuming two glasses of our best light port, which he stated was completely unfit for human consumption, and I wandered thoughtfully towards the first tee. There was no sign of Molly, though I thought I saw the flutter of something red in the distance, which might have been her. And then the professional strolled up.

'Hear there's a tenner on Colonel Thresher's game,' he said affably.

'There is,' I answered grimly. 'Did you see his opponent playing this morning?'

'I saw the gentleman doing his exercises on the seventeenth,' he said guardedly.

'That's my uncle, Jenkins,' I cried bitterly – 'or rather my wife's uncle. Can you as a man and a golfer give me the faintest shadow of hope that the match won't end on the tenth green?'

'Your uncle, is he,' he returned diplomatically. 'Peculiar style, sir, hasn't he?'

'Peculiar,' I groaned. 'He'd earn a fortune on the variety stage. By the way, you haven't seen my wife, have you?'

'Yes, sir. I thought she was playing with you. She's just bought a couple of old remakes.'

'What brand, Jenkins?' I asked slowly.

'Red-dot Silver Kings. Seemed very keen on 'em, though she generally uses Dunlops.'

I turned away lest he should see my face. I had more or less resigned myself to being cut out of Uncle James's will and to seeing his money go to a home for lost cats; but to be turned out of the club as well for Molly's nefarious scheme was a bit over the odds. What devilry she contemplated I did not know – I didn't even try to guess. But not for nothing had she invested in two remake red dots, and disappeared into the blue.

'Here they are,' said Jenkins. 'Odd sort of walk your uncle has got, sir.'

Now Uncle James has many peculiarities, but I had never noticed anything strange about his pedestrianism. The shock, therefore, was all the greater. To what portion of his anatomy he had attached his infernal machine factory I was in ignorance: but the net result was fierce. He looked like a cross between a king penguin and a trussed fowl suffering from an acute attack of locomotor ataxy. A perfect bevy of members had gathered outside the club house, and were watching him with awed fascination: his caddy, after one fearful convulsion of laughter, had relapsed into his customary after-luncheon hiccoughs. It was a dreadful spectacle – but worse, far worse, was to come.

The Colonel stalked to the tee in grim silence. His face was a little flushed: in his eyes was the light of battle.

'Ten pounds, you said, sir – I believe.'

'I will make it twenty, if you prefer,' said Uncle James loftily.

'Certainly,' snapped the Colonel, and addressed his ball.

Usually after lunch the Colonel fails to reach the fairway of the first hole. On this occasion, however, the ball flew quite a hundred yards down the middle of the course, and the Colonel stepped magnificently off the tee and proceeded to light a cigar.

The members drew closer as Uncle James advanced and even the caddy forbore to hiccough. The moment was tense with emotion: it still lives in my memory and ever will.

'Slow back,' had said Vardon; 'follow through,' had ordered Ray. Merciful heavens! they should have seen the result of their teaching. Uncle James achieved the most wonderful wind shot of modern times.

He lifted his driver like a professional weight-lifter, and at about the same velocity. Then, his face grim with determination, he let it down again. To say that he followed through would be to damn with faint praise. The club itself finished twenty yards in front of the Colonel's ball, and Uncle James fell over backwards.

'Very good,' said the Colonel. 'But the object of the game is to get your ball into the hole – not your club.'

'Another driver, boy,' said Uncle James magnificently when he was again in a vertical position, and at that moment I felt proud of being related to him. Once more Uncle James lifted his club; once more, under the combined influence of the 'to left wrist for follow through' rubber and his inflexible determination, the club descended. And this time he hit the ball. In cricket phraseology point would have got it in the neck. As it was, the Colonel's caddy sprang into the air with a scream of fear, and got it in the stomach, whence the ball rebounded into the tee box.

'Confound it, sir!' roared the Colonel. 'That's my boy.'

'Precisely, sir,' returned Uncle James complacently. 'It is therefore my hole.'

For a moment I feared for Colonel Thresher's reason. Even Jenkins, a most phlegmatic man, retired rapidly behind the starter's box, and laid his head on a cold stone. In fact, only Uncle James seemed unperturbed. He unwound himself, twanged faintly, and started for the second tee.

'I must adjust my "right elbow in" grip, Peter,' he remarked as I trailed weakly behind him. 'It prevents me raising my club with the freedom required for a perfect swing.'

'Do you mean to say, sir,' – the Colonel had at last found his voice – 'that you intend to claim that hole?'

'I presume that we are playing under the rules of golf.' Uncle James regarded him coldly. 'And the point is legislated for. Should a player's ball strike his opponent or his opponent's caddy the player wins the hole.'

'That doesn't apply to attempted murder off the tee,' howled the Colonel.

'You are not in the least degree funny, sir,' returned Uncle James still more coldly. 'In fact, I find you rather insulting. If you like, and care to forfeit the stakes, we will call the match off.'

'I'll be damned if I do,' roared the other. 'But before you drive next time, sir, I'll take precautions. I came out to play golf, not to be killed by a brass band.'

Uncle James turned white, but he controlled himself admirably. Even when he reached the second tee, and the Colonel, seizing his caddy, went to ground in a pot bunker, over the edge of which they both peered fearfully, Uncle retained his dignity.

'Straight down the middle is the line, I suppose,' he remarked to his caddy.

'Yus,' said the caddy from a range of twenty yards.

But unfortunately Uncle James did not go straight down the middle. It's a very nice five hole is our second: a drive, a full brassie and a mashie on to the green over a little hill. But you must get your drive – otherwise . . . And Uncle was otherwise.

I measured it afterwards. His driver hit the ground exactly eighteen inches behind the ball, travelling with all the force of 'to left wrist for follow through'. The shaft followed through: the head did not. It remained completely embedded in the turf.

'Have you finished?' demanded the Colonel, emerging from his dugout. Then he pointed an outraged finger at the broken head. 'This is a tee, sir, not a timber-yard. Would you be good enough to remove that foreign body, before I drive?'

I removed it: I was afraid Uncle would twang again if he stooped. And then the Colonel addressed his ball. From there by easy stages, with a fine-losing hazard off a tree, it travelled out of bounds.

'Stroke and distance, I presume,' murmured Uncle. 'Boy, another driver.'

And then ensued a spectacle which almost shattered my nerves. Uncle James got stuck. He got his club up but couldn't get it down. Both arms were wrapped round his neck, the club lay over his left shoulder pointing at the ground. And there he remained, saying the most dreadful things, and biting his sleeve.

'Posing for a statue?' asked the Colonel satirically.

'G-r-r-r – ' said Uncle, and suddenly something snapped. The club came down like a streak of lightning – there was a sweet, clear click, and even Duncan would have been satisfied with the result. Probably it was the most exquisite moment of Uncle's life. Heaven knows how it happened – certainly the performer didn't. But for the first time and – I feel tolerably confident – the last, Uncle James hit a perfect drive. It was three hundred yards if it was an inch, and the Colonel turned pale.

'That's two I've played,' said Uncle calmly. 'You play the odd, sir.'

It was then that the fighting spirit awoke in all its intensity in his opponent, and Uncle James followed him from bunker to bunker counting audibly until they came up with his drive.

'I'm playing one off ten,' he remarked genially.

'And you'll bally well play it,' snapped the Colonel.

Uncle James smiled tolerantly. 'Certainly. As you please. Boy, the wry-necked mashie.'

But it wasn't the wry-necked mashie's day in. Whatever Duncan might have thought about Uncle's drive, I don't think he'd have passed the wry-necked mashie. At the best of times it was a fearsome weapon – on this occasion it became diabolical. Turf and mud flew in all directions – only the ball remained *in statu quo*.

'That's like as we lie,' said the Colonel, as Uncle paused for breath.

'Confound you, sir – go away,' roared Uncle James, completely losing all vestige of self-control. And at that moment I saw Molly peering over the hill that guarded the green.

'The laid-back niblick, boy.' Uncle threw the wry-necked mashie into a neighbouring garden – and resumed the attack.

'Fourteen – fifteen – sixteen,' boomed the Colonel. 'Why not get a spade . . . Ah! congratulations. You've hit the ball, even if you have sliced it out of bounds. Perhaps you'd replace some of the turf – or shall I send for a "ground under repair" notice.'

'Your shot, sir,' said Uncle thickly.

'Let me see – I'm playing one off six,' remarked the Colonel. 'And you're out of bounds.'

'I may not be.' Uncle ground his teeth. 'I may have hit a tree and bounced back. G-r-r-r!'

There was a loud tearing noise, and Uncle James started as if an asp had stung him.

'Confound you, sir,' howled the Colonel, as he topped his ball, 'will you be silent when I'm playing?'

But Uncle James was beyond aid.

'My God, Peter!' he muttered. 'I've come undone.'

It was only too true: he was twanging all over like a jazz band. Portions of india-rubber were popping out of his garments like worms on a damp green, and every now and then the back of his coat was convulsed by some internal spasm.

'Can't you take it off altogether?' I asked feverishly.

'No. I can't,' he snapped. The beastly thing is sewn in.'

We heard the Colonel's voice from the green.

'I have played sixteen,' he began – then he stopped with a strangled snort. And as we topped the hill we saw him staring horror-struck at the hole, his lips moving soundlessly.

'That was a lucky shot of yours, Uncle,' came Molly's gentle voice from a shelter where she was knitting. 'Hit that log and bounced right back into the hole.'

And the brazen woman came across the green towards us literally staring me in the face.

'How does the game stand, Colonel Thresher?' she asked sweetly.

'The game, madam,' he choked. 'This isn't a game – it's an – an epidemic. He's murdered my caddy and dug a grave for him, and supplied the music – and now he's bounced into the hole.' He shook his putter in the air and faced Uncle James.

'You have that for a half,' said Uncle, dispassionately regarding a twenty-yard putt. Then he looked at the Colonel and frowned. 'What are you staring at, confound you, sir?'

But the Colonel was backing away, stealthily, muttering to himself.

'I knew it – I knew it,' he said shakingly. 'It's a monkey: the damned man's a musical monkey. He's got a tail – he's got two tails. He's got tails all over him. I've got 'em again: must have. What on earth will Maria say?'

'What the devil?' began Uncle James furiously.

'It's all right – quite all right, sir,' answered the Colonel. 'I'm not very well to-day. Touch of fever. Tails – scores of tails. Completely surrounded by tails. Some long – some short: some with loops – and some without. Great Heavens! there's another just popped out of his neck. Must go and see a doctor at once. Never touch the club port again, I swear it. Never – '

Still muttering, he faded into the distance, leaving Uncle James speechless on the green.

'What the devil is the matter with the fool?' he roared when he had partially recovered his speech.

'I don't think he's very well, Uncle,' said Molly chokingly.

'But isn't he going to play any more?' demanded Uncle. 'He'd never have holed that putt, and I'd have been two up.'

'I know, dear,' said Molly, slipping her arm through his

and leading him gently from the green. 'But I think he's a little upset.'

'Of course, if the man's ill,' began Uncle doubtfully.

'He is, Uncle James,' I said firmly – 'a touch of the sun.' I warily dodged two long streamers trailing behind him, and took his other arm. 'What about going home for tea?'

Uncle brightened.

'That reminds me,' he murmured, 'I've just perfected a small device for automatically washing dirty cups and saucers.'

'Splendid,' I remarked, staring grimly at Molly. 'You shall try it this afternoon.'

The Ooley-Cow

CHARLES E. VAN LOAN

AFTER the explanation, and before Uncle Billy Poindexter and Old Man Sprott had been able to decide just what had hit them, Little Doc Ellis had the nerve to tell me that he had seen the fuse burning for months and months. Little Doc is my friend and I like him, but he resembles many other members of his profession in that he is usually wisest after the post mortem, when it is a wee bit late for the high contracting party.

And at all times Little Doc is full of vintage bromides and figures of speech.

'You have heard the old saw,' said he. 'A worm will turn if you keep picking on him, and so will a straight road if you ride it long enough. A camel is a wonderful burden bearer, but even a double-humped ship of the desert will sink on your hands if you pile the load on him a bale of hay at a time.'

'A worm, a straight road, a camel and a sinking ship,' said I. 'Whither are we drifting?'

Little Doc did not pay any attention to me. It is a way he has.

'Think,' said he, 'how much longer a camel will stand up under punishment if he gets his load straw by straw, as it were. The Ooley-cow was a good thing, but Uncle Billy and Old Man Sprott did not use any judgment. They piled it on him too thick.'

'Meaning,' I asked, 'to compare the Ooley-cow with a camel?'

'Merely a figure of speech,' said Little Doc; 'but yes, such was my intention.'

'Well,' said I, 'your figures of speech need careful auditing. A camel can go eight days without a drink – '

Little Doc made impatient motions at me with both hands. He has no sense of humour, and his mind is a one-way track, totally devoid of spurs and derailing switches. Once started, he must go straight through to his destination.

'What I am trying to make plain to your limited mentality,' said he, 'is that Uncle Billy and Old Man Sprott needed a lesson in conservation, and they got it. The Ooley-cow was the easiest, softest picking that ever strayed from the home pasture. With care and decent treatment he would have lasted a long time and yielded an enormous quantity of nourishment, but Uncle Billy and Old Man Sprott were too greedy. They tried to corner the milk market, and now they will have to sign tags for their drinks and their golf balls the same as the rest of us. They have killed the goose that laid the golden eggs.'

'A minute ago,' said I, 'the Ooley-cow was a camel. Now he is a goose – a dead goose, to be exact. Are you all done figuring with your speech?'

'Practically so, yes.'

'Then,' said I, 'I will plaster up the cracks in your argument with the cement of information. I can use figures of speech myself. You are barking up the wrong tree. You are away off your base. It wasn't the loss of a few dollars that made Mr Perkins run wild in our midst. It was the manner in which he lost them. Let us now dismiss the worm, the camel, the goose and all the rest of the menagerie, retaining only the Ooley-cow. What do you know about cows, if anything?'

'A little,' answered my medical friend.

'A mighty little. You know that a cow has hoofs, horns and a tail. The same description would apply to many creatures, including Satan himself. Your knowledge of cows is largely academic. Now me, I was raised on a farm, and there were cows in my curriculum. I took a seven-year course in the gentle art of acquiring the lacteal fluid. Cow is my speciality, my long suit, my best hold. Believe it or not, when we christened old Perkins the Ooley-cow we builded better than we knew.'

'I follow you at a great distance,' said Little Doc. 'Proceed with the rat killing. Why did we build better than we knew when we did not know anything?'

'Because,' I explained, 'Perkins not only looks like a cow and walks like a cow and plays golf like a cow, but he has the predominant characteristic of a cow. He has the one distinguishing trait which all country cows have in common. If you have studied that noble domestic animal as closely as I have, you would not need to be told what moved Mr Perkins to strew the entire golf course with the mangled remains of the two old pirates before mentioned. Uncle Billy and Old Man Sprott were milking him, yes, and it is quite likely that the Ooley-cow knew that he was being milked, but that knowledge was not the prime cause of the late unpleasantness.'

'I still follow you,' said Little Doc plaintively, 'but I'm losing ground every minute.'

'Listen carefully,' said I. 'Pin back your ears and give me your undivided attention. There are many ways of milking a cow without exciting the animal to violence. I speak now of the old-fashioned cow – the country cow – from Iowa, let us say.'

'The Ooley-cow is from Iowa,' murmured Little Doc.

'Exactly. A city cow may be killed by machinery, and in a dozen different ways, but the country cow does not know anything about new-fangled methods. There is one thing – and one thing only – which will make the gentlest old mooley in Iowa kick over the bucket, upset the milker, jump a four-barred fence and join the wild bunch on the range. Do you know what that one thing is?'

'I haven't even a suspicion,' confessed Little Doc.

Then I told him. I told him in words of one syllable, and after a time he was able to grasp the significance of my remarks. If I could make Little Doc see the point, I can make you see it too. We go from here.

Wesley J Perkins hailed from Dubuque, but he did not hail from there until he had gathered up all the loose change in north-eastern Iowa. When he arrived in sunny Southern California he was fifty-five years of age, and at least fifty of those years had been spent in putting aside something for a rainy day. Judging by the diameter of his bankroll, he must have feared the sort of a deluge which caused the early settlers to lay the ground plans for the Tower of Babel.

Now, it seldom rains in Southern California – that is to say, it seldom rains hard enough to produce a flood – and as soon as Mr Perkins became acquainted with climatic conditions he began to jettison his ark. He joined an exclusive down-town club, took up quarters there and spent his afternoons playing dominoes with some other members of the I've-got-mine Association. Aside from his habit of swelling up whenever he mentioned his home town, and insisting on referring to it as 'the Heidelberg of America', there was nothing about Mr Perkins to provoke comment, unfavourable or otherwise. He was just one more Iowan in a country where Iowans are no novelty.

In person he was the mildest-mannered man that ever foreclosed a short-term mortgage and put a family out in the street. His eyes were large and bovine, his mouth dropped perpetually and so did his jowls, and he moved with the slow, uncertain gait of a venerable milch cow. He had a habit of lowering his head and staring vacantly into space, and all these things earned for him the unhandsome nickname by which he is now known.

'But why the Ooley-cow?' someone asked one day. 'It doesn't mean anything at all!'

'Well,' was the reply, 'neither does Perkins.'

But this was an error, as we shall see later.

It was an increasing waistline that caused the Ooley-cow to look about him for some form of gentle exercise. His physician suggested golf, and that very week the board of directors of the Country Club was asked to consider his application for membership. There were no ringing cheers, but he passed the censors.

I will say for Perkins that when he decided to commit golf he went about it in a very thorough manner. He had himself surveyed for three knickerbocker suits, he laid in a stock of soft shirts, imported stockings and spiked shoes, and he gave our professional *carte blanche* in the matter of field equipment. It is not a safe thing to give a Scotchman permission to dip his hand in your change pocket, and MacPherson certainly availed himself of the opportunity to finger some of the Dubuque money. He took one look at the novice and unloaded on him something less than a hundredweight of dead stock. He also gave him a lesson or two, and sent him forth armed to the teeth with wood, iron and aluminium.

Almost immediately Perkins found himself in the hands of Poindexter and Sprott, two extremely hard-boiled old gentlemen who have never been known to take any interest in a financial proposition assaying less than seven per cent, and that fully guaranteed. Both are retired capitalists, but when they climbed out of the trenches and retreated into the realm of sport they took all their business instincts with them.

Uncle Billy can play to a twelve handicap when it suits him to do so, and his partner in crime is only a couple of strokes behind him; but they seldom uncover their true form, preferring to pose as doddering and infirm invalids, childish old men, who only think they can play the game of golf, easy marks for the rising generation. New members are their victims; beginners are just the same as manna from heaven to them. They instruct the novice humbly and apologetically, but always with a small side bet, and no matter how fast the novice improves he makes the astounding discovery that his two feeble old tutors are able to keep pace with him. Uncle Billy and Old Man Sprott are experts at nursing a betting proposition along, and they seldom win any sort of a match by a margin of more than two up and one to go. Taking into account the natural limitations of age they play golf very well, but they play a cinch even better – and harder. It is common scandal that Uncle Billy has not bought a golf ball in ten years. Old Man Sprott bought one in 1915, but it was under the mellowing influence of the third toddy and, therefore, should not count against him.

The Ooley-cow was a cinch. When he turned up, innocent and guileless and eager to learn the game, Uncle Billy and his running mate were quick to realize that Fate had sent them a downy bird for plucking, and in no time at all the air was full of feathers.

They played the Ooley-cow for golf balls, they played him for caddie hire, they played him for drinks and cigars, they played him for luncheons and they played him for a sucker – played him for everything, in fact, but the locker rent and club dues.

How they came to overlook these items is more than I know. The Ooley-cow would have stood for it; he stood for everything. He signed all the tags with a loose and vapid grin, and if he suffered from writer's cramp he never mentioned the fact. His monthly bill must have been a thing to shudder at, but possibly he regarded this extra outlay as part of his tuition.

Once in a while he was allowed to win, for Poindexter and Sprott followed the system practised by other confidence men; but they never forgot to take his winnings away from him the next day, charging him interest at the rate of fifty per cent for twenty-four hours. The Ooley-cow was so very easy that they took liberties with him, so good-natured about his losses that they presumed upon that good nature and ridiculed him openly; but the old saw sometimes loses a tooth, the worm turns, the straight road bends at last, so does the camel's back, and the prize cow kicks the milker into the middle of next week. And, as I remarked before, the cow usually has a reason.

One morning I dropped into the down-town club which Perkins calls his home. I found him sitting in the reception-room, juggling a newspaper and watching the door. He seemed somewhat disturbed.

'Good morning,' said I.

'It is not a good morning,' said he. 'It's a bad morning. Look at this.'

He handed me the paper, with his thumb at the head of the Lost-and-Found column, and I read as follows:

LOST – *A black leather wallet, containing private papers and a sum of money. A suitable reward will be paid for the return of the same, and no questions asked. Apply to W. J. P., Argonaut Club, City.*

'Tough luck,' said I. 'Did you lose much?'

'Quite a sum,' replied the Ooley-cow. 'Enough to make it an object. In large notes mostly.'

'Too bad. The wallet had your cards in it?'

'And some papers of a private nature.'

'Have you an idea where you might have dropped it? Or do you think it was stolen?'

'I don't know what to think. I had it last night at the Country Club just before I left. I know I had it then, because I took it out in the lounging-room to pay a small bet to Mr Poindexter – a matter of two dollars. Then I put the wallet back in my inside pocket and came straight here – alone in a closed car. I missed it just before going to bed. I telephoned to the Country Club. No sign of it there. I went to the garage myself. It was not in the car. Of course it may have been there earlier in the evening, but I think my driver is honest, and – '

At this point we were interrupted by a clean-cut-looking youngster of perhaps seventeen years.

'Your initials are W J P, sir?' he asked politely.

'They are.'

'This is your ad in the paper?'

'It is.'

The boy reached in his pocket and brought out a black leather wallet. 'I have returned your property,' said he, and waited while

119

the Ooley-cow thumbed a roll of yellow-backed notes.

'All here,' said Perkins with a sigh of relief. Then he looked up at the boy, and his large bovine eyes turned hard as moss agates. 'Where did you get this?' he demanded abruptly. 'How did you come by it?'

The boy smiled and shook his head, but his eyes never left Perkins' face. 'No questions were to be asked, sir,' he said.

'Right!' grunted the Ooley-cow. 'Quite right. A bargain's a bargain. I – I beg your pardon, young man – Still, I'd like to know – Just curiosity, eh? – No? – Very well then. That being the case' – he stripped a fifty-dollar note from the roll and passed it over – 'would you consider this a suitable reward?'

'Yes, sir, and thank you, sir.'

'Good day,' said Perkins, and put the wallet into his pocket. He stared at the boy until he disappeared through the street door.

'Something mighty queer about this,' mused the Ooley-cow thoughtfully. 'Mighty queer. That boy – he looked honest. He had good eyes and he wasn't afraid of me. I couldn't scare him worth a cent. Couldn't bluff him – Yet if he found it somewhere, there wasn't any reason why he shouldn't have told me. He didn't steal it – I'll bet on that. Maybe he got it from someone who did. Oh, well, the main thing is that he brought it back – Going out to the Country Club this afternoon?'

I said that I expected to play golf that day.

'Come out with me then,' said the Ooley-cow. 'Poindexter and Sprott will be there too. Yesterday afternoon I played Poindexter for the lunches today. Holed a long putt on the seventeenth green, and stuck him. Come along, and we'll make Poindexter give a party – for once.'

'It can't be done,' said I. 'Uncle Billy doesn't give parties.'

'We'll make him give one,' chuckled the Ooley-cow. 'We'll insist on it.'

'Insist if you want to,' said I, 'but you'll never get away with it.'

'Meet me here at noon,' said the Ooley-cow. 'If Poindexter doesn't give the party, I will.'

I wasn't exactly keen for the Ooley-cow's society, but I accepted his invitation to ride out to the club in his car. He regaled me with a dreary monologue, descriptive of the Heidelberg of America, and solemnly assured me that the pretty girls one sees in Chicago are all from Dubuque.

It was twelve-thirty when we arrived at the Country Club, and Uncle Billy and Old Man Sprott were ahead of us.

'Poindexter,' said Perkins, 'you are giving a party today, and I have invited our friend here to join us.'

Uncle Billy looked at Old Man Sprott, and both laughed uproariously. Right there was where I should have detected the unmistakable odour of a rodent. It was surprise number one.

'Dee-lighted!' cackled Uncle Billy. 'Glad to have another guest, ain't we, Sprott?'

Sprott grinned and rubbed his hands. 'You bet! Tell you what let's do, Billy. Let's invite everybody in the place – make it a regular party while you're at it!'

'Great idea!' exclaimed Uncle Billy. 'The more the merrier!' This was surprise number two. The first man invited was Henry Bauer, who has known Uncle Billy for many years. He sat down quite overcome.

'You shouldn't do a thing like that, Billy,' said he querulously. 'I have a weak heart, and any sudden shock – '

'Nonsense! You'll join us?'

'Novelty always appealed to me,' said Bauer. 'I'm for ever trying things that nobody has ever tried before. Yes. I'll break bread with you, but – why the celebration? What's it all about?'

That was what everybody wanted to know and what nobody found out, but the luncheon was a brilliant success in spite of the dazed and mystified condition of the guests, and the only limit was the limit of individual capacity. Eighteen of us sat down at the big round table, and sandwich-and-milk orders were sternly countermanded by Uncle Billy, who proved an amazing host, recommending this and that and actually ordering Rhine wine cup for all hands. I could not have been more surprised if the bronze statue in the corner of the grill had hopped down from the pedestal to fill our glasses. Uncle Billy collected a great pile of tags beside his plate, but the presence of so much bad news waiting at his elbow did not seem to affect his appetite in the least. When the party was over he called the head waiter. 'Mark these tags paid,' said Uncle Billy, capping the collection with a yellow-backed note, 'and hand the change to Mr Perkins.'

'Yes sir,' said the head waiter, and disappeared.

I looked at the Ooley-cow, and was just in time to see the light of intelligence dawn in his big soft eyes. He was staring at Uncle Billy, his lower lip was flopping convulsively. Everybody began asking questions at once.

'One moment, gentlemen,' mooed the Ooley-cow, pounding on the table. 'One moment!'

'Now don't get excited, Perkins,' said Old Man Sprott. 'You got your wallet back, didn't you? Cost you fifty, but you got it back. Next time you won't be so careless.'

'Yes,' chimed in Uncle Billy, 'you oughtn't to go dropping your money round loose that way. It'll teach you a lesson.'

'It will indeed.' The Ooely-cow lowered his head and glared first at one old pirate and then at the other. His soft eyes hardened and the moss-agate look came into them. He seemed about to bellow, paw the dirt and charge.

'The laugh is on you,' cackled Poindexter, 'and I'll leave it to the boys here. Last night our genial host dropped his wallet on the floor out in the lounging-room. I kicked it across under the table to Sprott and Sprott put his foot on it. We intended to give it back to him today, but this morning there was an ad in the paper – reward and no questions asked – so we sent a nice bright boy over to the Argonaut Club with the wallet. Perkins gave the boy a fifty-dollar note – very liberal, I call it – and the boy gave it to me. Perfectly legitimate transaction. Our friend here has had a lesson, we've had a delightful luncheon party, and the joke is on him.'

'And a pretty good joke, too!' laughed Old Man Sprott.

'Yes,' said the Ooley-cow at last, 'a pretty good joke. Ha, ha! A mighty good joke.' And place it to his credit that he managed a very fair imitation of a fat man laughing, even to the shaking of the stomach and the wrinkles round the eyes. He looked down at the tray in front of him and fingered the few notes and some loose silver.

'A mighty good joke,' he repeated thoughtfully, 'but what I

can't understand is this – why didn't you two jokers keep the change? It would have been that much funnier.'

The Ooley-cow's party was generally discussed during the next ten days, the consensus of club opinion being that someone ought to teach Poindexter and Sprott the difference between humour and petty larceny. Most of the playing members were disgusted with the two old skinflints, and one effect of this senti-ment manifested itself in the number of invitations that Perkins received to play golf with real people. He declined them all, much to our surprise, and continued to wallop his way round the course with Uncle Billy and Old Man Sprott, apparently on as cordial terms as ever.

'What are you going to do with such a besotted old fool as that?' asked Henry Bauer. 'Here I've invited him into three four-somes this week – all white men, too – and he's turned me down cold. It's not that we want to play with him, for as a golfer he's a terrible thing. It's not that we're crazy about him personally, for socially he's my notion of zero minus; but he took his stinging like a dead-game sport and he's entitled to better treatment than he's getting. But if he hasn't any better sense than to pass his plate for more, what are you going to do about it?'

'"Ephraim is joined to idols,"' quoted Little Doc Ellis. 'Let him alone!'

'No, it's the other way round,' argued Bauer. 'His idols are joined to him – fastened on like leeches. The question naturally arises, how did such a man ever accumulate a fortune? Who forced it on him, and when, and where, and why?'

That very afternoon the Ooley-cow turned up with his guest, a large, loud person, also from Heidelberg of America, who addressed Perkins as 'Wesley' and lost no time in informing us that Southern California would have starved to death but for Iowa's capital. His name was Cottle – Calvin D Cottle – and he gave each one of us his card as he was introduced. There was no need. Nobody could have forgotten him. Some people make an impression at first sight – Calvin D Cottle made a deep dent. His age was perhaps forty-five, but he spoke as one crowned with Methuselah's years and Solomon's wisdom, and after each windy statement he turned to the Ooley-cow for confirmation.

'Ain't that so, Wesley? Old Wes knows, you bet your life! He's from my home town!'

It was as good as a circus to watch Uncle Billy and Old Man Sprott sizing up this fresh victim. It reminded me of two wary old dogs circling for position, manoeuvring for a safe hold. They wanted to know something about his golf game – what was his handicap, for instance?

'Handicap?' repeated Cottle. 'Is that a California idea? Something new, ain't it?'

Uncle Billy explained the handicapping theory.

'Oh!' said Cottle. 'You mean what do I go round in – how many strokes. Well, sometimes I cut under a hundred; sometimes I don't. It just depends. Some days I can hit 'em, some days I can't. That's all there is to it.'

'My case exactly,' purred Old Man Sprott. 'Suppose we dispense with the handicap?'

'That's the stuff!' agreed Cottle heartily. 'I don't want to have to give anybody anything; I don't want anybody to give me anything. I like an even fight, and what I say is, may the best man win! Am I right, gentlemen?'

'Absolutely!' chirped Uncle Billy. 'May the best man win!'

'You bet I'm right!' boomed Cottle. 'Ask Old Wes here about me. Raised right in the same town with him, from a kid knee-high to a grasshopper! I never took any the best of it in my life, did I, Wes? No, you bet not! Remember that time I got skinned out of ten thousand bucks on the land deal? A lot of fellows would have squealed, wouldn't they? A lot of fellows would have hollered for the police; but I just laughed and gave 'em credit for being smarter than I was. I'm the same way in sport as I am in business. I believe in giving everybody credit. I win if I can, but if I can't – well, there's never any hard feelings. That's me all over. You may be able to *lick* me at this golf thing – likely you will; but you'll never *scare* me, that's a cinch. Probably you gentlemen play a better game than I do – been at it longer; but then I'm a lot younger than you are. Got more strength. Hit a longer ball when I do manage to land on one right. So it all evens up in the long run.'

Mr Cottle was still modestly cheering his many admirable qualities when the Perkins party went in to luncheon, and the only pause he made was on the first tee. With his usual caution Uncle Billy had arranged it so that Dubuque was opposed to Southern California, and he had also carefully neglected to name any sort of a bet after he had seen the stranger drive.

Cottle teed his ball and stood over it, gripping his driver until his knuckles showed white under the tan. 'Get ready to ride!' said he. 'You're about to leave this place!'

The clubhead whistled through the air, and I can truthfully say that I never saw a man of his size swing any harder at a golf ball – or come nearer cutting one completely in two.

'Topped it, by gum,' ejaculated Mr Cottle, watching the maimed ball until it disappeared in a bunker. 'Topped it! Well, better luck next time! By the way, what are we playing for? Balls, or money, or what?'

'Whatever you like,' said Uncle Billy promptly. 'You name it.'

'Good! That's the way I like to hear a man talk. Old Wes here is my partner, so I can't bet with him, but I'll have a side match with each of you gentlemen – say, ten great, big, smiling Iowa dollars. Always like to bet what I've got the most of. Satisfactory?'

Uncle Billy glanced at Old Man Sprott, and for an instant the old rascals hesitated. The situation was made to order for them, but they would have preferred a smaller wager to start with, being petty larcenists at heart.

'Better cut that down to five,' said Perkins to Cottle in a low tone. 'They play a strong game.'

'Humph!' grunted his guest. 'Did you ever know me to pike in my life? I ain't going to begin now. Ten dollars or nothing!'

'I've got you,' said Old Man Sprott.

'This once,' said Uncle Billy. 'It's against my principles to play for money; but yes, this once.'

And then those two old sharks insisted on a foursome bet as well.

'Ball, ball, ball,' said the Ooley-cow briefly, and proceeded to follow his partner into the bunker. Poindexter and Sprott popped conservatively down the middle of the course and the battle was on.

Battle, did I say? It was a massacre of the innocents, a slaughter of babes and sucklings. Our foursome trailed along behind, and took note of Mr Cottle, of Dubuque, in his fruitless efforts to tear the cover off the ball. He swung hard enough to knock down a lamp-post, but he seldom made proper connections, and when he did the ball landed so far off course that it took him a dozen shots to get back again. He was hopelessly bad, so bad that there was no chance to make the side matches close ones. On the tenth tee Cottle demanded another bet – to give him a chance to get even, he said. Poindexter and Sprott each bet him another ten-dollar note on the last nine, and this time Uncle Billy did not say anything about his principles.

After it was all over Cottle poured a few mint toddies into his system and floated an alibi to the surface.

'It was those confounded sand greens that did it,' he said. 'I'm used to grass, and I can't putt on anything else. Bet I could take you to Dubuque and flail the everlasting daylights out of you!'

'Shouldn't be surprised,' said Uncle Billy. 'You did a lot better on the last nine – sort of got into your stride. Any time you think you want revenge – '

'You can have it,' finished Old Man Sprott, as he folded a crisp twenty-dollar note. 'We believe in giving a man a chance – eh, Billy?'

'That's the spirit!' cried Cottle enthusiastically. 'Give a man a chance; it's what I say, and if he does anything, give him credit. You beat me today, but I never saw this course before. Tell you what we'll do: Let's make a day of it tomorrow. Morning and afternoon both. Satisfactory? Good! You've got forty dollars of my dough and I want it back. Nobody ever made me quit betting yet, if I figure I have a chance. What's money? Shucks! My country is full of it! Now then, Wesley, if you'll come out on the practice green and give me some pointers on this sand thing, I'll be obliged to you. Ball won't run on sand like it will on grass – have to get used to it. Have to hit 'em harder. Soon as I get the hang of the thing we'll give these Native Sons a battle yet! Native Sons? Native Grandfathers! Come on!' Uncle Billy looked at Old Man Sprott and Old Man Sprott looked at Uncle Billy, but they did not begin to laugh until the Ooley-cow and his guest were out of earshot. Then they chuckled and cackled and choked like a couple of hysterical old hens.

'His putting!' gurgled Uncle Billy. 'Did he have a putt to win a hole all the way round?'

'Not unless he missed count of his shots. Say, Billy!'

'Well?'

'We made a mistake locating so far west. We should have stopped in Iowa. By now we'd have owned the entire state!'

I dropped Mr Calvin D Cottle entirely out of my thoughts; but when I entered the locker-room shortly after noon the next day something reminded me of him. Possibly it was the sound of his voice.

'Boy! Can't we have 'nother toddy here? What's the matter with some service? How 'bout you, Wes? Oh, I forgot – you never take anything till after five o'clock. Think of all the fun you're missing. When I get to be an old fossil like you maybe I'll do the same. Good rule. – You gentlemen having anything? No? Kind of careful, ain't you? Safety first, hey? – Just one toddy, boy, and if that mint ain't fresh, I'll – Yep, you're cagey birds, you are, but I give you credit just the same. And some cash. Don't forget that. Rather have cash than credit any time, hey? I bet you would! But I don't mind a little thing like that. I'm a good sport. You ask Wes here if I ain't. If I ain't a good sport I ain't anything – Still, I'll be darned if I see how you fellows do it! You're both old enough to have sons in the Soldiers' Home over yonder, but you take me out and lick me again – lick me and make me like it! A couple of dried-up mummies with one foot in the grave, and I'm right in the prime of life! Only a kid yet! It's humiliating, that's what it is, humiliating! Forty dollars apiece you're into me – and a flock of golf balls on the side! Boy! Where's the mint toddy? Let's have a little service here!'

I peeped through the door leading to the lounging-room. The Dubuque-California foursome was grouped at a table in a corner. The Ooley-cow looked calm and placid as usual, but his guest was sweating profusely, and as he talked he mopped his brow with the sleeve of his shirt. Uncle Billy and Old Man Sprott were listening politely, but the speculative light in their eyes told me that they were wondering how far they dared go with this out-lander from the Middle West.

'Why,' boomed Cottle, 'I can hit a ball twice as far as either one of you! 'Course I don't always know where it's going, but the main thing is I got the *strength*. I can throw a golf ball farther than you old fossils can hit one with a wooden club, yet you lick me easy as breaking sticks. Can't understand it at all – Twice as strong as you are – Why, say, I bet I can take one hand and out-drive you! *One hand*!'

'Easy, Calvin,' said the Ooley-cow reprovingly. 'Don't make wild statements.'

'Well, I bet I can do it,' repeated Cottle stubbornly. 'If a man's willing to bet his money to back up a wild statement, that shows he's got the right kind of a heart anyway. I ought to be able to stick my left hand in my pocket and go out there and trim two men of your age. I ought to, and I'll be damned if I don't think I can!'

'Tut, tut!' warned the Ooley-cow. 'That's foolishness.'

'Think so?' Cottle dipped his hand in his pocket and brought out a thick roll of notes. 'Well, this stuff here says I can do it – at least I can *try* – and I ain't afraid to back my judgment.'

'Put your money away,' said Perkins. 'Don't be a fool!'

Cottle laughed uproariously and slapped the Ooley-cow on the back.

'Good old Wes!' he cried. 'Ain't changed a bit. Conservative! Always conservative! Got rich at it, but me I got rich taking chances. What's a little wad of notes to me, hey? Nothing but chicken-feed! I'll bet any part of this roll – I'll bet *all* of it – and I'll play these sun-dried old sports with one hand. Now's the time to show whether they've got any sporting blood or not. What do you say, gentlemen?'

Uncle Billy looked at the money and moistened his lips with the tip of his tongue.

'Couldn't think of it,' he croaked at length.

'Pshaw!' sneered Cottle. 'I showed you too much – I scared you!'

'He ain't scared,' put in Old Man Sprott. 'It would be too much like stealing it.'

'I'm the one to worry about that,' announced Cottle. 'It's my money, ain't it? I made it, didn't I? And I can do what I damn please with it – spend it, bet it, burn it up, throw it away. When you've worried about everything else in the world, it'll be time for you to begin worrying about young Mr Cottle's money! This slim little roll – bah! Chicken-feed! Come get it if you want it!' He tossed the money on the table with a gesture which was an insult in itself. 'There it is – cover it! Put up or shut up!'

'Oh, forget it!' said the Ooley-cow wearily. 'Come in and have a bite to eat and forget it.'

'Don't want anything to eat!' was the stubborn response. 'Seldom eat in the middle of the day. But I'll have 'nother mint toddy – Wait a second, Wes. Don't be in such a rush. Lemme understand this thing. These – these gentlemen here, these two friends of yours, these dead-game old Native Sons have got eighty dollars of my money – not that it makes any difference to me, understand, but they've got it – eighty dollars that they won from me playing golf. Now I may have a drink or two in me and I may not, understand, but anyhow I know what I'm about. I make these – gentlemen a sporting proposition. I give 'em a chance to pick up a couple of hundred apiece, and they want to run out on me because it'll be like stealing it. What kind of a deal is that, hey? Is it sportsmanship? Is it what they call giving a man a chance? Is it – '

'But they know you wouldn't have a chance,' interrupted the Ooley-cow soothingly. 'They don't want a sure thing.'

'They've had one so far, haven't they?' howled Cottle. 'What are they scared of now? 'Fraid I'll squeal if I lose? Tell 'em about me, Wes. Tell 'em I never squealed in my life. I win if I can, but if I can't – 's all right. No kick coming. There never was a piker in the Cottle family, was there, Wes? No, you bet not! We're sports, every one of us. Takes more than one slim little roll to send us up a tree! If there's anything that makes me sick, it's a cold-footed, penny-pinching, nickel-nursing, sure-thing player!'

'Your money does not frighten me,' said Uncle Billy, who was slightly nettled by this time. 'It is against my principles to play for a cash bet – '

'But you and your pussy-footed old side-partner got into me for eighty dollars just the same!' scoffed Cottle. 'You and your principles be damned!'

Uncle Billy swallowed this without blinking, but he did not look at Cottle. He was looking at the roll of notes on the table.

'If you are really in earnest – ' began Poindexter, and glanced at Old Man Sprott.

'Go ahead, Billy,' croaked that aged reprobate. 'Teach him a lesson. He needs it.'

'Never mind the lesson,' snapped Cottle. 'I got out of school a long time ago. The bet is that I can leave my left arm in the club-house safe – stick it in my pocket – and trim you birds with one hand.'

'We wouldn't insist on that,' said Old Man Sprott. 'Play with both hands if you want to.'

'Think I'm a welsher?' demanded Cottle. 'The original proposition goes. 'Course I wouldn't really cut the arm off and leave it

130

in the safe, but what I mean is, if I use two arms in making a shot, right there is where I lose. Satisfactory?'

'Perkins,' said Uncle Billy, solemnly wagging his head, 'you are a witness that this thing has been forced on me. I have been bullied and brow-beaten and insulted into making this bet – '

'And so have I,' chimed in Old Man Sprott. 'I'm almost ashamed – '

The Ooley-cow shrugged his shoulders.

'I am a witness,' said he quietly. 'Calvin, these gentlemen have stated the case correctly. You have forced them to accept your proposition – '

'And he can't blame anyone if he loses,' finished Uncle Billy as he reached for the roll of notes.

'You bet!' ejaculated Old Man Sprott. 'He was looking for trouble, and now he's found it. Count it, Billy and we'll each take half.'

'That goes, does it?' asked Cottle.

'Sir?' cried Uncle Billy.

'Oh, I just wanted to put you on record,' said Cottle, with a grin. 'Wesley, you're my witness too. I mislaid a five-hundred-dollar note the other day, and it may have got into my change pocket. Might as well see if a big bet will put these safety-first players off their game! Anyhow, I'm betting whatever's there, I ain't sure how much it is.'

'I am,' said Uncle Billy in a changed voice. He had come to the five-hundred-dollar note, sandwiched in between two twenties. He looked at Old Man Sprott, and for the first time I saw doubt in his eyes.

'Oh, it's there, is it?' asked Cottle carelessly. 'Well, let it all ride. I never backed out on a gambling proposition in my life – never pinched a bet after the ball started to roll. Shoot the entire works – 's all right with me!'

Uncle Billy and Old Man Sprott exchanged significant glances, but after a short argument and some abuse from Cottle they toddled over to the desk and filled out two blank cheques – for five hundred and eighty dollars apiece.

'Make 'em payable to cash,' suggested Cottle. 'You'll probably tear 'em up after the game. Now the next thing is a stakeholder – '

'Is that – necessary?' asked Old Man Sprott.

'Sure!' said Cottle. 'I might run out on you. Let's have everything according to Hoyle – stakeholder and all the other trimmings. Anybody'll be satisfactory to me; that young fellow getting an earful at the door; he'll do.'

So I became the stakeholder – the custodian of eleven hundred and sixty dollars in coin and two cheques representing a like amount. I thought I detected a slight nervousness in the signatures, and no wonder. It was the biggest bet those old petty larcenists had ever made in their lives. They went in to luncheon – at the invitation of the Ooley-cow, of course – but I noticed that they did not eat much. Cottle wandered out to the practice green, putter in hand, forgetting all about the mint toddy, which, by the way, had never been ordered.

'You drive first, sir,' said Uncle Billy to Cottle, pursuing his usual system. 'We'll follow you.'

'Think you'll feel easier if I should hit one over into the eucalyptus trees yonder?' asked the man from Dubuque. 'Little nervous, eh? Does a big bet scare you? I was counting on that – Oh, very well, I'll take the honour.'

'Just a second,' said Old Man Sprott, who had been prowling about in the background and fidgeting with his driver. 'Does the stakeholder understand the terms of the bet? Mr Cottle is playing a match with each of us individually – '

'Separately and side by each,' added Cottle.

'Using only one arm,' said Old Man Sprott.

'If he uses both arms in making a shot,' put in Uncle Billy, 'he forfeits both matches. Is that correct, Mr Cottle?'

'Correct as hell! Watch me closely, young man. I have no moustache to deceive you – nothing up my sleeve but my good right arm. Watch me closely!'

He teed his ball, dropped his left arm at his side, grasped the driver firmly in his right hand and swung the club a couple of times in tentative fashion. The head of the driver described a perfect arc, barely grazing the top of the tee. His two-armed swing had been a thing of violence – a baseball wallop, constricted, bound up, without follow-through or timing, a combination of brute strength and awkwardness. Uncle Billy's chin sagged as he watched the easy, natural sweep of that wooden club – the wrist-snap applied at the proper time, and the long graceful follow-through which gives distance as well as direction. Old Man Sprott also seemed to be struggling with an entirely new and not altogether pleasant idea.

'Watch me closely, stakeholder,' repeated Cottle, addressing the ball. 'Nothing up my sleeve but my good right arm. Would you gentlemen like to have me roll up my sleeve before I start?'

'Drive!' grunted Uncle Billy.

'I'll do that little thing,' said Cottle, and this time he put the power into the swing. The ball, caught squarely in the middle of the clubface, went whistling toward the distant green, a perfect screamer of a drive without a suspicion of hook or slice. It cleared the cross-bunker by ten feet, carried at least a hundred and eighty yards before it touched grass, and then bounded ahead like a scared rabbit, coming to rest at least two hundred and twenty-five yards away. 'You like that?' asked Cottle, moving off the tee. 'I didn't step into it very hard or I might have had more distance. Satisfactory, stakeholder?' And he winked at me openly and deliberately.

'What – what sort of game is this?' gulped Old Man Sprott, finding his voice with an effort.

'Why,' said Cottle, smiling cheerfully, 'I wouldn't like to say offhand and so early in the game, but you might call it golf. Yes, call it golf, and let it go at that.'

At this point I wish to go on record as denying the rumour that our two old reprobates showed the white feather. That first tee shot, and the manner in which it was made, was enough to inform them that they were up against a sickening surprise party; but, though startled and shaken, they did not weaken. They pulled themselves together and drove the best they knew how, and I realized that for once I was to see their true golfing form uncovered.

Cottle tucked his wooden club under his arm and started down the course, and from that time on he had very little to say. Uncle Billy and Old Man Sprott followed him, their heads together at a confidential angle, and I brought up the rear with the Ooley-cow, who had elected himself a gallery of one.

The first hole is a long par four. Poindexter and Sprott usually make it in five, seldom getting home with their seconds unless they have a wind behind them. Both used brassies and both were short of the green. Then they watched Cottle as he went forward to his ball.

'That drive might have been a freak shot,' quavered Uncle Billy.

'Lucky fluke, that's all,' said Old Man Sprott, but I knew and they knew that they only hoped they were telling the truth.

Cottle paused over his ball for an instant, examined the lie and drew a wooden spoon from his bag. Then he set himself, and the next instant the ball was on its way, a long, high shot, dead on the pin.

'And maybe that was a fluke!' muttered the Ooley-cow under his breath. 'Look! He's got the green with it!'

From the same distance I would have played a full midiron and trusted in Providence, but Cottle had used his wood, and I may say that never have I seen a ball better placed. It carried to the little rise of turf in front of the putting green, hopped once, and trickled close to the cup. I was not the only one who appreciated that spoon shot.

'Say,' yapped Old Man Sprott, turning to Perkins, 'what are we up against here? Miracles?'

'Yes, what have you framed up on us?' demanded Uncle Billy vindictively.

'Something easy, gentlemen,' chucked the Ooley-cow. 'A soft thing from my home town. Probably he's only lucky.'

The two members of the SureThing Society went after their customary fives and got them, but Cottle laid his approach putt stone dead at the cup and holed out in four. He missed a three by the matter of half an inch. I could stand the suspense no longer. I took Perkins aside while the contestants were walking to the second tee.

'You might tell a friend,' I suggested. 'In strict confidence, what are they up against?'

'Something easy,' repeated the Ooley-cow, regarding me with his soft, innocent eyes. 'They wanted it and now they've got it.'

'But yesterday, when he played with both arms – ' I began.

'That was yesterday,' said Perkins. 'You'll notice that they didn't have the decency to offer him a handicap, even when they felt morally certain that he had made a fool bet. Not that he would have accepted it – but they didn't offer it. They're wolves, clear to the bones, but once in a while a wolf bites off more than he can chew.' And he walked away from me. Right there I began reconstructing my opinion of the Ooley-cow.

In my official capacity as stakeholder I saw every shot that was played that afternoon. I still preserve the original score card of that amazing golf round. There are times when I think I will have it framed and present it to the club, with red-ink crosses against the thirteenth and fourteenth holes. I might even set a red-ink star against the difficult sixth hole, where Cottle sent another tremendous spoon shot down the wind, and took a four where most of our Class-A men are content with a five. I might make a notation against the tricky ninth, where he played a marvellous shot out of a sand-trap to halve a hole which I would have given up as lost. I might make a footnote calling attention to his deadly work with his short irons. I say I think of all these things, but perhaps I shall never frame that card. The two men most interested will never forget the figures. It is enough to say that Old Man Sprott, playing such golf as I had never seen him play before, succumbed at the thirteenth hole, six down and five to go. Uncle Billy gave up the ghost on the fourteenth green, five and four, and I handed the money and the cheques to Mr Calvin D Cottle, of Dubuque. He pocketed the loot with a grin.

'Shall we play the bye-holes for something?' he asked. 'A drink – or a ball, maybe?' And then the storm broke. I do not pretend to quote the exact language of the losers. I merely state that I was surprised, yes, shocked at Uncle Billy Poindexter. I had no idea that a member of the Episcopal church – but let that pass. He was not himself. He was the biter bitten, the milker milked. It makes a difference. Old Man Sprott also erupted in an astounding manner. It was the Ooley-cow who took the centre of the stage.

'Just a minute, gentlemen,' said he. 'Do not say anything which you might afterward regret. Remember the stakeholder is still with us. My friend here is not, as you intimate, a crook. Neither is he a sure-thing player. We have some sure-thing players with us, but he is not one of them. He is merely the one-armed golf champion of Dubuque – and the Middle West.'

Imagine an interlude here for fireworks, followed by pertinent questions.

'Yes, yes, I know,' said Perkins soothingly. 'He can't play a lick with two arms. He never could. Matter of fact, he never learned. He fell off a haystack in Iowa – how many years ago was it, Cal?'

'Twelve,' said Mr Cottle. 'Twelve next July.'

'And he broke his left arm rather badly,' explained the Ooley-cow. 'Didn't have the use of it for – how many years, Cal?'

'Oh, about six, I should say.'

'Six years. A determined man can accomplish much in that length of time. Cottle learned to play golf with his right arm – fairly well, as you must admit. Finally he got the left arm fixed up – they took a piece of bone out of his shin and grafted it in – new-fangled idea. Decided there was no sense in spoiling a one-armed star to make a dub two-armed golfer. Country full of 'em already. That's the whole story. You picked him for an easy mark, a good thing. You thought he had a bad bet and you had a good one. Don't take the trouble to deny it. Gentlemen, allow me to present the champion one-armed golfer of Iowa and the Middle West!'

'Yes,' said Cottle modestly, 'when a man does anything, give him credit for it. Personally I'd rather have the cash!'

'How do you feel about it now?' asked the Ooley-cow.

Judging by their comments, they felt warm – very warm. Hot, in fact. The Ooley-cow made just one more statement, but to me that statement contained the gist of the whole matter.

'This,' said he, 'squares us on the wallet proposition. I didn't say anything about it at the time, but that struck me as a scaly trick. So I invited Cal to come out and pay me a visit – Shall we go back to the clubhouse?'

I made Little Doc Ellis see the point; perhaps I can make you see it now.

Returning to the original simile, the Ooley-cow was willing to be milked for golf balls and luncheons and caddie hire. That was legitimate milking and he did not resent it. He would have continued to give down in great abundance, but when they took fifty dollars from him, in the form of a bogus reward, he kicked over the bucket, injured the milkers and jumped the fence.

Why? I'm almost ashamed to tell you, but did you ever hear of a country cow – an Iowa cow – that would stand for being milked from the wrong side?

I think this will be all, except that I anticipate a hard winter for the golfing beginners at our club.

An Unlucky Golfer

A. A. MILNE

I AM the world's unluckiest golfer.

Yes, I know what you are going to say, but I don't mean what you mean. Of the ordinary bad luck which comes to us all at times I do not complain. It is the 'rub of the green'. When my best drive is caught by cover, or fielded smartly by mid-on with his foot; when I elect to run a bunker ten yards away and am most unfortunately held up by blown sand (or, as I generally call it, dashed sand); when I arrive at last on the green, and my only hope of winning the hole is that my opponent shall pick up a worm which he ought to have brushed away, or brush away one which he ought to have picked up . . . and there are no worms out this morning; on all these occasions I take my ill-luck with a shrug of the shoulders and something as nearly like a smile as I can manage. After all, golf would be a very dull game if it were entirely a matter of skill.

It is in another way altogether that I am singled out by Fate. Once I have driven off the first tee, she is no more unkind to me than to the others. By that time she has done her worst. But sometimes it is as much as I can do to get on to the first tee at all, so relentless is her persecution of me. Surely no other golfer is so obstructed.

I suppose my real trouble is that I take golf too seriously. When I arranged many years ago to be at St Margaret's at 2.30 on Wednesday, I *was* at St Margaret's at 2.30 on Wednesday. I didn't ring up suddenly and say that I had a cold, or that my dog wanted a run, or that a set of proofs had just arrived which had to be corrected quickly. No, I told myself that an engagement was an engagement. *'Wednesday, St Margaret's, 2.30'* – I turned up, and have never regretted it. If to-day my appointment is *'Sunningdale, Thursday, 10.45'*, it is as certain that I shall be there. But these other golfers, one wonders how they ever get married at all.

I am not saying that they are careless about their promises; not all of them; but that, in their case, the mere fact of making an important appointment seems to bring out something: spots or a jury-summons or a new baby. I suppose that, when they play with each other, they hardly notice these obstructions, for if A has to plead an unexpected christening on the Monday, B practically knows that he will have to have his tonsils removed suddenly on the Thursday, when the return match is to be played; wherefore neither feels resentment against the other. Only I, who take golf seriously, am surprised. 'Tonsils, juries, christenings,' I say to myself, 'but I thought we were playing *golf.'*

But not only am I a serious golfer, I am, as I have said, the world's unluckiest one. The most amazing things happen to the people who arrange to play with me. On the very morning of our game they are arrested for murder, summoned to Buckingham Palace, removed to asylums, sent disguised to Tibet, or asked to play the leading part in *Hamlet* at twenty-four hours' notice. Any actor out of work would be wise to fix up a game with me, for on that day he would almost certainly be sent for to start rehearsing. Of course he might have a fatal accident instead, but that is a risk which he would have to take.

However, it is time that you saw my golf in action. Here, then, is a typical day, unexaggerated.

On a certain Wednesday I was to play a couple of rounds with a friend. On Tuesday afternoon I rang him up on the telephone to remind him of our engagement, and in the course of a little talk before we hung our receivers up, I said that I had just been lunching with an actor-manager, and he said that he had just been bitten by a mosquito. Not that it mattered to the other in the least, but one must have one's twopennyworth.

Wednesday dawned, as it has a habit of doing, but never did it dawn so beautifully as now; the beginning of one of those lovely days of early autumn than which nothing is more lovely. That I was to spend the whole of this beautiful day playing golf, not working, was almost too good to be believed. I sang as I climbed into my knickerbockers; I was still singing as I arranged the tassels of my garters . . . And, as I went down to breakfast, the telephone bell began to sing.

I knew at once, of course. With all the experience I have had, I knew. I merely wondered whether it was the man himself who was dead, or one of his friends.

'Hallo!' said his voice. So he was alive.

'Yes?' I said coldly.

'Hallo! I say, you remember the mosquito?' (*Which mosquito?*) 'Well, my leg is about three times its ordinary size.' (*Does that matter? I thought. None of us is really symmetrical.*) 'I can hardly move it . . . Doctor . . . Nurses . . . Amputate . . . In bed for a year . . .' He babbled on, but I was not listening. I was wondering if I could possibly find somebody else. It is a funny thing, but somehow I cannot write in knickerbockers. Once I have put them on, I find it impossible to work. I *must* play golf. But alas! how difficult to find another at such short notice. As a last hope I decided to ring up Z. Z is almost as keen a golfer as myself. No such trifle as a lack of uniformity in his legs would keep *him* from his game. I cut off the other fellow as he was getting to the middle of his third operation, and got on to Z. Z, thank Heaven for him, would play.

I called for him. We drove down. We arrived. With each succeeding minute the morning became more lovely; with each succeeding minute I thanked Heaven more for Z. As we walked over to the caddie-master I was almost crying with happiness. Never was there day more beautiful. All this mosquito business had made us late, and there were no caddies left, but did I mind? Not a bit! On a morning like this, I thought to myself as I stepped on to the first tee, I couldn't mind anything.

The moment that Z stepped on to the first tee, I knew that I was mistaken. You will never believe it, but I give you my word that it is true. Z stepped on to the wrong bit of the first tee, uttered one loud yell . . . and collapsed on the grass with a broken ankle . . .

You say that I might have left him there and played a few holes by myself? I did. But it was necessary to give instructions for him to be removed before others came after me. I forget the exact rule about loose bodies on the tee, but a fussy player might easily have objected. So I had to go back and tell the secretary, and one way and another I was delayed a good deal. And of course it spoiled my day entirely.

But I was not surprised. As I say, I am the world's unluckiest golfer.

Beginner's Luck

A. G. MACDONELL

AFEW days after his curious experience on the cricket field, Donald's attention was drawn away from the problem of the Englishman's attitude towards his national game by a chance paragraph in a leading newspaper on the subject of Golf. And golf was a matter of grave temptation to Donald at this period of his life.

Both Sir Ethelred Ormerode, MP, and Sir Ludovic Phibbs, MP, had invited him to a day's golf at one or other of the large clubs near London to which they belonged; but Donald had made excuses to avoid acceptance, for the following reason. He had played no golf since he had been a lad of eighteen at Aberdeen, and as he had not enough money to join a club in the south and play regularly, he was unwilling to resurrect an ancient passion which he had no means of gratifying. Up to the age of eighteen golf had been a religion to him far more inspiring and appealing than the dry dogmatics of the various sections of the Presbyterian Church which wrangled in those days so enthusiastically in the North-East of Scotland. Since that time, of course, there has been a notable reunion of the sections and public wrangling has perforce come to an end, an end regretted so passionately that the phrase 'a peace-maker' in that part of the world is rapidly acquiring the sense of a busy-body or a spoil-sport. As one ancient soldier of the Faith, whose enthusiasm for the Word was greater than his knowledge of it, was recently heard to observe bitterly into the depths of his patriarchal beard, 'Isn't it enough for them to have been promised the Kingdom of Heaven, without they must poke their disjaskit nebs into Buchan and the Mearns?'

But whatever the rights and wrongs of the once indignant and now cooing Churches, it is a fact that Donald before the War was more interested in golf than in religion, and a handicap of plus one when he was seventeen had marked him out as a coming man. But first the War and then the work of farming the Mains of Balspindie had put an end to all that, and Donald was reluctant to awaken the dragon.

But one day he happened to read in one of the most famous newspapers in the world the following paragraph in a column written by 'Our Golf Correspondent':

'Our recent defeat at the hands of the stern and wild Caledonians was, no doubt, demnition horrid, as our old friend would have said, and had it not been for the amazing series of flukes by which the veteran Bernardo, now well advanced in decrepitude, not only managed to hang on to the metaphorical coat-tails of his slashing young adversary, but even to push his nose in front on the last green, the score of the Sassenachs would have been as blank as their faces. For their majestic leader was snodded on the fourteenth green, and even the Dumkins and the Podder of the team, usually safe cards, met their Bannockburn. And that was that. The only consolation for this unexpected "rewersal" lies in the fact that the Northerners consisted almost entirely of what are called Anglo-Scots, domiciled in England and products of English golf. For there is no doubt that the balance of golfing power has shifted to the south, and England is now the real custodian of the ancient traditions of the game. Which, as a consolation prize, is all wery capital.'

Donald read this through carefully several times, for it seemed to be a matter of importance to him and his work. He had seen, at very close quarters, the English engaged upon their ancient, indigenous national pastime, and he had been unable to make head or tail of it.

But it was worth while going out of his way to see how they treated another nation's national game which, according to the golf correspondent, they had mastered perfectly and had, as it were, adopted and nationalized.

The matter was easily arranged, and, on the following Sunday, he was picked up at the corner of Royal Avenue and King's Road by Sir Ludovic Phibbs in a Rolls-Royce limousine car. Sir Ludovic was wearing a superb fur coat and was wrapped in a superb fur rug. On the way down to Cedar Park, the venue of the day's golf, Sir Ludovic talked a good deal about the scandal of the dole. It appeared to be his view that everyone who took the dole ought to be shot in order to teach them not to slack. The solution of the whole trouble was the abolition of Trades Unionism and harder work all round, including Saturday afternoons and a half-day Sundays. This theme lasted most of the journey, and Donald was not called upon to contribute more than an occasional monosyllable.

Cedar Park is one of the newest of the great golf clubs which are ringed round the north, west, and south of London in such profusion, and what is now the club-house had been in earlier centuries the mansion of a venerable line of marquesses. High taxation had completed the havoc in the venerable finances which had begun in the Georgian and Victorian generations by high gambling, and the entire estate was sold shortly after the War by the eleventh marquess to a man who had, during it, made an enormous fortune by a most ingenious dodge. For, alone with the late Lord Kitchener, he had realized in August and September of 1914 that the War was going to be a very long business, thus providing ample opportunities for very big business, and that before it was over it would require a British Army of millions and millions of soldiers. Having first of all taken the precaution of getting himself registered as a man who was indispensable to the civil life of the nation during the great Armageddon, for at the outbreak of hostilities he was only thirty-one years of age, and, in order to be on the safe side, having had himself certified by a medical man as suffering from short sight, varicose veins, a weak heart, and incipient lung trouble, he set himself upon his great task of cornering the world's supply of rum. By the middle of 1917 he had succeeded, and in 1920 he paid ninety-three thousand pounds for Cedar Park, and purchased in addition a house in Upper Brook Street, a hunting-box near Melton, a two-thousand-ton motor-yacht, Lochtarig Castle, Inverness-shire, and the long leases of three luxurious flats in Mayfair in which to entertain, without his wife knowing, by day or night, his numerous lady friends. He was, of course, knighted for his public services during the War. It was not until 1925 that the rum-knight shot himself to avoid an absolutely certain fourteen years for fraudulent conversion, and Cedar Park was acquired by a syndicate of Armenian sportsmen for the purpose of converting it into a country club.

An enormous man in a pale-blue uniform tricked out with thick silver cords and studded with cartwheel silver buttons, opened the door of the car and bowed Sir Ludovic, and a little less impressively, Donald Cameron into the clubhouse. Donald was painfully conscious that his grey flannel trousers bagged at the knee and that his old blue 1914 golfing-coat had a shine at one elbow and a hole at the other.

The moment he entered the clubhouse a superb spectacle met his dazzled gaze. It was not the parquet floor, on which his nail-studded shoes squeaked loudly, or the marble columns, or the voluptuous paintings on the ceiling, or the gilt-framed mirrors on the walls, or the chandeliers of a thousand crystals, or even the palms in their gilt pots and synthetic earth, that knocked him all of a heap. It was the group of golfers that was standing in front of the huge fire-place. There were purple jumpers and green jumpers and yellow jumpers and tartan jumpers; there were the biggest, the baggiest, the brightest plus-fours that ever dulled the lustre of a peacock's tail; there were the rosiest of lips, the gayest of cheeks, and flimsiest of silk stockings, and the orangest of finger-nails and probably, if the truth were known, of toe-nails too; there were waves of an unbelievable permanence and lustre; there were jewels, on the men as well as on the women, and foot-long jade and amber cigarette-holders and foot-long cigars with glistening cummerbunds; and there was laughter and gaiety and much bending, courtier-like, from the waist, and much raising of girlish, kohl-fringed eyes, and a great chattering. Donald felt like a navvy, and when, in his agitation, he dropped his clubs with a resounding clash upon the floor and everyone stopped talking and looked at him, he wished he was dead. Another pale-blue-and-silver giant picked up the clubs, held them out at arm's length and examined them in disdainful astonishment – for after years of disuse they were very rusty – and said coldly, 'Clubs go into the locker-room, sir,' and Donald squeaked his way across the parquet after him amid a profound silence.

The locker-room was full of young gentlemen who were discarding their jumpers – which certainly competed with Mr Shelley's idea of Life Staining the White Radiance of Eternity – in favour of brown leather jerkins fastened up the front with that singular arrangement which is called a zipper. Donald edged in furtively, hazily watched the flunkey lay the clubs down upon a bench, and then fled in panic through the nearest open door and found himself suddenly in a wire-netted enclosure which was packed with a dense throng of caddies. The caddies were just as surprised by his appearance in their midst as the elegant ladies and gentlemen in the lounge had been by the fall of the clubs, and a deathly stillness once again paralysed Donald.

He backed awkwardly out of the enclosure, bouncing off caddy after caddy like a cork coming over a rock-studded sluice, and was brought up short at last by what seemed to be a caddy rooted immovably in the ground. Two desperate backward lunges failed to dislodge the obstacle and Donald turned and found it was the wall of the professional's shop. The caddies, and worse still, an exquisitely beautiful young lady with a cupid's-bow mouth and practically no skirt on at all, who had just emerged from the shop, watched him with profound interest. Scarlet in the face, he rushed past the radiant beauty, and hid himself in the darkest corner of the shop and pretended to be utterly absorbed in a driver which he picked out at random from the rack. Rather to his surprise, and greatly to his relief, no one molested him with up-to-date, go-getting salesmanship, and in a few minutes he had pulled himself together and was able to look round and face the world.

Suddenly he gave a start. Something queer was going on

inside him. He sniffed the air once, and then again, and then the half-forgotten past came rushing to him across the wasted years. The shining rows of clubs, the boxes of balls, the scent of leather and rubber and gripwax and pitch, the club-makers filing away over the vices and polishing and varnishing and splicing and binding, the casual members waggling a club here and there, the professional listening courteously to tales of apocryphal feats, all the old familiar scenes of his youth came back to him. It was eleven years since he had played a game of golf, thirteen years since he had bought a club. Thirteen wasted years. Dash it, thought Donald, damn it, blast it, I can't afford a new club – I don't want a new club, but I'm going to buy a new club. He spoke diffidently to one of the assistants who was passing behind him, and enquired the price of the drivers.

'It's a new lot just finished, sir,' said the assistant, 'and I'm not sure of the price. I'll ask Mr Glennie.'

Mr Glennie was the professional himself. The great man, who was talking to a member, or rather was listening to a member's grievances against his luck, a ritual which occupies a large part of a professional's working day, happened to overhear the assistant, and he said over his shoulder in the broadest of broad Scottish accents, 'They're fufty-twa shullin' and cheap at that'.

Donald started back. Two pounds twelve for a driver! Things had changed indeed since the days when the great Archie Simpson had sold him a brassy, brand-new, bright yellow, reful-gent driver with a lovely whippy shaft, for five shillings and nine-pence.

His movement of Aberdonian horror brought him out of the dark corner into the sunlight which was streaming through the window, and it was the professional's turn to jump.

'It's Master Donald!' he exclaimed. 'Yes mind me, Master Donald – Jim Glennie, assistant that was at Glenavie to Tommy Anderson that went to the States?'

'Glennie!' cried Donald, a subtle warm feeling suddenly invading his body, and he grasped the professional's huge red hand.

'Man!' cried the latter, 'but I'm glad to see ye. How lang is't sin' we used to ding awa at each other roon' Glenavie? Man, it must be years and years. And fit's aye deein' wi' yer game? Are ye plus sax or seeven?'

'Glennie,' said Donald sadly, 'I haven't touched a club since those old days. This is the first time I've set foot in a professional's shop since you took me that time to see Alec Marling at Balgownie the day before the War broke out.'

'Eh, man, but you're a champion lost,' and the professional shook his head mournfully.

'But, Glennie,' went on Donald, 'where did you learn that fine Buchan accent? You never used to talk like that. Is it since you came south that you've picked it up?'

The big professional looked a little shamefaced and drew Donald back into the dark corner.

It's good for trade,' he whispered in the pure English of Inverness. 'They like a Scot to be real Scottish. They think it makes a man what they call "a character". God knows why, but there it is. So I just humour them by talking like a Guild Street carter who's having a bit of back-chat with an Aberdeen fish-wife. It makes the profits something extraordinary.'

'Hi! Glennie, you old swindler,' shouted a stoutish, red-faced man who was smoking a big cigar and wearing a spectroscopic suit of tweeds. 'How much do you want to sting me for this putter?'

'Thirty-twa shullin' and saxpence, Sir Walter,' replied Glennie over his shoulder, 'but ye'll be wastin' yer siller, for neither that club nor any ither wull bring ye doon below eighteen.'

A delighted laugh from a group of men behind Sir Walter greeted this sally.

'You see,' whispered Glennie, 'he'll buy it and he'll tell his friends that I tried to dissuade him, and they'll all agree that I'm a rare old character, and they'll all come and buy too.'

'But fifty-two shillings for a driver!' said Donald. 'Do you mean to say they'll pay that?'

'Yes, of course they will. They'll pay anything so long as it's more than any other professional at any other club charges them. That's the whole secret. Those drivers there aren't a new set at all. They're the same set as I was asking forty-eight shillings for last week-end, but I heard during the week from a friend who keeps an eye open for me, that young Jock Robbie over at Addingdale Manor had put his drivers and brassies up from forty-six shillings to fifty, the dirty young dog. Not that I blame him. It's a new form of commercial competition, Master Donald, a sort of inverted price-cutting. Na, na, Muster Hennessey,' he broke into his trade voice again, 'ye dinna want ony new clubs. Ye're playin' brawly with yer auld yins. Still, if ye want to try yon spoon, tak it oot and play a couple of roons wi' it, and if ye dinna like it put it back.'

He turned to Donald again.

'That's a sure card down here. They always fall for it. They take the club and tell their friends that I've given it to them on trial because I'm not absolutely certain that it will suit their game, and they never bring it back. Not once. Did you say you wanted a driver, Master Donald?'

'Not at fifty-two shillings,' said Donald with a smile.

Glennie indignantly waved away the suggestion.

'You shall have your pick of the shop at cost price,' he said, and then, looking furtively round and lowering his voice until it was almost inaudible, he breathed in Donald's ear, 'Fifteen and six.'

Donald chose a beautiful driver, treading on air all the while and feeling eighteen years of age, and then Sir Ludovic Phibbs came into the shop.

'Ah! There you are, Cameron,' he said genially; 'there are only two couples in front of us now. Are you ready? Good morning, Glennie, you old shark. There's no use trying to swing the lead over Mr Cameron. He's an Aberdonian himself.'

As Donald went out, Glennie thrust a box of balls under his arm and whispered, 'For old time's sake!'

On the first tee Sir Ludovic introduced him to the other two players who were going to make up the match. One was a Mr Wollaston, a clean-shaven, intelligent, large, prosperous-looking man of about forty, and the other was a Mr Gyles, a very dark man, with a toothbrush moustache and a most impressive silence. Both were stockbrokers.

'Now,' said Sir Ludovic heartily, 'I suggest that we play a four-ball foursome, Wollaston and I against you two, on handicap, taking our strokes from the course, five bob corners, half a crown

for each birdie, a dollar an eagle, a bob best ball and a bob aggregate and a bob a putt. What about that?'

'Good!' said Mr Wollaston. Mr Gyles nodded, while Donald, who had not understood a single word except the phrase 'four-ball foursome' – and that was incorrect – mumbled a feeble affirmative. The stakes sounded enormous, and the reference to birds of the air sounded mysterious, but he obviously could not raise any objections.

When it was his turn to drive at the first tee, he selected a spot for his tee and tapped it with the toe of his driver. Nothing happened. He looked at his elderly caddy and tapped the ground again. Again nothing happened.

'Want a peg, Cameron?' called out Sir Ludovic.

'Oh no, it's much too early,' protested Donald, under the impression that he was being offered a drink. Everyone laughed ecstatically at this typically Scottish flash of wit, and the elderly caddy lurched forward with a loathsome little contrivance of blue and white celluloid which he offered to his employer. Donald shuddered. They'd be giving him a rubber tee with a tassel in a minute, or lending him a golf-bag with tripod legs. He teed his ball on a pinch of sand with a dexterous twist of his fingers and thumb amid an incredulous silence.

Donald played the round in a sort of daze. After a few holes of uncertainty, much of his old skill came back, and he reeled off fairly good figures. He had a little difficulty with his elderly caddy at the beginning of the round, for, on asking that functionary to hand him 'the iron', he received the reply, 'Which number, sir?' and the following dialogue ensued:

'Which number what?' faltered Donald.

'Which number iron?'

'Er – just the iron?'

'But it must have a number, sir.'

'Why must it?'

'All irons have numbers.'

'But I've only one.'

'Only a number one?'

'No. Only one.'

'Only one what, sir?'

'One iron!' exclaimed Donald, feeling that this music-hall turn might go on for a long time and must be already holding up the entire course.

The elderly caddy at last appreciated the deplorable state of affairs. He looked grievously shocked and said in a reverent tone:

'Mr Fumbledon has eleven.'

'Eleven what?' enquired the startled Donald.

'Eleven irons.'

After this revelation of Mr Fumbledon's greatness, Donald took 'the iron' and topped the ball hard along the ground. The caddy sighed deeply.

Throughout the game Donald never knew what the state of the match was, for the other three, who kept complicated tables upon the backs of envelopes, reckoned solely in cash. Thus, when Donald once timidly asked his partner how they stood, the taciturn Mr Gyles consulted his envelope and replied shortly, after a brief calculation, 'You're up three dollars and a tanner.'

Donald did not venture to ask again, and he knew nothing more about the match until they were ranged in front of the bar in the clubroom, when Sir Ludovic and Mr Wollaston put down the empty glasses which had, a moment ago, contained double pink gins, ordered a refill of the four glasses, and then handed over to the bewildered Donald the sum of one pound sixteen and six.

Lunch was an impressive affair. It was served in a large room, panelled in white and gold with a good deal of artificial marble scattered about the walls, by a staff of bewitching young ladies in black frocks, white aprons and caps, and black silk stockings. Bland wine-stewards drifted hither and thither, answering to Christian names and accepting orders and passing them on to subordinates. Corks popped, the scent of the famous club fish-pie mingled itself with all the perfumes of Arabia and Mr Coty, smoke arose from rose-tipped cigarettes, and the rattle of knives and forks played an orchestral accompaniment to the sound of many voices, mostly silvery, like April rain, and full of girlish gaiety.

Sir Ludovic insisted on being host, and ordered Donald's half-pint of beer and double whiskies for himself and Mr Gyles. Mr Wollaston, pleading a diet and the strict orders of Carlsbad medicos, produced a bottle of Berncastler out of a small brown handbag, and polished it off in capital style.

The meal itself consisted of soup, the famous fish-pie, a fricas-see of chicken, saddle of mutton or sirloin of roast beef, sweet, savoury, and cheese, topped off with four of the biggest glasses of hunting port that Donald had ever seen. Conversation at lunch was almost entirely about the dole. The party then went back to the main club-room where Mr Wollaston firmly but humorously pushed Sir Ludovic into a very deep chair, and insisted upon taking up the running with four coffees and four double kümmels. Then after a couple of rubbers of bridge, at which Donald managed to win a few shillings, they sallied out to play a second round. The golf was only indifferent in the after-noon. Sir Ludovic complained that, owing to the recrudescence of what he mysteriously called 'the old trouble', he was finding it very difficult to focus the ball clearly, and Mr Wollaston kept on over-swinging so violently that he fell over once and only just saved himself on several other occasions, and Mr Gyles developed a fit of socketing that soon became a menace to the course, causing, as it did, acute nervous shocks to a retired major-general whose sunlit nose only escaped by a miracle, and a bevy of beauty that was admiring, for some reason, the play of a well-known actor-manager.

So after eight holes the afternoon round was abandoned by common consent, and they walked back to the clubhouse for more bridge and much-needed refreshment. Donald was handed seventeen shillings as his inexplicable winnings over the eight holes. Later on, Sir Ludovic drove, or rather Sir Ludovic's chauffeur drove, Donald back to the corner of King's Road and Royal Avenue. On the way back, Sir Ludovic talked mainly about the dole.

Seated in front of the empty grate in his bed-sitting-room, Donald counted his winnings and reflected that golf had changed a great deal since he had last played it.

Is a Golfer a Gentleman?

A. P. HERBERT

Rex v. Haddock (before the Stipendiary)

THIS case, which raised an interesting point of law upon the meaning of the word 'gentleman', was concluded today.

The Stipendiary, giving judgment, said: 'In this case the defendant, Mr Albert Haddock, is charged, under the Profane Oaths Act, 1745, with swearing and cursing on a Cornish golf-course. The penalty under the Act is a fine of one shilling for every day-labourer, soldier or seaman, two shillings for every other person under the degree of gentleman, and five shillings for every person of or above the degree of gentleman – a remarkable but not, unfortunately, unique example of a statute which lays down one law for the rich and another (more lenient) for the poor. The fine, it is clear, is leviable not upon the string or succession of oaths, but upon each individual malediction (see *Reg.* v. *Scott*, (1863) 33 L.J.M. 15). The curses charged, and admitted, in this case are over four hundred in number, and we are asked by the prosecution to inflict a fine of one hundred pounds, assessed on the highest or gentleman's rate at five shillings a swear. The defendant admits the offences but contends that the fine is excessive and wrongly calculated, on the curious ground that he is not a gentleman when he is playing golf.

'He has reminded us, in an able argument, that the law takes notice, in many cases, of such exceptional circumstances as will break down the normal restraints of a civilized citizen and so powerfully inflame his passions that it would be unjust and idle to apply to his conduct the ordinary standards of the law, as for example where without warning or preparation he discovers another man in the act of molesting his wife or family. The law recognizes that under such provocation a reasonable man ceases for the time being to be a reasonable man; and the defendant maintains that in the special circumstances of his offence a gentleman ceases to be a gentleman and should not be judged or punished as such.

'Now what were these circumstances? Broadly speaking, they were the 12th hole on the – Mullion golf-course, with which most of us in this court are familiar. At that hole the player drives (or does not drive) over an inlet of the sea, which is enclosed by cliffs some sixty feet high. The defendant has told us that he never drives over, but always into, this inlet or Chasm, as it is locally named. A moderate if not sensational player on other sections of the course, before this obstacle his normal powers invariably desert him. This, he tells us, has preyed upon his mind; he has registered, it appears, a kind of a vow, and year after year, at Easter and in August, he returns to this county, determined ultimately to overcome the Chasm.

'Meanwhile, unfortunately, his tenacity has become notorious. It is the normal procedure, it appears, if a ball is struck into the Chasm, to strike a second, and, if that should have no better fate, to abandon the hole. The defendant tells us that in the past he has struck no fewer than six or seven balls in this way, some rolling gently over the cliff and some flying far and high out to sea. But recently, grown fatalistic, he has not thought it worth while to make even a second attempt, but has immediately followed his first ball into the Chasm, and there, among the rocks, small stones and shingle, has hacked at his ball with the appropriate instrument until some lucky blow has lofted it on to the turf above, or, in the alternative, until he has broken his instruments or suffered some injury from flying fragments of rock. On one or two occasions a crowd of holiday-makers and local residents has gathered on the cliff and foreshore to watch the defendant's indomitable struggles and to hear the verbal observations which have accompanied them. On the date of the alleged offences a crowd collected of unprecedented dimensions, but so intense was the defendant's concentration that he did not, he tells us, notice their presence. His ball had more nearly traversed the gulf than ever before; it struck the opposing cliff but a few feet from

156

the summit, and nothing but an adverse gale of exceptional ferocity prevented success. The defendant therefore, as he conducted his customary excavations among the boulders of the Chasm, was possessed, he tells us, by a more than customary fury. Oblivious of his surroundings, conscious only of the will to win, for fifteen or twenty minutes he lashed his battered ball against the stubborn cliffs until at last it triumphantly escaped. And before, during, and after every stroke he uttered a number of imprecations of a complex character which were carefully recorded by an assiduous caddie and by one or two of the spectators. The defendant says that he recalls with shame a few of the expressions which he used, that he has never used them before, and that it was a shock to him to hear them issuing from his own lips; and he says quite frankly that no gentleman would use such language.

'Now this ingenious defence, whatever may be its legal value, has at least some support in the facts of human experience. I am a golf-player myself – (*Laughter*) – but, apart from that, evidence has been called to show the subversive effect of this exercise upon the ethical and moral systems of the mildest of mankind. Elderly gentlemen, gentle in all respects, kind to animals, beloved by children and fond of music, are found in lonely corners of the Downs hacking at sand-pits or tussocks of grass and muttering in a blind ungovernable fury elaborate maledictions which could not be extracted from them by robbery with violence. Men who would face torture without a word become blasphemous at the short fourteenth. And it is clear that the game of golf may well be included in that category of intolerable provocations which may legally excuse or mitigate behaviour which is not otherwise excusable, and that under that provocation the reasonable or gentle man may reasonably act like a lunatic or lout, and should be judged as such.

'But then I have to ask myself, What does the Act intend by the words *"of or above the degree of gentleman"*? Does it intend a fixed social rank or a general habit of behaviour? In other words, is a gentleman legally always a gentleman, as a duke or a solicitor remains unalterably a duke or a solicitor? For if this is the case the defendant's argument must fail. The prosecution say that the word "degree" is used in the sense of "rank". Mr Haddock argues that it is used in the sense of an university examination, and that, like the examiners, the Legislature divides the human race, for the purposes of swearing, into three vague intellectual or moral categories, of which they give certain rough but not infallible examples. Many a First-Class man has taken a Third, and many a day-labourer, according to Mr Haddock, is of such a high character that under the Act he should rightly be included in the First "degree". There is certainly abundant judicial and literary authority for the view that by "gentleman" we mean a personal quality and not a social status. We have all heard of "Nature's gentlemen". "Clothes do not make the gentleman," said Lord Arrowroot in *Cook* v. *The Mersey Docks and Harbour Board*, (1897) 2 Q.B., meaning that a true gentleman might be clad in the foul rags of an author. In the old maxim "Manners makyth man" (see *Charles* v . *The Great Western Railway*), there is no doubt that by "man" is meant "gentleman", and that "manners" is contrasted with wealth or station. Mr Thomas, for the prosecution, has quoted against these authorities an observation of the poet SHAKESPEARE that

"The Prince of Darkness is a gentleman,"

but quotations from SHAKESPEARE are generally meaningless and always unsound. This one, in my judgment, is both. I am more impressed by the saying of another author (whose name I forget) that the King can make a nobleman, but he cannot make a gentleman.

'I am satisfied therefore that the argument of the defendant has substance. Just as the reasonable man who discovers his consort in the embraces of the supplanter becomes for the moment a raving maniac, so the habitually gentle man may become in a bunker a violent unmannerly oaf. In each case the ordinary sanctions of the law are suspended; and, while it is right that a normally gentle person should in normal circumstances suffer a heavier penalty for needless imprecations than a common seaman or cattle-driver, for whom they are part of the tools of his trade, he must not be judged by the standards of the gentle in such special circumstances as provoked the defendant.

'That provocation was so exceptional that I cannot think it was contemplated by the framers of the Act; and had golf at that date been a popular exercise I have no doubt that it would have been dealt with under a special section. I find therefore that this case is not governed by the Act. I find that the defendant at the time was not in law responsible for his actions or his speech, and I am unable to punish him in any way. For his conduct in the Chasm he will be formally convicted of Attempted Suicide while Temporarily Insane, but he leaves the court without a stain upon his character.'

Beautiful Husbands

JOHN UPDIKE

S PENCER Ridgeway had always liked Kirk Matthews, and
even while, in the messy wake of his affair with Dulcie
Matthews, he was being legally battered by him, Spencer
found something to admire, something warriorlike and sterling,
in the barrage of registered letters, hand-delivered summonses,
and grim-voiced, telephoned ultimatums – all intended, Spencer
felt, less to discomfit him than to panic Dulcie into an easy
divorce settlement. Spencer had been noticing Kirk, indeed – on
the train, downtown on Saturdays – long before Dulcie made
any impression on him. He was taller than Spencer, with a full
and fluffy head of hair gray in just the right places (temples, side-
burns, a collielike frosting above the collar), whereas Spencer
was going thin on top and combing the remaining strands across
his pate from a parting closer and closer to the tip of one ear. Kirk
had a year-round tan and one of those thin no-nonsense mouths,
with two little tense buttons of muscle underneath that Spencer
envied; he had always been embarrassed by his own big, soft-
looking lips. As the men and their wives happened to be, more
and more, at the same cocktail parties and on adjacent tennis
courts at the club, and in the same conservation groups, the
couples drew closer. Kirk laughed at Spencer's jokes – Kirk himself could not make jokes, his tongue wasn't hinged that way –
and took him on as a golf partner, though he was a solid 8 and
Spencer a courtesy 20.

Dulcie was a steady, up-the-middle 13 – from the women's
tees, of course. She had oodles of honey-gold curly hair held in
place by her visor, and tidy brown legs exposed to mid-thigh

by her taut khaki golf skirt. The one time Doris, Spencer's unfortunate first wife, showed up to make a Sunday-afternoon foursome, she horrified the other three by wearing blue-jean cutoffs, with the shadow of a Sixties-style heart-patch on the backside, and muddy Adidases in place of golf shoes. All of Dulcie's costumes were impeccably Eighties-suburban. When she and Spencer first began to meet illicitly, her broad-shouldered, waistless wool suits and summer frocks of fine-striped ticking, or her scoop-necked georgette blouse with a flickering skirt of pleated crêpe de chine, gave him the thrilling impression that Kirk himself had dressed her; Spencer could picture him, sitting with his intent, humorless handsomeness in the clothing store, surrounded by multiple reflections of his fluffy, frosty hair, as Dulcie strutted out of the dressing room in one smart outfit after another. And when her furtive luncheons with Spencer blossomed into intimacy, this impression spread to her underwear – lace-trimmed bras, bikini-style panties, sexy yet not really frivolous, in military tones of beige or black – and even to her skin, which was silky-smooth with lotions that perhaps Kirk's hands had spread, especially on that unreachable itchy area just under the shoulder blades.

In the Matthews house, after the figurative roof fell in, Spencer would stretch his tired body and ease his battered spirit amid Kirk's heavy, leathery furniture. He admired the matching plaid walnut suite in the den lined with Books of the Month, the stereo and record cabinets expertly cut and mortised by Kirk's sharp-toothed array of power equipment in the basement, and, upstairs, the monolithic bed that consisted simply of an airfoam mattress on a low wooden platform. Perfect-seeming Kirk had had a bad back, Dulcie revealed; another unsuspected debility was that, according to her, he had been incredibly boring.

Spencer always tried to defend him. 'I always found him pleasant. Not a laugh a minute, exactly . . . '

'Like incredibly darling and amusing you,' she interrupted, giving him such a hug that the wooden platform creaked beneath the airfoam.

He found her adoration unexpected and, he could not but feel, undeserved. Spencer had some trouble understanding how he had come to be in this other man's wife's embrace, trying to pick a prong of her tumbling golden hair out of his eye. '. . . but hearty,' he finished. 'Good-natured.'

'He was rigid and brutal,' Dulcie insisted. 'This tactic with the eviction notices is so typical; he knows how terrified I am of the police.'

In truth, it was an impressive sight, to see the sheriff's new Chevrolet Celebrity coupé, with its twirling blue light and silver lettering, pull up the driveway to deliver the latest beribboned, notarized document.

'Just getting a parking ticket used to make me cry.' This kind of small revelation, this little glimpse of her feminine softness, had had a slightly different quality when she was still Kirk's lawful wife. Then, it had been a peek into paradise; now it was a mere datum. 'Whereas *he* scoffed at tickets and used to rip them off the windshield and throw them into the gutter. I used to pick them up when he wasn't looking and Scotch-tape them together and pay them.'

'He did?' Spencer said. 'That's fascinating.'

'It used to make me hysterical. He liked that. That's why he's doing all this now, to make me hysterical. It's his way of still interacting.' He felt her skin take on an oily, preening texture as he mechanically rubbed below her shoulder blades.

'Oh now,' he said comfortingly. 'Don't forget he's hurting. We've badly hurt him.'

'Pooh,' she said, her face unseen beneath her heap of hair, except for a corner of her painted lips, where a bubble of saliva had popped with the exclamation. 'I don't know,' she went on woefully. 'It's horrible, being a woman. Sometimes I feel you're both against me. Everything he does, you seem to defend.'

'I just think we should be fair, and try to understand Kirk. All this suing and so on is just his way of dealing. We have each other and he has nothing.'

'He has his own precious pretty carcass, and that's all he ever cared about anyway.'

'Yes, it was pretty,' Spencer had to agree.

Even when the lawsuit for alienation of affections was far advanced, Spencer imagined he could glimpse through the swirl of correspondence and the hours of stilted conferences with dapper lawyers, a twinkle in Kirk's eye. At one point in the actual proceedings, he found himself bumping through the padded courtroom doors at the same time as the plaintiff and made a joke ('Must have been part of a padded cell') at which Kirk curtly, grudgingly chuckled. Away from Dulcie's calorie-and-fiber-conscious cooking, the man had put on weight and looked, in the witness box, a bit jowly. He looked grim and unsympathetic; between responses, he clenched his teeth and did a lot of blinking. Spencer (who had lost seven pounds) felt disappointed by Kirk's deterioration and further disappointed by the verdict of not guilty and no damages. The judge was a woman to whom the very charge savored of a bygone sexism. In this day and age wasn't a woman free to change men if she so desired? Was she some sort of chattel for men to bandy back and forth?

'It was sad,' Spencer confided to Dulcie, 'to see him come such a cropper.'

'Why?' she asked wide-eyed. 'I thought it served him right. Now he says he's going after custody of the children.'

There had been something lovable, Spencer had thought, in the erect dignity with which Kirk had marched away at the head of his little team of legal advisers, none of them quite so tall nor so gravely tan nor so tastefully grayed as he.

'Poor guy. I'm afraid he doesn't have much of a chance.'

'Not if you make me an honest woman, he doesn't.'

Married, and reduced to impecuniousness by their legal fees, Spencer and Dulcie resigned from the club and played at public courses, she giving him three strokes a side. Kirk got fatter and uglier and his legal attentions became a mere embarrassment. When he sullenly, silently came to pick up the children on alternate weekends, Spencer would spy on him from the upstairs window, or from behind the library curtains, probing his old admiration much as the tongue warily probes the socket of an extracted tooth. His heart would flutter, his face get hot. It took a long time for Kirk's silvery magic to tarnish entirely.

He loved hearing from Dulcie details of her other marriage,

especially the early years – the rainy honeymoon in Bermuda, the quarrels with his possessive upstate mother, the progressively larger and less shabby living quarters spiralling out from the heart of the city into increasingly affluent and spacious suburbs. Kirk at first was almost painfully thin, a beanpole, and totally innocent about alcohol, among other things. Then there was a period of problem drinking, and flirtations with these tarty, man-hungry junior account execs at his office. But such a dear father, at least in the beginning, when the children were little and thought he was God, before this obsession with his own career, his own condition, even his clothes. 'You see, Spencer dear – don't tickle like that – they didn't have the word "yuppie" in those days, so Kirk didn't know exactly what he was until he was forty, and it was almost too late.'

Spencer's own early married life had been spent in exotically different circumstances, on the other coast, in rebellion and riot, experimenting with drugs and organic farming. Doris had been a perfect hippie, hairy all over and serenely stoned. Even the divorce she had been laid-back and philosophical about. He begged Dulcie, 'Tell me about the pajamas again.'

'Well, darling, there's really nothing much to tell. I think I began to hate the marriage when he insisted I iron his pajamas. When we were first married, he was still such a boy he would sleep in the underwear he had worn that day, the way he would in college, and then for years he used these simple dacron pajamas with a drawstring, no monogram or anything, and it was plenty good enough if I simply folded them when they were fresh out of the dryer, before the wrinkles really, you know, set. But then we got into a-hundred-percent sea-island cotton that he said had to be hand-washed in lukewarm water, and he wanted sharp *creases* just to put himself between the covers in. And the eyeshades, and the ear stopples – I felt utterly shut out.'

'And the shoes,' Spencer prompted. 'Did he have shoes?'

'Did he have *shoes*? They covered the entire floor of his closet row on row, and went right up one wall. He had a separate pair for every suit, and then on the weekend, if he raked leaves it would be the suede Hush Puppies, but if I asked him to haul just one load of mulch over to the rose bed he would go back in the house and put on the shitkickers. It was like his skis, he had the pair for corn and the pair for icy conditions, and then a third kind for deep powder. And the *gloves*: if he couldn't find one certain pair of gloves, with grease stains already on them, he wouldn't touch the engine of the car, even just to add windshield-washer fluid.'

'And did he take a long time in the bathroom, or a short time?' Spencer asked, knowing full well the answer. Eventually he knew all the answers, had extracted every molecule of the departed husband from his wife's memory – Kirk's odors and deodorants his habits both annoying and endearing, the quarrels they had and the orgasms he gave her or, increasingly during the last years, failed to.

'I love kissing you,' she confided to Spencer. 'With him it was like putting your mouth against an automatic bank teller, where it swallows your credit card. And his hair! You had to be so careful not to muss his hair. That fluffiness wasn't natural, you know. It was *set*.' There was a limit to this sort of information. Kirk slowly became boring. The wraps of her first husband fell from her, so that Dulcie at last stood naked, fit to be loved.

Spencer loved her. Warming the dawn and evening of every day, the source and goal of every commute, the light and animator of every weekend, Dulcie was his treasure, the gold from which Kirk's dull residue had been panned away. He loved her cascading hair, her sturdy legs, her sweet, steady golf swing, which never strayed from the fairway in an ill-advised attempt to achieve more distance. They rejoined the golf club, their finances again permitting and Kirk having long ago resigned.

It was there, at the post-fourball barbecue, in the fullness of the happiness of Dulcie's team's having won the women's division, that a copper-haired woman approached Spencer. 'Hi there,' she said, speaking just like a name tag, 'I'm Deirdre.' Her handshake was a little too firm, and her gaze a shade too level. 'Ol' Dulce was terrific out there, though I was the one got the gross par on the dogleg eleventh, which what with my twenty handicap made a net eagle for the team.'

Dulcie had come up behind the other woman, and gave her a comradely hug. Their two curly heads were side by side, their tan faces with pale laugh crinkles at the corners of their eyes. 'Isn't she terrific?' Dulcie asked, though Spencer couldn't see quite how. But then, years ago, he remembered he had been insensitive to Dulcie's charm. 'The Greenfields have just moved to town and I've promised to have them over.'

Deirdre glanced around, rather urgently. 'Let me find Ben.' She hurried into the crowd, which was dressed with facetious country-club gaudiness – scarlet pants, straw hats – under the hanging cloud of mesquite-flavored smoke. Spencer felt a fateful sliding in his stomach.

'I don't want to meet any new people,' he told his wife.

'You'll like him,' Dulcie promised.

The aggressive copper-haired woman was dragging a man toward them – a tall, dazed sacrificial lamb with a sheepish air, an elegantly narrow and elevated nose, slicked-down black hair, and a seersucker suit that gave him, with his blue button-down shirt and striped necktie, an endearingly old-fashioned, vaguely official ambience. He was, in his way, beautiful.

Spencer, his face heating up, hardly had time to protest, 'I don't want to like him.'

Farrell's Caddie

JOHN UPDIKE

WHEN Farrell signed up, with seven other ageing members of his local Long Island club, for a week of golf at the Royal Caledonian Links, in Scotland, he didn't foresee the relationship with the caddies. Hunched little men in billed tweed caps and rubberized rainsuits, they huddled in the misty gloom as the morning foursomes got organized, and reclustered after lunch, muttering, as unintelligibly as sparrows, for the day's second eighteen.

Farrell would never have played thirty-six holes a day in America, let alone walked the distance, but here in Scotland golf was not an accessory to life, drawing upon one's marginal energy; it *was* life, played out of the center of one's being. At first, stepping forth on legs one of which had been broken in a college football game forty years before, and which damp weather or a night of twisted sleep still provoked to a reminiscent twinge, he missed the silky glide and swerve of the accustomed electric cart, its magic-carpet suspension above the whispering fairway; he missed the rattle of spare balls in the retaining shelf, and the round plastic holes to hold drinks, alcoholic or carbonated, and the friendly presence on the seat beside him of another gray-haired sportsman, another warty pickle blanching in the brine of time, exuding forbearance and the expectation of forbearance, and resigned, like Farrell, to a golfing mediocrity that would gradually make its way down the sloping dogleg of decrepitude to the level green of death.

Here, however, on the heather-rimmed fairways, cut as close as putting surfaces back home, yet with no trace of mower tracks, and cheerfully marred by the scratchings and burrows of the nocturnal rabbits that lived and bred beneath the impenetrably thorny, waist-high gorse, energy came up through the turf, as if Farrell's cleats were making contact with primal spirits beneath the soil, and he felt he could walk forever. The rolling and treeless terrain, the proximity of the wind-whipped sea, the rain that came and went with the suddenness of thought composed the ancient matrix of the game, and the darkly muttering caddies were also part of this matrix.

That first morning, in the drizzly shuffle around the golf bags, his bag was hoisted up by a hunched shadow who, as they walked together in pursuit of Farrell's first drive (good contact, but pulled to the left, toward some shaggy mounds), muttered half to himself, with those hiccups or glottal stops the Scots accent inserts, 'Sandy's wha' they call me.'

Farrell hesitated, then confessed 'Gus.' His given name, Augustus, had always embarrassed him, but its shortened version seemed a little short on dignity, and at the office, as he had ascended in rank, his colleagues had settled on his initials, 'A.D.'

'Here, ye want tae geh oover the second boosh fra'the'laift,' Sandy said, handing Farrell a 7-iron. The green was out of sight behind the shaggy mounds, which were covered with long tan grass that whitened in waves as gusts flattened it.

'What's the distance?' Farrell was accustomed to yardage markers – yellow stakes, or sprinkler heads.

The caddie looked reflectively at a sand bunker not far off, and then at the winking red signal light on the train tracks beyond, and finally at a large bird, a gull or a crow, winging against the wind beneath the low, tattered, blue-black clouds. 'Ah hunnert thirty-eight tae the edge of the green, near a hunnert fifty tae the pin, where they ha't.'

'I can't hit a 7-iron a hundred fifty. I can't even hit it even one forty, against this wind.'

Yet the caddie's fist, in a fingerless wool glove, did not withdraw the offered club. 'Seven's what ye need.'

As Farrell bent his face to the ball, the wet wind cut across his eyes and made him cry. His tears turned the ball into two; he supposed the brighter one was real. He concentrated on taking the club head away slowly and low, initiating his downswing with a twitch of the left hip and suppressing his tendency to dip the right shoulder. The shot seemed sweet, soaring with a gentle draw up precisely over the second bush. He looked toward the caddie, expecting congratulations or at least some small sign of shared pleasure. But the man, his creased face weathered the strangely even brown of a white actor playing Othello, followed the flight of the ball as he had that of the crow, reflectively. 'Yer right hand's a wee bit forward,' he observed, and the ball – they saw as they climbed to the green – was indeed pulled to the left, in a deep pot bunker. Further more, it was fifteen yards short. The caddie had underclubbed him, but showed no sign of remorse as he handed Farrell the sand wedge. In Sandy's dyed-looking face, pallid gray eyes showed like touches of morning light; it shocked Farrell to realize that the other man, weathered though he was, and bent beneath the weight of a perpetual golf bag, was younger than himself – a prematurely wizened Celt, or Pict, serving one of Northeast America's tall, bloated Anglo-Saxons.

The side of the bunker toward the hole was as tall as Farrell and sheer, built up of bricks of sod in a way never seen at Long Island courses. Rattled, irritated at having been unrepentantly underclubbed, Farrell swung five times into the damp, brown sand, darker than any sand on Long Island. With each swing, the ball thudded beneath the trap's high lip and dribbled back at his feet. 'Hit at it well beheend,' the caddie advised, 'and dinna stop the cloob.' Farrell's sixth swing brought the ball bobbling up onto the green, within six feet of the hole.

His fellow Americans lavished ironical praise on the shot, but the caddie, with deadpan solemnity, handed him his putter. 'Ae ball tae th' laift,' he advised, and Farrell was so interested in this peculiar phrase – the ball as a unit of measure – that his putt stopped short. 'Ye forgot tae hit it, Gus,' Sandy told him. Farrell tersely nodded. Tingling with nervousness, he felt onstage and obliged to keep up a show of the stoic virtues. Asked for his score, he said loudly, in a theatrical voice, 'That was an honest ten.'

'We'll call it a six,' said the player keeping score, in the forgiving American way.

As the round progressed, through a rapid alternation of brisk showers and silvery sunshine, with rainbows springing up around them and tiny white daisies gleaming underfoot, Farrell and his caddie began to grow into each other, as a foot in damp weather grows into a shoe. Sandy consistently handed Farrell a club too short to make the green, but Farrell came to accept the failure as his; his caddie was handing the club to the stronger golfer latent in Farrell, and it was Farrell's job to let this superior performer out, to release him from his stiff, soft, more than middle-aged body. On the twelfth hole, called 'Dunrobin' – a seemingly endless par 5 with a broad stretch of fairway, bleak and vaguely restless like the surface of the moon, receding over a distant edge marked by two small pot bunkers and a pale-green arm of gorse that extended from the rabbit-under-mined thickets on the left – his drive clicked. Something about the ghostly emptiness of this particular hole's terrain, the feature-lessness of it, removed Farrell's physical inhibitions; he felt the steel shaft of the driver bend in an elastic curve at his back, and a corresponding springiness awaken in his knees, and knew, as his weight smoothly moved from the right foot to the left, that he would bring the club face squarely into the ball, and indeed did, so that the ball – the last of his new Titleists, the others having disappeared in gorse and heather and cliffside scree – was melt-ing into the drizzle straight ahead almost before he looked up, his head held sideways, as if pillowed on his right ear, just like the heads of the pros on television. 'O.K.?' he asked Sandy, mock-modest but also genuinely fearful of some hazard, some trick of the layout, that he had missed taking into account.

'Bonnie shot, sir,' the caddie said and his face, as if touched by a magic wand, crumpled into a smile full of crooked gray teeth, his constantly relit cigarette adhering to one corner. Small matter that Farrell, striving for a repetition of this scarcely precedented distance, topped the following 3-wood, hit a 5-iron fat, and skulled his wedge shot clear across the elevated green. He had for a second awakened the golf giant sleeping among his muscles, and imagined himself vindicated in the other man's not quite colorless, not quite indifferent eyes.

Dinner, for this week of excursion, was a repeating male event, the same eight Long Island males, their hair growing curly and their faces ruddy away from the dry Manhattan canyons and air-conditioned compartments where they had accumulated their little fortunes. They discussed their caddies as men, extremely unbuttoned, might discuss their mistresses. 'Come on, Freddie, hit it fer once!' the very distinguished banker Frederic R. Panoply boasted his had cried out to him in frustration as, on the third day of his cautious, down-the-middle banker's game, he painstakingly addressed his ball.

Another man's caddie, when asked what he thought of Mrs Thatcher, had responded with a twinkle, 'She'd be a good hump.'

Farrell, prim and reserved by nature, had relatively little to offer of his caddie. He worried about the man's incessant smoking, and whether at the end of a round he tipped him too much less than what a Japanese golfer would have given. As the week went by, their relationship had become more intuitive. 'A 6-iron?' Farrell would now say and without a word would be handed the club. Once, he had dared decline an offered 6, asked for the 5, and sailed his unusually well-struck shot into the sedge beyond the green. On the greens, where he at first had been bothered by the caddie's explicit directives, so that he forgot to stroke the ball firmly, he had come to depend upon Sandy's advice, and would expertly tilt his ear close to the caddie's mouth and try to envision the curve of the ball into the center of the hole from 'an inch an' a fingernail tae th' laift.' Farrell began to sink putts. He began to get pars, as the whitecaps flashed on one side of the links and on the other the wine-red electric commuter trains swiftly glided up to Glasgow and back. This was happiness, on this wasteland between the tracks and the beach, and freedom of a wild and windy sort. On the morning of his last day, having sliced his first drive into the edge of the rough, between a thistle and what appeared to be a child's weathered tombstone, Farrell bent his ear close to the caddie's mouth for advice, and heard, 'Ye'd be better leavin' 'er.'

'Beg pardon?' Farrell said, as he had all week, when the glottal, hiccupping accent had become opaque. Today the acoustics were specially bad; a near-gale off the sea was making his rain pants rattle like machine guns, and deformed his eyeballs with air pressure as he tried to squint down. When he could stop seeing double, his lie looked fair – semi-embedded.

'Yer missus,' Sandy clarified, passing over the 8-iron. 'Ere it's tae late, mon. She was never yer type. Tae proper.'

'Shouldn't this be a wedge?' Farrell asked uncertainly.

'Nay, it's sitting' up guid enough,' the caddie said, pressing his foot into the heather behind the ball, so it rose up like ooze out of mud. 'Ye kin reach with th' 8,' he said. 'Go fer yer par. Yer fauts er a' in yer mind; ye tend t' play defensive.'

Farrell would have dismissed his previous remarks as a verbal mirage amid the clicks and skips of windblown Scots had they not seemed so uncannily true. 'Too proper' was exactly what his college friends had said of Sylvia, but he had imagined that her physical beauty had been the real thing, and her propriety a pose she would outgrow, whereas thirty-five married years had revealed the propriety as enduring and the beauty as transient. As to leaving her, this thought would never have entered his head until recently; the mergers-and-acquisitions branch had recently taken on a certain Irma Finegold, with heavy-lidded eyes, full lips painted sharply red, and a curious presumptuous way of teasing Farrell in the eddies of chitchat before and after a conference. She had recently been divorced, and when she talked to Farrell she tapped her lower lip with a pencil eraser and shimmied her shoulders beneath their pads. On nights when the office worked late – he liked occasionally to demonstrate that, far along though he was, he could still pull an all-nighter with the young bucks – there had been between him and Irma shared Chinese meals from greasy take-out cartons, and a shared limo home in the dawn light. On one undreamed-of occasion, there had even been an invitation, which he did not refuse, to interrupt his return to Long Island with an hour at her apartment in Brooklyn.

The 8-iron pinched the ball clean, and the Atlantic gale brought the soaring shot left-to-right toward the pin. 'Laift edge, but dinna gi' the hole away,' Sandy advised of the putt, and Farrell sank it, for the first birdie of his week of golf.

Now, suddenly, out of the silvery torn sky, sleet and sunshine descended simultaneously, and as the two men walked at the same tilt to the next tee, Sandy's voice came out of the wind, 'An' steer clear o' the MiniCorp deal. They've leveraged th' company tae death.'

Farrell studied Sandy's face. Rain and sleet bounced off the brown skin as if from a waxy preservative coating. Metallic gleams showed as the man surveyed, through narrowed eyelids, the water horizon. Farrell pretended he hadn't heard. On the tee he was handed a 3-wood with the advice, 'Ye want tae stay short o' th' wee burn. The wind's come aroond behind bringin' the sun with it.'

As the round wore on, the sun did struggle through, and a thick rainbow planted itself over the profile of the drab town beyond the tracks, with its soot-black steeples and distillery chimneys. By the time of the afternoon's eighteen, there was actually blue sky, and oblique solar rays. Pockets of lengthening shadows showed the old course to be everywhere curvacious, crest and swale, like the body of a woman. Forty feet off the green on the fourteenth ('Whinny Brae'), Farrell docilely accept-ed the caddie's offer of a putter, and rolled it up and over the close-mowed irregularities to within a gimme of the hole. His old self would have skulled or fluffed a chip. 'Great advice,' he said, and in his flush of triumph challenged the caddie: 'But Irma *loves* the MiniCorp deal.'

'Aye, 't keeps the twa o' you togither. She's fairful ye'll wander off, i'th' halls o' corporate power.'

'But whatever does she see in me?' 'Lookin' fer a faither, the case may be. Thet first husband o' hers was meikle immature. And also far from yer own income bracket.'

Farrell felt his heart sink at the deflating shrewdness of the analysis. His mind elsewhere – absented by bitter-sweet sorrow, he hit one pure shot after another. Looking to the caddie for praise, however, he met the same impassive, dour, young-old visage, opaque beneath the billed tweed cap. Tomorrow, the man would caddie for someone else, and Farrell would be belted into a business-class seat within a 747. On the home stretch of holes – one after the other strung out along the tracks, as the Victorian brick clubhouse, with its turrets and neo-Gothic arches, drew closer and closer – Farrell begged for advice. 'The 5-wood, or the 3-iron? The three keeps it down out of the wind, but I feel more confident with the wood, the way you've got me swinging.'

'The five'll be ower and gone, ye're a' pumped up. Take the 4-iron. Smooth it on, laddie. Aim fer th' little broch.'

'Broch?'

'Wee stone fortress, frae th' days we had our own braw king.' He added, 'An' ye might be thinkin', Gus, aboot takin' early retirement. The severance deals won't be so sweet aye. Ye kin free yerself up an' tak on some consults, fer th' spare change.'

'Just what I was thinking, if Irma's a will-o'-the-wisp.'

'Will-o'-the-wisp, do ye say? Ye're a speedy lairner.'

Farrell felt flattered and windscoured, here in this surging universe of green and gray. 'You think so, Sandy?'

'I ken sae. Ye can tell a' aboot a man, frae th' way he gowfs.'

Miss Hogg and Miss Cairns

FRED URQUHART

'W HEN you go to the supermarket on Saturday,' Mrs Hogg said, 'don't forget to get one of those Bakewell tarts.'

'I won't be going to the supermarket on Saturday,' her daughter said. 'You know perfectly well, Mother, I never go to the supermarket on Saturdays. I haven't been near the supermarket on a Saturday for years.'

'Oh no, of course, it's your golfing day,' Mrs Hogg said. 'I can't see why you have to spend your entire Saturday playing golf. I've told you often enough, and I'll tell you again, Babbie Hogg, golfing is not a suitable game for a woman.'

'And I've told you often enough, Mother, that I don't spend the entire Saturday playing golf,' Miss Hogg said. 'I only play golf in the morning with Miss Cairns. You know fine that I always spend the whole of Saturday evening with you, watching the telly.'

'Well, if you change your mind, or if your dear Miss Cairns can't play golf, you can go to the supermarket and get me a Bakewell tart,' Mrs Hogg said.

'I'll ask the Gilchrist girl next door to get your Bakewell tart,' Miss Hogg said. 'And any other messages you may want; so you'd better get a list ready. But I shall not be getting them; I'm meeting Miss Cairns at nine-thirty sharp, and we're going to play at Muirfield this week. Miss Cairns says Muirfield's a much better course than Longniddry. Miss Cairns used to play at Muirfield quite a lot.'

'Miss Cairns! Miss Cairns! It's never anything else but Miss Cairns,' Mrs Hogg said. 'I'm sick and tired of the sound of it.

She's got another name, hasn't she? Why can't you say "Mabel Cairns" and be done with it?'

'I always call her Miss Cairns,' Miss Hogg said. 'I never remember that her name is Mabel. She's always called Miss Cairns in the office, and when she signs a letter she signs "M Cairns".'

'Well, for your information, my girl, her name is Mabel,' Mrs Hogg said. 'And fine you know it, too.'

'Why should I? She's "Miss Cairns" to me and always will be "Miss Cairns".'

'It was Mabel Cairns when you went to school together.'

'That's a long time ago. Times change, Mother.'

'Not as much as all that,' Mrs Hogg said.

'I don't remember much about my schooldays,' Miss Hogg said. 'I had quite forgotten that Miss Cairns went to Broughton Secondary until you brought it up. Miss Cairns never mentions school.'

'I suppose she's too busy talking about her golf handicap. What is it again? Not that I care a button. I disapprove of golf, as you well know. I disapprove of it for men as well as for women.'

'But everybody plays golf, Mother. I don't see what you have against it.'

'Well, for one thing, it keeps you on the links when you'd be better employed keeping me company or doing the shopping.'

'I need the exercise and the fresh air, Mother, after being cooped up in the office all day.'

'And being forced to keep me company on Saturday nights,' Mrs Hogg said. 'Go on, say it. It's written all over your sour puss. My God, Babbie, you've turned into a right auld maid and no mistake about it. You look fifty-five if you look a day. And you've got no right to. You're only forty-six.'

'Forty-five, Mother. Let us be accurate seeing you're being so acrimonious.'

'You seem to have lost a year somewhere, Babbie. My God, I should know how long it is after all the trouble I had having you. But let bygones be bygones and get back to the subject of golf.'

'I thought you weren't interested in golf, Mother.'

'I'm not. It's a daft game and all you people carting around those heavy bags of clubs are even dafter. If I was the Prime Minister I'd prohibit it.'

'The Prime Minister plays golf, too, Mother.'

'No wonder the country's in the state it's in,' Mrs Hogg said. 'The Scottish Parliament put a ban on golf in the 15th century. It's a pity we haven't as sensible a Parliament as that today.'

'It's a good job people like you are in the minority, Mother. You're living in the Dark Ages. Nobody would have any fun if you had your way.'

'What fun is there in putting a wee ball?' Mrs Hogg said. 'I don't know what it is about Scotsmen, but they're never happy unless they're playing with their balls. And now women are as bad. They must be after balls the whole time, too.'

After they left Broughton Secondary School, Babbie Hogg and Mabel Cairns did not see each other for twenty-five years. Miss Hogg lived at Comely Bank, Miss Cairns lived at Newington; their paths never crossed until Miss Cairns came to work as an executive's secretary in the large legal firm in St Andrew Square where Miss Hogg had worked since she was nineteen. Miss Hogg was now one of the main pivots of the firm, and the rest of the staff gave her due respect. As a chief secretary, Miss Cairns had no need to be more than ordinarily polite to her ex-schoolmate, but they often came into contact, and before long the two women became such bosom pals they were referred to behind their backs as 'Burke and Hare.' The nickname was not inappropriate, for the two ladies were adept at doing hatchet jobs on workers they considered to be dead wood in the firm.

For the past five or six years Miss Cairns and Miss Hogg had lunched together every working day. Every Wednesday evening they went together to either the cinema, the theatre or a concert. Every Saturday morning they met and played golf until the early afternoon. And every year they went abroad together, to a golfing holiday in the Algarve. But never once had Miss Hogg visited the flat in Newington where Miss Cairns had lived with her Aunt Ellen since the death of her parents; nor had Miss Cairns ever been to the small villa in Comely Bank where Miss Hogg lived with her mother. Often Mrs Hogg complained: 'Why don't you ask Mabel Cairns to come for her tea? Or why can't you ask her to lunch on a Sunday? I know you must be fed up with the sight of her, but I like to see a new face occasionally. I get very lonely here on my own with nothing to entertain me but television or that glaikit lassie Gilchrist, who can never be depended on to get even a few messages without getting at least one thing wrong. And then there's you, of course, but even you could never claim to be the life and soul of the party, could you, Babbie? Good grief, the evenings I sit here and wait for you to tell me a few wee bits of what's happening in your precious office, and you never open your mouth to talk unless it's about your beloved Miss Cairns.'

'Well, if that's that way you look on her, Mother, I don't see why you're so anxious to invite her here.'

'It would be a change from your sour-plumed mouth and the clank of your brogues, Babbie *dear*.' Mrs Hogg gave a derisive skirl. 'I can't see why you don't wear decent-like high-heeled shoes like other girls and not those *sensible* flat-heeled ones.'

'Now, don't let's have an argument, Mother. And for the last time I'm telling you that I've asked Miss Cairns often enough to come here and meet you, but she has always declined. You know perfectly well she spends every Saturday night with her old auntie who's lived with her ever since her father died. Aunt Ellen has phlebitis in both legs, and she walks with two sticks. Miss Cairns feels she has to sacrifice herself for Aunt Ellen's benefit, so she makes the supper and then sits and watches TV with her, as I make the supper and watch TV with you.'

'And I suppose that's your sacrifice?' Mrs Hogg said. 'Your good deed of the week? Your errand of mercy? Oh, I can see your halo shining, Babbie Hogg. You'll go straight to the front row of the stalls when you get to Heaven.'

'There's no need to be blasphemous, Mother. I'm only doing my duty.'

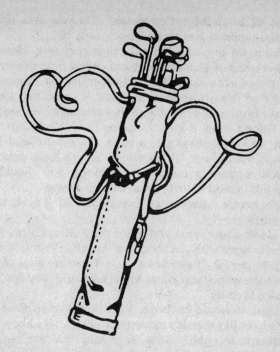

'I'm doin' my doooty! I'm doin' my doooty!' Mrs Hogg sang.
'For I am doin' my doooty like a solider and a man!

'God be with the day when we had those good old songs,'
she said. 'I can't be fashed with the dirt they dish out nowadays. Silly young creatures clutching a microphone and near
swallowing it while they moan a lot of blethers. Give me the
good old days of Florrie Forde and Nellie Wallace. They didn't
need microphones. They belted it out in the voices God gave
them. If I had them on the telly on Saturday nights, Babbie,
I'd never ask for your company. Not that I ask for it, as it is. If
you want to go out on a Saturday night, I'm not stopping you.
I'm perfectly content to sit and watch the telly on my own. It might
be a bit lonely, but I'm better to be lonely than to look at your
sour physiog.'

* * *

One day at lunch Miss Cairns said: 'Do you ever read the Personal Column in *The Weekly Pibroch*, Miss Hogg?'

'I wouldn't. I think it's beneath contempt,' Miss Hogg said, taking her order of water biscuits and cheese from the waitress. 'I'm surprised at an old established paper like *The Pibroch* printing such stuff. It's not respectable. In fact, it's positively indecent for people to advertise like that so they can have illicit sex.'

'Oh, I don't think it goes as far as that,' Miss Cairns said, beaming as the waitress put a plate of icecream and tinned apricots in front of her. 'Thank you, Effie, this looks delicious. I think you've made a mistake, Miss Hogg, you should have ordered this instead of that plastic-looking cheese.'

'I prefer cheese, Miss Cairns,' her friend said. 'I'm not one for sweet things.'

'You don't know what you're missing,' Miss Cairns said. 'I don't really agree with you about *The Pibroch*'s Personal Column. It seems to me that it satisfies a need. There are a lot of lonely people in the world, you know, Miss Hogg, and they don't often make friends easily.'

'I'd think it would be better to be lonely than flaunt it in people's faces like that. It's indecent. It's like . . . it's like going to the bathroom in public,' Miss Hogg said, lowering her voice. 'They should be ashamed to admit they can't make friends.'

'I see your point,' Miss Cairns said. 'Still, I do feel sorry for people who are alone in the world. And the Personal Column is a way for lonely people and shy people to make contacts. Listen to this: "Gentleman, fifty-five, tall and good-looking, would like to meet lady, forty-five to fifty, for companionship with a view to a lasting relationship. Widower, keen on travel, theatre, sport and good food." It's a Box number.'

'It's dreadful,' Miss Hogg said. 'It's just a dirty old man wanting free sex.'

'Oh, I wouldn't go so far as that,' Miss Cairns said. 'I don't think sex comes into it. After all, it's not mentioned, is it?'

'It's not mentioned because it's unmentionable, Miss Cairns. I think people who talk about sex are beyond the pale. Did you see that programme on TV last night? About married couples and their sexual problems going to a psychologist and then

182

being sent to classes in sexual therapy. It was so awful, I didn't know which way to look. I wanted to switch it off, but Mother insisted we watch it to the bitter end. I can't see what pleasure she got out of it. Sex is disgusting enough, anyway, but when old people talk about it it's absolutely monstrous.'

Miss Hogg reached out her hand and said: 'Let me have a look at that paper for a minute, Miss Cairns. Let's have a decka, as we used to say at Broughton, remember?' Her prim lips pursed as her eyes travelled down the column, then she read: '"Nice bloke, age nineteen, wishes to meet nice girl, aged eighteen to twenty-five, for outings and social occasions. Photo and phone number appreciated". It's outrageous! What that young man needs is a stern hand.'

'Probably he's just lonely,' Miss Cairns said. 'He may become tongue-tied when he meets a girl.'

'It doesn't sound like it.' Miss Hogg dropped the paper on the table as if it smeared her hands. 'I bet that if anybody answers and gives her phone number he'll never stop making obscene calls. And if anybody does answer that advert, they deserve all they get. The ones that answer are even worse than the ones who put them in. They should be shot.'

Mrs Hogg sang: 'Beebaw, Babbity! Babbity! Babbity! Beebaw, Babbity! You were a bonnie wee lassie.'

'What do you want now, Mother?' Miss Hogg said.

'When you go to the supermarket tomorrow, could you get me one of their nice cherry cakes? I fancy a cherry cake for my tea on Sunday.'

'I shall not be going to the supermarket tomorrow, Mother. You know perfectly well that I never go to the supermarket on Saturdays.'

'Oh no, of course not,' Mrs Hogg said. 'On Saturdays you go and play golf with your dear friend Miss Cairns, and tomorrow I've no doubt you'll be busy making plans for your annual holiday in the Algarve.'

'We will not be going to the Algarve this year, Mother. Miss Cairns has got a better post in Glasgow.'

'Well, fancy that!' Mrs Hogg said. 'Good for her. There's nothing like a change. I'm glad she's got the gumption. I thought she was like you in that office, built in with the bricks. When does she leave?'

'She left tonight at five o'clock, Mother,' Miss Hogg said. 'She starts her new job on Monday.'

'My goodness, that was quick work,' Mrs Hogg said. 'Why did you not tell me before this that she was leaving?'

'I didn't know myself until a few days ago, Mother. Miss Cairns has been very deceitful about the whole business. She never breathed a word to a soul, and when she told me she made me a promise not to breathe a word either. The staff are all very upset because they didn't have time to subscribe to a going-away present for her. There's been a lot of talk about it, and quite a few have said there's something fishy about her quick departure. However, I happen to know there's nothing underhand about it, no matter how underhand she may have been about hiding it from everybody. She gave her week's notice fair and square to Mr Gillespie last Friday, but she never said anything until she informed me on Wednesday lunchtime.'

'Informed,' Mrs Hogg said. 'Informed? Well, well.'

Then she said: 'I daresay you'll miss her. You and she have been bosom pals for such a long time. You'll have to look around for somebody else now, Babby. Or do you think you'll be able to content yourself with your poor old mother?'

What Miss Hogg never told her mother was that Miss Cairns did not tell her she was leaving until exactly half an hour before she left.

At four-thirty that Friday afternoon she had come into Miss Hogg's office and said: 'I've got some news for you, Miss Hogg. I'm leaving tonight to get married.'

'What do you mean, Miss Cairns? Is this some kind of joke?'

'It's no joke,' Miss Cairns said. 'But I'm full of fun and laughter about being able to tell you. Thank God this is the last time I'm ever likely to see your crabbit old face, and I'm glad I'll never need to listen again to you raving about some lassie you fancied as she drove off the sixteenth tee. And I'll tell you something that'll make you choke with laughing – I'm marrying a man I found through the Personal Column of *The Weekly Pibroch*.'

'You mean to say you have the audacity to confess that you answered one of those awful advertisements?'

'I do, and I'm glad I did it. I've met a super bloke – a right nice, gentle, kind man who thinks the world of me – and we've been living together – cohabiting, as they call it – for the past six months.'

'But what about your Aunt Ellen? What's she got to say to this?

'My Aunt Ellen died ten years ago,' Miss Cairns said. 'Before I came to work here. I kept her up my sleeve as a good excuse whenever I wanted to get shot of you.'

'You should be ashamed to admit such a deception, Miss Cairns. You're a deceitful . . . Oh, words fail me, you awful liar!'

'That advert I read out to you seven months ago – about a widower, aged fifty-five, tall and good-looking – that's the one I answered. And Billy's everything he said. And more. And do you know this: We've been doing the football pools together, and a couple of weeks ago we won a hundred thousand pounds. So we thought the time had come: We're going to shake the dust of Auld Reekie off our feet and go and live in the Algarve.'

'The Algarve?' Miss Hogg said.

'Ay, the Algarve. I thought that would make your hair stand on end, Lizzie Burke.'

'What do you mean? Lizzie Burke?'

'Did you not know?' Miss Cairns said. 'But of course you didn't, you're so wrapped up in yourself. Did you not know that the staff call us "the two Lizzies" and "Burke and Hare" after the famous body-snatchers of the 19th century who took corpses from their coffins and sold them to Dr Knox right here in our fair city of Edinburgh? They call you Burke, and I'm Hare because I'm the one that gets chased. It was that pug-nosed little cow, Peggy Pringle, who told me. You know the one you used to suck up to? She told me in a tantrum after

I got Mr Gillespie to give her the boot for inefficiency. Oh, you're not loved in this office, Lizzie Burke.'

'Get out of my sight, you awful creature,' Miss Hogg said.

'Nothing will give me greater pleasure,' Miss Cairns said.

She went to the door, opened it, looked back and said, 'Stymied!' Then she closed the door quietly behind her.

McAuslan in the Rough

GEORGE MACDONALD FRASER

M<small>Y</small> tough granny – the Presbyterian MacDonald one, not the pagan one from Islay – taught me about golf when I was very young. Her instruction was entirely different from that imparted by my father, who was a scratch player, gold medallist and all, with a swing like de Vicenzo; he showed me how to make shots, and place my feet, and keep calm in the face of an eighteen-inch putt on a downhill green with the wind in my face and the match hanging on it. But my granny taught me something much more mysterious.

Her attitude to the game was much like her attitude to religion; you achieved grace by sticking exactly to the letter of the law, by never giving up, and by occasional prayer. You replaced your divots, you carried your own clubs, and you treated your opponent as if he was a Campbell, and an armed one at that. I can see her now, advanced in years, with her white hair clustered under her black bonnet, and the wind whipping the long skirt round her ankles, lashing her drives into the gale; if they landed on the fairway she said 'Aye', and if they finished in the rough she said 'Tach!' Nothing more. And however unplayable her lie, she would hammer away with her niblick until that ball was out of trouble, and half Perthshire with it. If it took her fifteen strokes, no matter; she would tot them up grimly when the putts were down, remark, 'This and better may do, this and waur will never do', and stride off to the next tee, gripping her driver like a battle-axe.

As an opponent she was terrifying, not only because she played well, but because she made you aware that this was a personal duel in which she intended to grind you into the turf without pity; if she was six up at the seventeenth she would still attack that last hole as if life depended on it. At first I hated playing with her, but gradually I learned to meet her with something of her own spirit, and if I could never achieve the killer instinct which she possessed, at least I discovered satisfaction in winning, and did so without embarrassment.

As a partner she was beyond price. Strangely enough, when we played as a team, we developed a comradeship closer than I ever felt for any other player; we once even held our own with my father and uncle, who together could have given a little trouble to any golfers anywhere. Even conceding a stroke a hole they were immeasurably better than an aged woman and an erratic small boy, but she was their mother and let them know it; the very way she swung her brassie was a wordless reminder of the second commandment, and by their indulgence, her iron will, and enormous luck, we came all square to the eighteenth tee.

Counting our stroke, we were both reasonably close to the green in two, and my granny, crouching like a bombazine vulture with her mashie-niblick, put our ball about ten feet from the pin. My father, after thinking and clicking his tongue, took his number three and from a nasty lie played a beautiful rolling run-up to within a foot of the hole – a real old Fife professional's shot.

I looked at the putt and trembled. 'Dand,' said my grandmother. 'Never up, never in.'

So I gulped, prayed, and went straight for the back of the cup. I hit it, too, the ball jumped, teetered, and went in. My father and uncle applauded, granny said 'Aye', and my uncle stooped to his ball, remarking, 'Halved hole and match, eh?'

'No such thing,' said granny, looking like the Three Fates. 'Take your putt.'

Nowadays, of course, putts within six inches or so are frequently conceded, as being unmissable. Not with my grandmother; she would have stood over Arnold Palmer if he had been on the lip of the hole. So my uncle sighed, smiled, took his putter, played – and missed. His putter went into the nearest bunker, my father walked to the edge of the green, humming to himself, and my grandmother sniffed and told me curtly to pick up my bag and mind where I was putting my feet on the green.

As we walked back to the clubhouse, she grimly silent as usual, myself exulting, while the post-mortem of father and uncle floated out of the dusk behind us, she made one of her rare observations.

'A game,' she said, 'is not lost till it's won. Especially with your Uncle Hugh. He is –' and here her face assumed the stern resignation of a materfamilias who has learned that one of the family has fled to Australia pursued by creditors, '– a *trifling* man. Are your feet wet? Aye, well, they won't stay dry long if you drag them through the grass like that.'

And never a word did she say about my brilliant putt, but back in the clubhouse she had the professional show her all the three irons he had, chose one, beat him down from seventeen and six to eleven shillings, handed it to me, and told my father to pay for it. 'The boy needs a three iron,' she said. And to me: 'Mind you take care of it.' I have taken care of it.

But all this was long ago, and has nothing much to do with the story of Private McAuslan, that well-known military disaster, golfing personality and caddy extraordinary. Except for the fact that I suppose something of that great old lady's personality stayed with me, and exerted its influence whenever I took a golf club in hand. Not that this was often; as I grew through adolescence I developed a passion for cricket, a love–hate relationship with Rugby, and some devotion to soccer, so that golf faded into the background. Anyway, for all my early training, I wasn't much good, a scratching, turf-cutting 24-handicapper whose drives either went two hundred yards dead straight or whined off at right angles into the wilderness. I was full of what you might call golfing lore and know-how, but in practice I was an erratic slasher, a blasphemer in bunkers, and prone to give up round about the twelfth hole and go looking for beer in the clubhouse.

In the army there was less time than ever for golf, but it chanced that when our Highland battalion was posted back to Scotland from North Africa shortly after the war we were stationed on the very edge of one of those murderous east coast courses where the greens are small and fast, the wind is a howling menace, and the rough is such that you either play straight or you don't play at all. This, of course, is where golf was born, where the early giants made it an art before the Americans turned it into a science, and whence John Paterson strode forth in his blacksmith's apron to partner the future King James II in the first international against England. (That was a right crafty piece of gamesmanship on James's part, too, but it won the match, so there you are.)

In any event, the local committee made us free of their links, and the battalion had something of a golfing revival. This was encouraged by our new Colonel, a stiffish, Sandhurst sort of man who had decided views on what was sport and what was not. Our old Colonel had been a law unto himself: boxing, snooker, billiards-fives, and working himself into hysterics at battalion football matches had been his mark, but the new man saw sport through the pages of *Country Life*. Well, I mean, he rode horses, shot grouse, and belonged to some ritzy yacht club on the Forth where they drank pink gin and wore handkerchiefs in their sleeves. To a battalion whose notions of games began and ended with a football, this was something rich and strange. But since he approved of golf, and liked to see his officers taking advantage of the local club's hospitality, those of us who could play did so, and a fairly bad showing we made. Subalterns like myself plowtered our way round and rejoiced when we broke 90; two of our older majors set a record in lost balls for a single round (23, including five found and lost again); the Regimental Sergeant-Major played a very correct, military game in which the ball seldom left the fairway but never travelled very far either; and the M.O. and Padre set off with one set of clubs and the former's hip flask – their round ended with the Padre searching for wild flowers and the M.O. lying in the bracken at the long fourteenth singing 'Kishmul's Galley'. It was golf of a kind, if you like, and only the Adjutant took it at all seriously.

This was probably because he possessed a pair of pre-war plus fours and a full set of clubs, which enabled him to put on tremendous side. Bunkered, which he usually was, he would affect immense concern over whether he should use a seven or eight iron – would the wind carry his chip far enough? should he apply top spin?

'What do you think, Pirie?' he would ask his partner, who was the officers' mess barman but in private life had been assistant pro. at a course in Nairn and was the only real golfer in the battalion. 'Should I take the seven or the eight?'

'For a' the guid ye are wi' either o' them ye micht as weel tak' a bluidy bulldozer,' Pirie would say. Upon which he would be sternly reprimanded for insubordination, the Adjutant would seize his blaster, and after a dozen unsuccessful slashes would snatch up the ball in rage and hurl it frenziedly into the whins.

'It's a' one,' Pirie would observe. 'Ye'd have three-putted anyway.'

'I can't understand it,' I once heard the Adjutant say in the mess bar, in that plaintive, self-examining tone which is the hall-mark of the truly bum golfer. 'I've tried the overlap grip, I've tried the forefinger down the shaft; I've stood up from the ball and I've crouched over it; I've used several stances, with my feet together, my feet apart, and my knees bent – everything! But the putts simply won't go down. Pirie here will confirm me. I don't understand it at all. What do you think, Pirie?'

'Ye cannae bluidy well putt,' said the unfeeling Pirie. 'That's a' there is to it.'

Mess barmen, it need hardly be added, are privileged people, and anyway the Adjutant and Pirie had once stood back to back in an ambush on the Chocolate Staircase, and had an understanding of their own. It was something which the new Colonel would not have fully appreciated, for he had not served with the regiment since before the war, and was as big a stickler for military discipline as long service on the staff could make him. He did not understand the changes which six years of war had wrought, most especially in a Highland regiment, which is a curious organization in the first place.

It looks terribly military, and indeed it is, but under the surface a Highland unit has curious currents which are extremely irregular. There is a sort of unspoken yet recognized democracy which may have its roots in clanship, or in the

Scottish mercenary tradition, and which can play the devil with rank and authority unless it is properly understood. The new Colonel obviously was unaware of this, or he would not have suddenly ordained, one fine bright morning, that whenever an officer played golf he should have a soldier to caddy for him.

In feudal theory, even in military theory, this was all very well. In the egalitarian atmosphere of a Highland battalion, circa 1947, it was simply not on; our old Colonel wouldn't even have thought of it. Quite apart from the fact that every man in the unit, in that Socialist age, knew his rights and was well aware that caddying wasn't covered by the Army Act – well, you can try getting a veteran of Alamein and Anzio to carry golf clubs for a pink-cheeked one-pipper, but when that veteran has not only learned his political science at Govan Cross but is also a member of an independent and prideful race, you may encounter difficulties. However, the Colonel's edict had gone forth, and after it had been greeted in the mess with well-bred whistles and exclamations of 'I *say*!' and 'Name o' the wee man!', I was left, as battalion sports officer, to arrange the impressment of suitable caddies.

'The man's mad,' I told the Adjutant. 'There'll be a mutiny.'

'Oh, I don't know,' he said. 'You could try picking on the simple-minded ones.'

'The only simple-minded ones in this outfit are in our own mess,' I said. 'Can you imagine Wee Wullie's reaction, for example, if he's told to caddy for some of our young hopefuls? He'll run amuck.' Wee Wullie was a giant of uncontrolled passions and immense brawn whose answer to any vexing problem was usually a swung fist. 'And the rest of them are liable to write to their M.P.s. You don't know the half of it in Headquarter Company; out where the rest of us live it's like a Jacobin literary society.'

'Use tact,' advised the Adjutant, 'and if that fails, try blackmail. But whatever you do, for God's sake don't provoke a disciplinary crisis.'

In other words, perform the impossible, and the only normal way to do that was to enlist the Regimental Sergeant-Major, the splendid Mr Mackintosh. But I hesitated to do this; like a scientist on the brink of some shattering experiment, I was fearful of releasing powers beyond my control. So after deep thought I decided to confine my activities to my own platoon, whom I knew, and made a subtle approach to the saturnine Private Fletcher, who was the nearest thing to a shop steward then in uniform. We were soon chatting away on that agreeable officerman basis which is founded on mutual respect and makes the British Army what it is.

'Fletcher,' I said casually, 'there are a limited number of openings for Jocks to caddy for the officers when they play golf. It's light work, in congenial surroundings, and those who are fortunate enough to be selected will receive certain privileges, etc., etc. Now those loafers up in Support Company would give their right arms for the chance, but what I say is, what's the use of my being sports officer if I can't swing a few good things for my own chaps, so–'

'Aye, sir,' said Fletcher. 'Whit's the pey?'

'The pay?'

'Uh-huh. The pey. What's the rate for the job?'

This took me aback. It hadn't occurred to me to suggest paying Jocks to caddy, and I was willing to bet it hadn't occurred to the Colonel either. Fall in the loyal privates, touching their forelocks by numbers, would be his idea. But I now saw a way through this embarrassing problem – after all, I did have a sports fund at my disposal, and a quarter-master who could cook a book to a turn.

'Well, now,' I said, 'we ought to be able to fix that easily enough. Suppose we say about a shilling an hour . . .' The fund ought to be able to stand that, under 'miscellaneous'.

'Aw, jeez, come aff it, sir,' said Fletcher respectfully. '*Two* bob an hour, an' overtime in the evenin's. Double time Setterdays an' Sundays, an' a hardship bonus for whoever has tae carry the Adjutant's bag. Yon's a bluidy disgrace, no kiddin'; the man's no fit tae play on the street. Ye'll no' get anyone in his right mind tae caddy for him; it'll hae tae be yin o' the yahoos.' He fumbled in his pocket. 'I've got a wee list here, sir, o' fellas that would do, wi' the rates I was mentionin' just now. Wan or two o' them have played golf theirsel's, so they mebbe ought tae get two an' six an hour – it'll be kinda professional advice, ye see. But we'll no' press it.'

I looked dumbly at him for a moment. 'You knew about this? But, dammit, the Adjutant only mentioned it half an hour ago . . .'

He looked at me pityingly as I took his list. Of course, I ought to have known better. All this stuff about Highlanders' second sight is nonsense; it's just first-class espionage, that's all.

'Well,' I said, studying the list, 'I don't know about this. I'm sure it's all very irregular . . .'

'So's the employment o' military personnel ootwith military duties,' said Fletcher smugly. 'Think if somebody frae the *Daily Worker* wis tae get word that wee shilpit Toamy frae the Q.M. store – him wi' the bad feet – wis humphin' the Adjutant's golf-sticks a' ower the place. They might even get a picture of him greetin'–'

'Quite, quite,' I said. 'Point taken. All right, two bob an hour, but I want respectable men, understand?'

'Right, sir.' Fletcher hesitated. 'Would there be a wee allowance, mebbe, for wear an' tear on the fellas' civvy clothes? They cannae dae the job in uniform, and it's no fair tae expect a fella tae spile his glamour pants and long jaicket sclimmin' intae bunkers–'

'They can draw white football shirts and long khaki drills from the sports store,' I said. 'Now go away, you crimson thief, and see that nobody who isn't on this list ever hears that there's payment involved, otherwise we'll have a queue forming up. I want this thing to work nice and smoothly.'

And of course it did. Fletcher had picked eight men, including himself, of sober habit and decent appearance, and the sight of them in their white shirts and khaki slacks, toting their burdens round the links, did the Colonel's heart good to see. It all looked very military and right, and he wasn't to know that they were being subsidized out of battalion funds. In fact, I had quietly informed the Adjutant that if those officers who played golf made an unofficial contribution to the sports kitty, it would be welcome, and the result was that we actually showed a profit.

The Jocks who caddied were all for it. They made money, they missed occasional parades, and they enjoyed such privileges as watching the Adjutant have hysterics while standing thigh-deep in a stream, or hearing the Padre addressing heaven from the midst of a bramble patch. It was all good clean fun, and would no doubt have stayed that way if the new Colonel, zealous for his battalion's prestige, hadn't got ambitious.

He didn't play golf himself, but he took pride in his unit's activities, and it chanced that on one of his strolls across the course he saw Pirie the barman playing against the better of our elderly majors. The major must have been at his best, and Pirie's game was immaculate as usual, so the Colonel, following them over the last three holes, got a totally false impression of the standard of golf under his command. This, he decided, was pretty classy stuff, and it seems that he mentioned this to his friend who commanded the Royals, who inhabited that part of the country. Colonels are forever boasting to each other in this reckless way, whereby their underlings often suffer most exquisitely.

Anyway, the Colonel of the Royals said he had some pretty fair golfers in his mess, and how about a game? Our Colonel, in his ignorance, accepted the challenge. I privately believe that he had some wild notion that because we had caddies in nice white shirts we would have a built-in advantage, but in any event he placed a bet with the Royals' C.O. and then came home to tell the Adjutant the glad news. We were to field ten players in a four-somes match against the Royals, and we were to win.

Now, you may think an inter-regimental golf match is fairly trivial stuff, but when a new and autocratic Colonel is involved, puffed up with regimental conceit, and when the opposition is the Royals, it is a most serious matter. For one thing, the Royals are unbearable. They are tremendously old, and stuffed with tra-dition and social graces, and adopt a patronizing attitude to the rest of the army in general, and other Scottish units in particular. Furthermore, they can play golf – or they could then – and of this the Adjutant was painfully aware.

However, like the good soldier he was, he set about mar-shalling his forces, which consisted of making sure that he personally partnered Pirie.

'We know each other's game, you see,' he told me. 'We blend, as it were.'

'You mean he'll carry you round on his back,' I said. 'You don't fool me, brother. You see that partnering Pirie is the one chance you've got of being in a winning pair.'

'Look,' he said. 'I've got to work with the Colonel; I see him every day, don't I? I've got to salvage something from what is sure to be a pretty beastly wreck. Now, how about the second pair? The Padre and the M.O., eh? They always play together.'

'They'll be good for a laugh, anyway,' I said. 'Unless the Royals go easy on them out of respect for the clerical cloth, or the M.O. can get his opponents drunk, they don't stand a prayer.'

'Then there's young Macmillan – he's not bad,' said the Adjutant hopefully. 'I saw him hole a putt the other day. You could partner him yourself.'

'Not a chance,' I said. 'The best he's ever gone round in is 128, with a following wind. Furthermore he giggles. I want to succumb with dignity; either I partner the R.S.M. or you can get yourself another boy.'

'Old man Mackintosh, eh?' said the Adjutant. 'Well, he's a steady player, isn't he? Can't think I've ever seen him in the rough.'

'That's why I want him,' I said. 'I want to play a few of my shots from a decent lie.'

'You've got a rotten, defeatist attitude,' said the Adjutant severely.

'I'm a rotten, defeatist golfer,' I said. 'So are you, and so are the rest of us, bar Pirie.'

'Ah, yes, Pirie,' said the Adjutant, smirking. 'He and I should do not too badly, I think. If I can remember not to overswing; and I think I'll get the pro. to shave my driver just a teeny fraction – for balance, you know – and get in a bit of practice with my eight iron . . .'

'Come back to earth, Sarazen,' I said. 'You've still got two couples to find.'

We finally settled on our two elderly majors, Second-Lieutenant Macmillan, and Regimental Quartermaster Bogle, a stout and imposing warrant officer who had been known to play a few rounds with the pipe-sergeant. No one knew how they scored, but Bogle used to say off-handedly that his game had rusted a wee bitty since he won the Eastern District Boys' Title many years ago – heaven help us, it must have been when Old

Tom Morris was in small clothes – and the pipey would nod sagely and say:

'Aye, aye, Quarters, a wee thing over par the day, just a wee thing, aye. But no' bad, no' bad at all.'

Personally I thought this was lying propaganda, but I couldn't prove it.

'It is,' admitted the Adjutant, 'a pretty lousy team. Oh, well, at least our caddies will look good.'

But there he was dead wrong. He was not to know it but lurking in the background was the ever-present menace of Private McAuslan, now preparing to take a hand in the fate of the battalion golf team.

He was far from my mind on the afternoon of the great match, as the R.S.M. and I stood waiting outside the clubhouse to tee off. Presently my own batman, the tow-headed McClusky, who was caddying for me, arrived on the scene, and shambling behind him was the Parliamentary Road's own contribution to the pollution problem, McAuslan himself.

'What's he doing here?' I demanded, shaken.

'He's come tae caddy,' explained McClusky. 'See, there's only eight caddies on the list, an' ten o' ye playin', so Fletcher picked anither two. Him an' Daft Bob Broon.'

'Why him?' I hissed, aware that our visitors from the Royals were casting interested glances towards McAuslan, whose grey-white shirt was open to the waist, revealing what was either his skin or an old vest, you couldn't tell which. His hair was tangled and his mouth hung open; altogether he looked as though he'd just completed a bell-ringing stint at Notre Dame.

'Fletcher said it would be a'right.'

'I'll talk to Master Fletcher in due course,' I said. 'But you ought to have known better, at least. Well, you can darn your own socks after this, my lad.' I turned to McAuslan. 'You,' I hissed, 'button your shirt and try to look half-decent.'

'Ah cannae, sir, but.' He pawed unhappily at his insanitary frontage. 'The buttons his come aff.'

I'd been a fool to mention it, of course. I wondered momentarily if there was time to dismiss him and get a replacement, but the first foursome was already on the tee. 'Well, tuck the damned thing in at least, and get hold of yourself. You're caddying for the Regimental Sergeant-Major.'

I don't know which of them was hit hardest by this news; probably no two men in the battalion were as eager to shun each other's company. McAuslan went in fear and horror of the majestic Mackintosh; the R.S.M., on the other hand, who had been brought up in the Guards, regarded McAuslan as a living insult to the profession of arms, and preferred to ignore his existence. Now they were in enforced partnership, so to speak. I left them to renew old acquaintance, and went to watch the first shots being exchanged on the tee.

Pirie and the Adjutant were our openers, and when Pirie hit his drive out of sight you could see the Adjutant smirking approval in a way which invited the onlookers to believe that he, too, was cast in the same grand mould. Poor sap, he didn't seem to realize that he would shortly be scooping great lumps out of the fairway while Pirie gritted his teeth and their opponents looked embarrassed. Not that the Royals looked as though pity was their long suit; it is part of their regimental tradition to look as much like army officers as possible – the type who are to be seen in advertisements for lime juice, or whisky, or some splendid out-of-doors tobacco. They were brown, leathery, moustached upper-crust Anglo-Scots, whose well-worn wind-cheaters and waterproof trousers could have come only from Forsyth's or Rowan's; their wooden clubs had little covers on their heads, their brogues had fine metal spikes, and they called each other Murdoch and Doug. Nowadays they broke stocks or manage export concerns, and no doubt they still play golf extremely well.

Our second pair were Damon and Pythias, the two elderly majors, who took the tee with arthritic moans. Rivals for the same girl when they had been stationed at Kasr-el-Nil before the war, they disliked each other to the point of inseparability, and lived in a state of feud. If they could manage to totter round the eighteen holes they would at least put up a show, which was more than I expected from our third couple, the Padre and the M.O.

They were a sight to see. The M.O., eating pills and wearing gym shoes, was accompanied by a caddy festooned with impedimenta – an umbrella, binoculars, flask, sandwich case and the like. Golf, to the M.O., was not to be taken lightly. The Padre, apart from his denim trousers, was resplendent in a jersey embroidered for him by the market mammies of some St Andrew's Kirk in West Africa, a souvenir of his missionary days. A dazzling yellow, it had his name in scarlet on the front – 'Rev. McLeod', it said – while on the back, in many colours, was the Church of Scotland emblem of the burning bush, with 'Nec tamen consumebatur' underneath. The Padre wouldn't have parted with it for worlds; he had worn it under his battledress on D-Day, and intended to be buried in it.

The M.O., breathing heavily, drove off, which consisted of swinging like a Senlac axe-man, overbalancing, and putting up a ball which, had he been playing cricket, would have been easily caught at square leg.

'"Gregory, remember thy swashing blow",' quoted the Padre. 'Man, but there's power there, if it could be harnessed. Don't you worry, Lachlan, I'll see to it', and he wandered off towards the ball to play the second shot after his opponents had driven off – which they did, very long and very straight.

Second-Lieutenant Macmillan and R.Q.M.S. Bogle were next, Macmillan scraping his drive just over the brow of the hill fifty yards in front of the tee. Then the MacNeill-Mackintosh combo took the stage, and as we walked on to the tee with the Colonels and attendant minions watching from the clubhouse verandah, I could hear the R.S.M.'s muttered instructions to the shuffling McAuslan: '. . . those are the wooden clubs with the wooden heads; the irons have metal heads. All are numbered accordin' to their purpose. When I require a parteecular club I shall call oot the number, and you will hand it to me, smertly and with care. Is that clear?'

God help you, you optimistic sergeant-major, I thought, and invited him to tee off – whoever fell flat on his face in front of the assembled gallery, it wasn't going to be me. He put a respectable drive over the hill, our opponents drove immaculately, and we were off, four golfers, three caddies, and McAuslan shambling behind, watching the R.S.M. fearfully, like a captured slave behind a chariot.

Looking back, I can't say I enjoyed that match. For one thing, I was all too conscious of what was happening in the foursomes ahead of us, and over the first nine at least it wasn't good. From time to time they would come into view, little disheartening tableaux: the M.O. kneeling under a bush, swearing and wrestling with the cap of his flask; R.Q.M.S. Bogle trying to hit a ball which was concealed by his enormous belly, while Macmillan giggled nervously; our elderly majors beating the thick rough with their clubs and reviling each other; the Adjutant's plaintive bleat drifting over the dunes: 'I'm awfully sorry, Pirie, I can't imagine what's happened to my mid-irons today; either it's the balance of the clubs or I'm over-swinging. What do you think, Pirie, am I over-swinging?' And so on, while the whin blew gently over the sunlit course, ruffling the bent grass, and the distant sea glittered from its little choppy wavelets; it was a brisk, beautiful backdrop totally out of keeping with the condition of the tortured souls trudging over the links, recharging all their worst emotions and basest instincts in the pursuit of little white balls. It makes you think about civilization, it really does.

I refer to the emotions of our own side, of course. The Royals, for all I know, were enjoying it. My own personal opponents seemed to be, at any rate. They were of the type I have already described, trim, confident men called Hamilton and Dalgliesh – or it may have been Melville and Runcieman, I can't be sure. They played a confident, rather showy game, with big, erratic drives and carefully-considered chips and putts – which, oddly enough, didn't give them much edge on us. Mackintosh was a steady, useful player, and I'd been worse; we weren't discontented to reach the turn one down.

I had arranged for the pipe-sergeant to station himself at the ninth green, to give progress reports on the other games, and he was bursting with news.

'Sir, sir, the Adjutant and Pirie iss in the lead! They're wan hole up, sir, an' Pirie playin' like God's anointed. The Adjutant iss a shambles, poor soul, and him such a charmin' dancer, but Pirie is carryin' the day. His drives iss like thunderbolts, and his putts is droppin' from wherever. Oh, the elegance of it, and the poor Adjutant broke his driver at the eighth an' him near greetin'. But they're wan up, sir.'

'How about the others?'

'The majors is square, but failin' rapidly. I doot Major Fleming'll be to carry home; the endurance is not in him. Bogle an' the boy – Mr Macmillan, that is – are two doon, an' lucky at that, for Bogle's guts is a fearful handicap. They hinder his swing, ye see, and he's vexed. But he's game, for a' that, an' wan o' the Royals he's playin' against has ricked his back, so there's hope yet.'

Ahead in one game, square in one, behind in two; it could have been worse. 'How about the Padre and the M.O.?'

The pipe-sergeant coughed delicately. 'Seven doon, sir, and how they contrived to save two holes, God alone knows. It's deplorable, sir; the M.O. has been nippin' ahint a bush after every hole for a sook at his flask, and iss as gassed as a Ne'erday tinker. The poor Padre has gone awa' into one o' they wee broon things–'

'Into what?'

'Into a dwalm, sir, a revaree, like a trance, ye ken. He wanders, and keeks intae bunkers, and whistles in the Gaelic There's nae sense in either o' them, sir; they're lost to ye.' He said it much as a Marshal of France might have reported the defeat of an army to Napoleon, sad but stern. 'And yerself, sir? One doon? What is that to such men as yerself and the Major, see the splendid bearin' of him! Cheer up, sir, a MacNeill never cried barley; ye had your own boat in the Flood.'

'That was the MacLeans, pipey,' I said sadly. The Colonel, I was thinking, wasn't going to like this; by the same process of logic, he wasn't going to like his sports officer. Well, if Pirie kept his winning streak, and the two old majors lasted the distance – it was just possible that the R.S.M. and I might achieve something, who knew? But the outlook wasn't good, and I drove off at the tenth in no high spirits.

And it was at this point that Private McAuslan began to impose his personality on the game. Knowing about McAuslan, you might think that an odd way of putting it – interfere with something, yes; wreck, frustrate or besmirch – all these things he could do. But even with his talent for disaster, he had never been what you could call a controlling influence – until the R.S.M., playing our second shot at the tenth, for once hooked, and landed us deep in tiger country.

We thrashed about in the jungle searching, but there wasn't a hope, and with the local five-minute rule in operation we had to forfeit the hole. Personally, if it had been our opponents, I'd have suggested they drop a new ball and forfeit a stroke, but there it was. We were two down, and the R.S.M. for once looked troubled.

'I'm extremely sorry aboot that, sir,' he confided to me. 'Slack play. No excuse. I'm extremely sorry.'

I hastened to reassure him, for I guessed that perhaps to the R.S.M. this match was even more important than to the rest of us. When your life is a well-ordered, immaculate success, as his was, any failure begins to look important. Perfection was his norm; being two down was not perfection, and losing a ball was inexcusable.

Meanwhile, I was aware of voices behind us, and one of them was McAuslan's. He had been quiet on the outward half, between terror of the R.S.M. and his own inability to distinguish one club from another – for he was illiterate, a rare but not unknown thing in the Army of those days. Perhaps his awe of Mackintosh had diminished slightly – the serf who sees his over-lord grunting in a bunker gets a new slant on their relationship, I suppose. Anyway, the fearful novelty of his situation having worn off, he was beginning to take an interest, and McAuslan taking an interest was wont to be garrulous.

'Hey, Chick,' I heard him say, addressing my caddy. 'Whit we no' finishing this hole fur?'

'We've loast it,' said McClusky. 'We lost wir ba'.'

'So whit? Hiv we no' got anither yin?'

'Aye, we've got anither yin, but if ye lose a ba' ye lose the hole. It's the rules.'

A pause. Then: 'Ah, – the rules. It's no' fair. Sure it's no' fair, huh, Chick?'

'Aw, Goad,' said McClusky, 'Ah'm tellin' ye, it's the rule, ye dope. Same's at fitba'.'

'Weel, Ah think it's daft,' said McAuslan. 'Look, at fitba', if a man kicks the ba' oot the park–'

'All right, McAuslan, pipe down,' I said. I knew that one of the few abstract ideas ever to settle in that neanderthal mind was a respect for justice – his sense of what was 'no fair' had once landed him in a court martial – but this was no time for an address by McAuslan, Q.C. 'Just keep quiet, and watch the ball. If you'd done it last time we might not have lost the hole.' Which wasn't strictly fair, but I was punished for it.

'Quaiet, please,' said one of our opponents. 'No tocking on the tee, if you don't mind.' And he added, 'Thenk-you.'

The crust of it was, he hadn't even teed up. Suddenly I realized what had been wrong with this game so far – I'd had half my mind on the other matches, half on my own play: I hadn't really noticed our opponents. And that's no good. Ask Dr Grace or Casey Stengel or my Highland granny – you've *got* to notice the opposition, and abominate them. That totally unnecessary 'Quaiet, please' had made it easy.

Our opponents drove off, respectably, and Mackintosh, sub-consciously trying to redeem his lost ball, tried a big one, instead of his usual cautious tee-shot. It soared away splendidly, but with slice written all over it; it was going to land well among the whins.

'Keep your eye on it!' I shouted, and McAuslan, full of zeal, bauchled masterfully across the tee, dragging his bag, his eyes staring fixedly into the blue, roaring:

'Ah see it! Ah've spotted the b–! Don't worry, sir! Ah see–'

Unfortunately it was one of those high plateau tees with a steep drop to whins and rough grass at the start of the fairway. McAuslan, blind to everything except the soaring ball, marched into the void and descended with a hideous clatter of clubs and body, to which presently he added flowers of invective picked up on the Ibrox terracing. He crawled out of the bushes blaspheming bitterly, until he realized the R.S.M's cold eye was on him; then he rose and limped after the ball.

The opponent who had rebuked me – I think of him as Melville – chuckled.

'Thet's a remarkable individual,' he said to me. 'Wherever did you get him?' A fair enough question, from anyone meeting McAuslan for the first time, but with just a hint of patronage, perhaps. 'You ott to keep an aye on him, before he hurts himself,' went on Melville jocularly. 'Aye don't think he's doing anything for your partner's peace of mind, eether.'

It might have been just loud enough for Mackintosh to hear; I may have been wrong, but I think I know gamesmanship when I hear it. Coming on top of the 'Quaiet, please', it just settled my hate nicely; from that moment the tension was on, and I squared up to that second shot in the deep rough, determined to hit the green if it killed me. Four shots later we were in a bunker, con-ceding a hole that was hopelessly lost. Three down and seven to play.

Not a nice position, and McAuslan didn't help things. Perhaps his fall had rattled him, or more probably his brief sally into the limelight had made him more than normally self-conscious. He accidentally trod in the tee-box at the twelfth, and had to have his foot freed by force (the fact that Melville muttered something about 'accident prone' did nothing for my temper). Then he upended the R.S.M.'s bag, and we had to wait while he retrieved the clubs, scrabbling like a great beast with his shirt coming out. I forced myself to be calm, and managed a fairish drive to the edge of the short twelfth green; Mackintosh chipped on well, and we halved in three.

The thirteenth was one of those weird hole by which games of golf are won and lost. Our position was fairly hopeless – three down and six – possible because of that we played it like champions. The R.S.M. drove straight, and for once he was long; I took my old whippy brassie with its wooden shaft, drove from my mind the nameless fear that McAuslan would have an apoplectic fit or shoot me in the back while I was in the act of swinging, and by great good luck hit one of those perfect shots away downhill. It flew, it bounced, it ran, trickling between the bunkers to lie nicely just a yard on to the green.

Melville and Co. were in dire straits. They took three and were still short of the green, and I was counting the hole won when Melville took out his number seven iron and hit the bonniest chip I ever hope to see; of course it was lucky, landing a yard short of the flag with lots of back spin, and then running straight as a die into the cup, but that's golf. They were down in four, we were on in two, and Mackintosh had a fifteen-yard putt.

He strode ponderously on to the green, looked at the ball as though to ask its name, rank and number, and held out his hand for his putter. McAuslan rummaged carefully, and then announced tremulously:

'It's no' here, sir.'

And it wasn't. Sulphurous question and whimpering answer finally narrowed the thing down to the point where we realized it must have fallen out when McAuslan, Daedalus-like, had tried to defy gravity at the eleventh tee. He was driven, with oaths and threats, to fetch it, and we waited in the sunlight, Melville and his friend saying nothing pointedly, until presently McAuslan hove in view again, looking like the last survivor of Fort Zinderneuf staggering home, dying of thirst. But he had the club.

'Ah'm awfu' sorry, sir. It must hiv fell oot.' He wiped his

sweating grey nose audibly, and the R.S.M. took the putter with-out a word, addressed the ball briefly, and sent it across the huge waste of green dead true, undeviating, running like a pup to its dinner, plopping with a beautiful mellow sound into the tin.

(It's a strange thing, but when I think back to that heroic, colossal putt – or to any other moment in that game, for that matter – I see in my imagination the R.S.M., not clothed in the mufti which I known he must have been wearing, but resplen-dent in full regimentals, white spats, kilt, dress tunic and broadsword, with a feather bonnet on top. I *know* he wasn't wearing them, but he should have been.)

And as we cried our admiration, I thought to myself, we're only two down now. And five holes to go. And `I heard again that old golfing maxim: 'Two up and five never won a match.' Well, it might come true, given luck.

It certainly began to look like it, for while our drives and approaches were level at the fourteenth, the R.S.M. played one of his canny chips while our opponents barely found the green. Their putt was feebly short, and mine teetered round the hole, took a long look in, and finally went down. One up and four.

The fifteenth was a nightmare hole, a par-three where you played straight out to sea, hoping to find a tiny green perched above the beach, with only a ribbon of fairway through the jungle. This was where Mackintosh's cautious driving was beyond price; I trundled on a lamentable run-up that missed the guarding bunker by a whisker, and then Melville, panicking, put his approach over the green and, presumably, into the North Sea. All square with three to play.

For the first time I was enjoying myself; I felt we had them on the run, whereupon my Presbyterian soul revolted and slapped me on the wrists, urging me to be calm. So I drove cautiously and straight, the R.S.M. put us within pitching distance, and my chip just stayed on the back of the green. Melville played the like into a bunker, they took three to get pin-high, and the R.S.M.'s putt left me nothing to do but home a twelve-incher. For the first time we were in front. And only two holes remained.

The seventeenth was the first half of a terribly long haul to the

clubhouse. It and the eighteenth were par fives, where our opponents' longer hitting ought to tell. But Melville's partner duffed his drive, and while we broke no records in getting to the edge of the green in five, he and his partner undertook a shocking safari into the rough on both sides, and were still off the green in six. I was trembling slightly as I chipped on, and more by luck than judgement I left it within a foot of the cup. Unless they sank their approach, which was unthinkable, we had the match won. I glanced at the R.S.M. His face was wooden, as usual, but as we waited for their shot his fingers were drumming on the shaft of his putter.

Melville's partner, hand it to him, was ready to die game. 'This goes in,' he said, shaping up to his ball, which was on the wrong side of a bunker, fifteen yards from the flag. 'Pin out, please.'

And Private McAuslan, the nearest caddy, ambled across the green to remove the flag.

I should have known, of course; I should have taken thought. But I'd forgotten McAuslan in the excitement of the game;

vaguely I had been aware of his presence, when he sniffed, or grunted, or dropped the clubs or muttered, 'Aw, jeez, whit a brammer' when we hit a good shot, or 'Ah, –', when our opponents did. But he hadn't broken his leg, or gone absent, or caught beri-beri, or done anything really McAuslan-like. Now he tramped across to the flag, his paw outstretched, and I felt my premonition of disaster too late.

He claimed afterwards it was a wasp, but as the Adjutant said, it must have been a bot-fly, or maybe a vulture: no sane wasp would have gone near him, in his condition. Whatever it was, he suddenly leaped, swatting and cursing, he stumbled, and his great, flat, ugly, doom-laden foot came down on our ball, squashing it into the turf.

I think I actually screamed. Because the law is the law, and if your caddy touches your ball in play, let alone tries to stamp the damned thing through to Australia, you forfeit the hole. Even Melville, I'll swear, had compassion in his eyes.

'Dem bed luck,' he said to me. 'Aym offly sorry, but thet puts us all square again.'

McAuslan, meanwhile, was gouging our ball out of the green, as a hungry boar might root for truffles. Presently, from the exclamations around, he gathered that somehow he had erred; when he understood that he had cost us the hole, and probably the game, his distress was pitiful to see and disgusting to hear. But what could you say to him? It had all been said before, anyway, to no avail. Poor unwashed blundering soul, it was just the way he was made.

So certain victory had been taken from us, and now all was to play for at the last hole, where the pipe sergeant was skipping with excitement on the tee. On hearing how we stood he sent a runner post-haste to Aix with the news, and then delivered himself.

Unbelievably, of the other four games we had won two and lost two, and but for the M.O.'s drunken folly we might even have been ahead 3–1. Pirie and the Adjutant had won, two and one ('and oh, the style of yon Pirie, sir! Whaur's yer Wullie Turnesa noo, eh?'). The two elderly majors, against all the odds, had triumphed at the eighteenth by one hole; it appeared that the corpulent Major Fleming, about to give up the struggle at the fifteenth, had been roused by his partner's taunt that the girl in Kasr-el-Nil had said that she couldn't abide fat men, and had told him (the partner) that she could never love a man as overweight as Fleming, who would certainly be dead of a stroke before he was forty. Inflamed, Fleming had carried all before him, and even with the Padre and M.O. going down to cataclysmic defeat, 9 and 7, the overall prospects had looked not bad. Macmillan and Bogle had fought back to level terms ('and auld Bogle wi' his guts in a sling and pechin' sore, sore') and at the sixteenth one of their opponents, whom the pipey had earlier reported as suffering from muscle strain, had wrenched his shoulder. He had been about to give up and concede the game, when the Padre, happening by from the scene of his own rout, had suggested that our M.O., who had taken his flask for a sleep in the rough, be summoned to examine the sufferer. They roused the M.O. from beneath a bush, and after focusing unsteadily on the affected part he had announced: 'In my professional opinion this man cannot be moved without imperilling his life. Call an ambulance.' Alarmed, they had asked him what the Royal was suffering from, and he had replied: 'Alcoholic poisoning', and then collapsed himself into a bunker. So indignant had the injured Royal – a senior and extremely stiffish company commander – been that he had insisted on carrying on, and Bogle and Macmillan had lost, two down.

So it was up to the R.S.M. and me to win or lose the whole shooting-match, and as I looked at the huge eighteenth, with its broad fairway just made for the big driving of our opponents, I almost gave up hope. The worst of it was, if it hadn't been for that grubby moron's great flat feet we would have been walking home now, with the thing in the bag; he was mumping dolefully somewhere in the background. I knew I was silly, feeling so upset over a mere game, but what would you? One does.

I watched Melville drive off, and he must have been feeling the pressure, for he hooked shockingly into clump of firs. Now's your chance, I thought joyfully, and taking a fine easy swing I topped my drive a good twenty yards down the fairway. Shattered, I watched the R.S.M. prepare to play the second; he had said not a word during the McAuslan débâcle, but for once there was the beginning of a worried frown on the great brow, and with cause, for he sliced his shot away to the high outcrop of rock which ran between the fairway and the sea. The ball pinged among the crags, and then vanished on to the crest, far out in badman's territory. To make it worse, Melville's partner hit a colossal spoon from the trees, leaving them only a longish iron to the green.

This was plainly the end, I thought, as I set off up the bluff in search of the ball, with McClusky trailing behind. We tramped what seemed miles over the springy turf, and found the ball, nicely cocked up on a tuft with the ground falling away sharply ahead to the wide fairway, and three hundred yards off the green, hemmed in by broad deep bunkers. It was a lovely lie, downhill and wide open save for a clump of boulders about two hundred yards off on the right edge of the fairway; there was a following wind, the sea was sparkling, the sun was warm, and everything was an invitation to beat that ball to kingdom come and beyond. Anyway, there was nothing to lose, so I unshipped the old brassie, did everything wrong, lifted my heel, raised my head, turned my body, and lashed away for dear life. And so help me I leaned upon that ball, and I smote it, so that it rose like a dove in the Scriptures, whining away with an upward trajectory beyond the ken of man, and flew screaming down the wind.

I've never hit one like it, and I never will again. It was the Big One, the ultimate, and no gallery thundering with applause could have acknowledged it more appropriately than my own ruptured squawk of astonishment and McClusky's reverent cry of: 'Jayzus!' For one fearful moment I thought it was going to develop a late slice, but it whanged into the clump of rocks, kicked magnificently to a huge height as it skidded on, fell within thirty yards of the green, and rolled gently out of sight somewhere beside the right-hand bunker.

We hurried down to join the others on the fairway, where Melville was unlimbering his three iron. He hit a reasonable shot, but was well short; his partner's seven was way too high, and plumped into the short rough just off the green to left. My spirits soared; we were in business again with a stroke in hand, assuming the R.S.M. had a reasonable lie, which seemed probable. We made for the right-hand bunker; I thought I must be just short of it – and then my heart sank. We were in it; right in.

Foul trolls from the dark ages had dug that bunker. It was just off the green, a deep, dark hideous pit fringed by gorse, with roots straggling under its lips, and little flat stones among the powdery sand. My great, gorgeous brassie shot had just reached it, so that the ball was nestling beside a root, with just room for a man to swing, and eight feet of bank baring its teeth five yards in front of him. I've seen bunkers, and bad lies in them, but this was the nadir.

We looked, appalled, and then that great man the R.S.M. climbed down into the depths. McAuslan, hovering on the bunker's edge, clubs at the high port, dropped everything as usual, but the R.S.M. simply snapped: 'Number nine'; even he looked like one on whom the doom has come. He waited, hand out, eyes fixed on the barely-visible tip of the flag, while McAuslan rummaged among the irons on the grass, and handed one down to him. The R.S.M. took the club, and addressed the ball.

It was hopeless, of course; Nicklaus might have got out in one, but I doubt it. The R.S.M. was just going through the motions; he addressed the ball, swung down, and then I saw his club falter in mid-descent, an oath such as I had never heard sprang to his lips, but he was too late to stop. The club descended in a shower of sand, the ball shot across the bunker with frightful speed, hit a root, leaped like a salmon, curved just over the lip of the bunker, bounced, hung, and trickled away down the steep face of the bank on to the green. For a minute I thought it was going in, but it stopped on the very lip of the hole while the sounds of joy and grief from the people wildly rose.

For a moment I could only stare, amazed. I was aware that Melville was chipping on a yard short, and that his partner was holing the putt; they were down in six. I had a tiny putt, two inches at most, for a five and victory, and for the first time in that game the shade of my grandmother asserted herself, reminding me of Uncle Hugh, and chickens unwisely counted. 'Never up, never in,' I thought, and crouched over the ball; I tapped it firmly in, and that was the ball game.

The Royals were extremely nice about it; splendid losers they were, and there was much good-natured congratulation on the green itself, from our immediate opponents and the other players as well. I detached myself and looked for the R.S.M., but he was not in sight; I went over to the scene of his great shot, and there he was, still standing in the bunker, like a great tweed statue, staring at the club in his hand. And before him, Caliban to Prospero, McAuslan crouched clutching the bag.

'McAuslan,' the R.S.M. was saying. 'You gave me this club.'

'Aye – eh, aye, sir.' He was snuffling horribly.

'What club did I require you to give me?'

'Ra number nine, sir.'

'And what club did you give me?'

McAuslan, hypnotized, whimpered: 'Oh, Goad, Ah dunno, sir.'

'This, McAuslan,' said the R.S.M. gravely, 'is nott a number nine. It is, in fact, a number two. What is called a driving iron. It is not suitable for bunker shots.'

'Zat a fact, sir?'

The R.S.M. took a deep breath and let it out again. He was looking distinctly fatigued.

'Return this club to the bag,' he said, 'put the bag in my quarters, go to the sergeants' mess – the back door – and tell the barman on *my* instructions to supply you with one pint of beer. That's all for now – right, move!'

McAuslan hurled himself away, stricken dumb by fear and disbelief. As he clambered out of the bunker the R.S.M. added:

'Thank you for bein' my caddy, McAuslan.'

If McAuslan heard him, I'm sure he didn't believe what he heard.

The R.S.M. climbed out heavily, and gave me his slight smile. 'Thank you, sir, for a most enjoyable partnership; a very satisfactory concluding putt, if I may say so.'

'Major,' I said – my emotion and admiration were such that I had slipped into the old ranker's form of address – 'any infant could have holed it. But that bunker shot – man, that was incredible!'

'Incredible indeed, sir. Did you see what I played it wi'? A number two iron – a flat-faced club, sir! Dear me, dear me. By rights I should be in there yet – and I would have been thanking McAuslan for that, I can tell you!'

'Well, thank goodness he did give you the wrong club. You couldn't have played a finer shot, with a nine or anything else.'

'Indeed I couldn't. Indeed I couldn't.' He shook his head. 'By George, Mr MacNeill, we had the luck with us today.'

'Hand of providence,' I said lightly.

'No, sir,' said the R.S.M. firmly. 'Let us give credit where it is due. It was the hand of Private McAuslan.'

Golfers

ROBIN JENKINS

A famous professional recently stressed the importance to golfers of shutting out the world and concentrating only on the game. That this is sound advice is known even to bunglers with handicaps of twenty-four. Whenever one of these muffs a shot and the ball stots feebly in the wrong direction he will nevertheless have been trying very hard to think of absolutely nothing else but hitting it straight and far: his crude technique has simply let him down. Those figures in bright pullovers and spiked shoes, which can be seen walking about a golf course as determined as ants, are not human beings, they are golfers, concentrating on ball, stance and swing, to the exclusion of everything else. The best jokes in clubhouses celebrate this fanatical but necessary single-mindedness.

Of the three hundred members of Auchenskeoch Golf Club, on the west coast of Scotland, none appreciated the necessity of total concentration more than a threesome that played together every Saturday morning. It consisted of William Lossit, manager of the local branch of the Caledonia Bank, Jack Killeyan, principal teacher of geography at Auchenskeoch High School, and Donald McLairg, proprietor of the Clydeview Hotel. They had met on the golf course and had taken care to keep their acquaintance purely a golfing one. They did not visit one another's houses and were not interested in one another's affairs. Their wives knew one another to nod to in the main street but were too well-trained ever to stop and gossip. Instinctively they knew that in some mysterious way their husbands' golf would suffer if they got to know one another well. Thus, after five years of playing together, the three men remained staunchly strangers.

Unless the rain was tempestuous or snow blanketed the course, they would meet on the first tee at half-past nine. After exchanging nods and good-mornings, they would toss to see who should have the honour of driving off first, and immediately begin. During the game they might mention, perfunctorily, some tournament of world-famous professionals taking place elsewhere, and the other two might grunt in commendation if the third brought off some spectacularly good shot; but for the most part they kept quiet and concentrated on the golf.

William Lossit had been a bank manager for ten years. Headquarters in Edinburgh, and some of his customers, now and then were not satisfied with his management, but in a time of fallen standards anyone not downright incompetent was secure. So he was content in his red-tiled bungalow with its fine view of Arran. He liked to work in the garden, taking care not to get calluses on his hands that might interfere with the proper gripping of his golf clubs. His grown-up son, happily married, was flourishing in Inverness as a chartered accountant. He had only one worry, if it could be called that. It concerned his wife, Agnes. For months on end she would be the perfect wife, obedient, dutiful, thrifty and self-effacing; then suddenly she would go and do something odd. It was never anything sensational, indeed it was always trifling. For instance, he would plant some gladioli in some spot he had carefully chosen. In a day or two he would discover she had dug them up and replanted them in some other place quite unsuitable. Then again, he was fond of a certain brand of sauce. Once when the bottle was empty she replaced it with a different brand altogether, one she must have known he would not like. Over the years there had been many such oddities of behaviour on her part. Sometimes he wondered if their purpose could be to spite him, perhaps in revenge for his devoting more time to golf than to her.

* * *

As a teacher, Jack Killeyan was no more and no less successful than the majority of his colleagues. Given a bright class, he got good results; given a dull one, his results were poor.

He had been glad when he had got the post at Auchenskeoch: there was an increase in salary; the troublemakers of Auchenskeoch were less vicious and enterprising than those of Glasgow, whence he had come and where he had been born; the seaside air was healthier for his two daughters, and the golf course at Auchenskeoch was a splendid one, running alongside the sea.

After eight years at Auchenskeoch, his contentment was ruined when he noticed, or rather when his wife Bessie noticed, that contemporaries of his, in no observable way superior, were being promoted to headmasterships. He thereupon began to apply for every appropriate post he saw advertised, from Thurso in the north to Kelso in the south. Bessie helped him to fill in the forms. Unfortunately, she could not be with him at his interviews, to tell him what to say and, still more important, what not to say. Unknown to him, she wrote to their daughters, one by this time a nurse in Glasgow and the other a student in Edinburgh, that Dad was getting a bit depressed about being rejected so often, but they weren't to mention it, and anyway he had his golf to console and sustain him.

Donald McLairg had inherited Clydeview Hotel from his father. It was large, and occupied an enviable position near the harbour, though the roses in its front gardens seemed to smell of seaweed. Like Auchenskeoch itself, it was a little run down, suffering, like all Clydeside hotels, from the preference of Glaswegians for the sunshine of Majorca to the rain and midges of the Scottish Riviera.

In his young days Donald loved to go off to watch the Open Championship wherever it was being played. He had stayed in the same five-star hotels as some of the famous competitors, and spent a lot of money. He had also been fond of pinching the bottoms of the Clydeview maids. Since then he had unaccountably married Martha, as skinny as she was devout. There was no mention of golf in the Bible, so she couldn't make up her mind whether or not the Lord approved of it. Consequently, Donald

was allowed to continue, though he was obliged to wear less flamboyant pullovers and hats. After a while, his bottom-pinching was resumed, furtively.

On a certain Sunday in early September, with the sun shining mellowly and the course in delectable condition, the threesome met on the first tee, making practice swings with customary zest, and handling their golf balls with the same old delight and anticipation. Or so it appeared. The truth was, none of the three that morning was going to find it easy to shut out the world and concentrate on the game.

* * *

On the previous afternoon, Mrs Lossit had come into her husband's office at the bank, carrying her shopping-bag. There was no stated rule, but he did not approve of her bothering him at work. Besides, he had a customer coming in to discuss Unit Trusts.

While he was hinting as fondly as he could about the inconvenience of her intrusion, she made things worse by taking out of her bag, and setting down on his desk, such absurd objects as a bobbin of purple thread, a card of white elastic, a packet of needles, and a tin of ointment. For a few moments he gave his attention to this assortment. He jaloused she intended to replace the elastic in her knickers, say, and he tried to remember if she had a pair purplish in colour. The ointment baffled him. He was about to ask her to take them off his desk when she remarked, casually, that she hadn't paid for them, she had just shoplifted them out of Woolworth's. She didn't know whether anyone had seen her.

Immediately he saw his career in jeopardy. At any moment there would be a knock on the door and in would come Jim Chapman, manager of Woolworth's, followed by Sergeant Moffat and a constable. Agnes would be charged. The case would go before Bob Aitchison, the Sheriff, a member of the Golf Club. If a plea of temporary insanity was put forward she might get off with a fine or even an admonition. But there would be a full account in the *Auchenskeoch Observer*. The whole town, nay the whole county, would wonder if a man whose wife had been found guilty of shoplifting was fit to manage a bank. Everybody would think he had been mean with the housekeeping money.

With an effort he turned his concern from himself to poor Agnes, still surveying with silly pride her pathetic booty. He hated her then, but he also loved her more poignantly than he had done for years. She was so familiar and yet so strange. He saw pain in her eyes where, that very morning, at breakfast, he had seen only wilful obtuseness. He noticed now how thin and shaky her hands were in their black gloves. He had looked after his golf clubs more carefully than he had her. Whatever her present condition, he was partly to blame for it.

* * *

That same Friday, Jack Killeyan was in Aberdeen for an interview. Always, before those interviews, and alas during them, he was so worked up that he could scarcely force words past his lips, and they were never his best words. Once again he did not do himself justice; but this time his failure left him sickened and demoralized. Among the other candidates was a man he'd worked beside in Glasgow years ago, a notorious work-dodger with a glib tongue. Saunders had been the one appointed. The Aberdeen councillors were not to blame. They had been hoodwinked. The system was at fault, allowing the best man to be passed over and the worst chosen.

Returning in his car to Auchenskeoch, he wept. Tears dribbled down his cheeks. Not even Bessie would ever know about them. He would as always pretend he wasn't a bit hurt or downhearted. His sense of humour, he would say, enabled him, thank God, to laugh at the absurdity of a scrimshanker like Harry Saunders being made a headmaster.

That night Bessie was unable to comfort him. Like the unjealous wife she was, she hoped golf would do it, as it had done often in the past.

About three months before a new barmaid had been engaged for the Clydeview cocktail bar. Since his wife was the hirer, Donald was astonished to find that the new employee was the kind of woman he yearned for. Nancy Cameron was big, with magnificent bosom and ample buttocks. But it was the quality of her flesh that thrilled him, it was so soft, luscious and perfumed. His own melted at the sight of it, more so at the feel of it, for in the closed space behind the bar his haunch could hardly avoid nudging hers. He found himself pouring drams of unprecedented generosity. Suddenly the lounge with its few poinsettias bloomed like Eden. He was in love. Her blonde hair was dyed, but it didn't matter.

She was divorced and living in a rented room-and-kitchen in the working-class end of the town. One wet night he offered to run her home in his car. Her street was deserted. Hand on his knee, she asked him up. He mumbled his car would be seen. She suggested he could drive it to the front nearby, where it would never be noticed among the cars of holiday makers.

Here was a situation overwhelming for a furtive bottom-pincher. Mumbling what he thought was a rejection of her offer, but which she took to be an acceptance, he drove off, intending to head straight for the safe dullness of home, but finding himself, to his alarm, on the sea-front.

He crouched in his car for ten minutes, trying to fight off the temptation. He saw how abominably foolish it would be for him to put in peril his respectability as a citizen and church-goer and husband, not to mention his career as a golfer. He recalled his triumphs on the golf course, especially his winning of the Auchenskeoch Trophy. That had been the proudest time in his life. He smiled bravely and told himself that the man who had then received the silver cup from Provost Paible, with dozens applauding, would hardly be so stupid as to ruin himself for the sake of half an hour in the company of a woman who, however luscious, was nevertheless just a barmaid, and divorced at that. All the time he knew, as men in such situations nearly always do, that he would in the end sneak through the rain to No. 53 Westfield Street.

She was expecting him in the little kitchen. She wore a short pink négligé and furry slippers. A whisky bottle and glasses were on the table. There was a blazing coal fire. There was also a set-in bed.

Speaking in a soothing yet cheerful voice, she encouraged him to talk at length about his ambitions and achievements as a golfer. She had heard, she said, he had been a great player in his day, and still was a pretty good one, considering his age. Not that he was too old for golf, or for anything else she could think of.

He stayed three hours, and made love to her in the set-in bed. So kind her voice, and so hospitable her body, his fears and scruples were, for the short time it took, easily routed by joy.

Martha was asleep when he crept into their bedroom. She woke up and, to his amazement, swallowed his lie that he had been golfing with friends. Yawning, she went back to sleep. He felt greatly relieved, but also, so irrepressible is self, a little displeased and disappointed that she should so readily consider him incapable of any tremendous defiance of respectability. Before falling asleep, he lay and shuddered, knowing that he might have put himself into a blackmailer's power; but amidst the shudders were little shivers of remembered joy.

During the following week he kept out of Nancy's way. She made it easy by not pursuing him. When they did meet she merely winked. If she thought she had a claim on him, she was going to take her time about asserting it. Then, suddenly, she was gone, sacked by Martha. 'I'm not saying she was brazen, but she's the kind could be.' He waited, in terror, for Nancy to come and demand that he speak up for her, otherwise she'd tell; but she was content with a smile, on her way out. He watched her go, with relief and regret chasing each other round his mind.

Discreetly speiring, he heard she'd left the town and gone to Greenock.

Then, on the same Friday that Mrs Lossit took to shoplifting and Jack Killeyan saw the triumph of the unworthy, Donald was called to the telephone. To his horror, the voice was Nancy's, as kind and cheerful as ever. She wanted to see him. She had something interesting to tell him. He'd find her on a seat near the paddling pool.

He went, with twenty pounds in his pocket to buy her off. He whimpered to himself what a reckless, trusting fool he had been.

On the green bench she looked beautiful in a bright red costume and red shoes. She seemed relaxed, and gave him a wave that couldn't have been more friendly or even loving.

'Hello, Daddy,' she whispered, cheerily.

No greeting could have flummoxed him more. He and Martha had no children, and never would have. He was fond of children, though. Nancy must have seen him joking with them at the hotel.

She laid her hand on her stomach. 'I'm pregnant, love.'

People were passing. Beyond them shone the sea. If she was telling the truth he would have to drown himself. The view from the seventh tee flashed into his mind. There were cliffs and seabirds. A badly hooked drive could land you in the sea.

He recovered his wits. 'You can't be.'

'I may be divorced, love, but I've still got my ovaries.'

'Are you sure? Have you seen a doctor?'

'Missed twice, love. No doctor could tell better than that.'

'All right. But what's it got to do with me?'

She laughed, but not sarcastically. 'Quite a lot. It's yours.'

'So you say. It could be some other man's.'

'When it's born you'll see it's got sandy hair and big ears.'

Lots of men had sandy hair and big ears, he could have told her, but didn't, she would have found it funny. He had never seen a woman so carefree.

'You don't look at all worried.'

'Why should I be worried, love? A wee sister, or a wee brother, for Melinda. That's how I look at it.'

'Who's Melinda?'

'My girl. She's eight. That's her, in the blue coat.'

The little girl was neat and bonny. He would have been proud to be her father.

'I didn't know you had a daughter.'

'Donald, you and me are practically strangers, more's the pity, even if we've been intimate, as they say in the divorce courts.'

But from the way she laughed she bore no more spite against those courts than she did against him.

'What do you want me to do?'

'Nothing, love. You've got your wife to think of. She needs you. I just thought you should know. Some day, maybe, if you'd like, I could bring him or her and let you have a look.'

It was too astonishing a prospect for him to know whether he would like it or not.

'Don't worry, love. I'll not embarrass you. I like you too much. You're my kind of fellow. You and me could have made a great pair. Well, here's Melinda. Melinda, this is my friend, Mr McLairg.'

He exchanged smiles with the little girl. He wondered if her half-brother or half-sister would look like her.

Nancy rose. She seemed just a little agitated. 'Got to go, love. Best of luck.'

He watched them ambling along the sea-front, hand-in-hand, the big fine-looking woman in the red costume, and the dainty little girl in the blue coat. They turned twice to wave. He was almost in tears. He suspected he was losing something more valuable than gold or golf.

No golfer, or golfer's wife, will marvel that men with such burdens on their minds should turn up that Saturday morning to hit a small white ball from one distant hole to another. Golf is not so much a game as an addiction.

It never occurred to William Lossit not to play that morning. He had left Agnes alone so often that it had become a habit. In any case, he felt that with his clubs in his hands he would be better able to steady his mind, so that afterwards he would know what to do about Agnes. It could well be that if he was a little more.overt in his displays of affection, she would cease her pathetic attempts to persecute him. Or it could be that firmness was required, or at least a determination to stop her from hiding herself from him in the depths of her mind. She ought not to have given up golf. For a woman of her build she had played not badly.

Well, he thought, as he got out of his car, rejoicing to see the course shining in the sun, he was only her husband after all, not the keeper of her soul.

Jack Killeyan was tenderly kissed by his wife at the door. 'Don't take it too sorely to heart,' she whispered. Just like a woman, he reflected, as he drove to the course. He had been given proof of a rottenness in society, and she wanted him not to let it bother him. Bessie was a good woman and a loyal wife, she cleaned his shoes and knitted his pullovers, but she had no understanding of principle. When he had said he was minded to write to the *Glasgow Herald*, exposing the injustices inherent in the present system of promoting teachers, she had been horrified. All the authorities in Scotland would read it, she'd whispered. His name would be marked. There would be no use his applying ever again, anywhere. No one would say he'd done it out of principle; everybody would say it was sour grapes. Best write nothing. Best give the impression you thought the system was fair enough. Best keep applying and hoping. That had been her advice, and he found it all the more insulting because of course he intended to follow it.

Several other players were at the first tee waiting their turn. They looked on with interest as our threesome prepared to drive off. McLairg, Lossit and Killeyan were known to have been very low handicap men in their heyday, McLairg's name in fact was up on the champions' board in the clubhouse, and they all still played off four or five. They were scrutinized therefore, not as men and citizens, but as golfers whose swings were still worth analysing.

Lossit and Killeyan watched too as their partner drove off. For the first time in years they saw him as a man. To Lossit he was the husband of a sensible, business-like woman. To Killeyan he was the owner of a substantial hotel, independent therefore, and removed from the rat-race of promotion.

As McLairg's ball flew straight down the fairway for a good two hundred and thirty yards, his partners, nodding appreciation, at the same time thought how unfair it was that this red-checked, unimaginative native of Auchenskeoch hadn't a care between his big ears. It gave him a three-stroke advantage, at least.

Killeyan, watching Lossit drive, thought the bank manager too was lucky, in that he belonged to a profession where promotion depended on merit, not on chance or glibness. He attributed therefore to a jerky swing the surprising rightward deviation of Lossit's ball, which landed in the midst of whins, where it could well be lost.

Watching Killeyan's ball fly far and true, Lossit thought gloomily how he too could have hit a good shot if, at the moment of striking, he had had a picture of his wife smiling adoringly, like Killeyan's, instead of hurrying into Auchenskeoch as soon as his back was turned, for some more shoplifting, or worse.

As he strode over the turf, McLairg was hardly aware of his two companions, even as golfers. He had satisfied himself that there was no danger of Martha's ever finding out about his child. Therefore he felt free to savour the joy and glory of becoming a father. Under his shoes were tiny violet flowers he had seen dozens of times before but had never really noticed until now. He wished he knew their name. Then, when he was poking among the whins in search of Lossit's ball, and saw there were still a few yellow flowers on the bushes, he recalled the saying that kissing would be out of favour when the whins were out of flowers. He felt so delighted that he did not search as diligently as he ought, and neither, he observed, did Killeyan, with the result that Lossit, visibly peeved at so poor a beginning, had to declare his ball lost and go all the way back to the tee and drive another.

They always played for a stake. Each man put a pound into the kitty and the winner took all. It was a small amount for prosperous men, and never before had brought temper or grudge into the game. McLairg therefore was surprised when, on the sixth green, Killeyan pulled to within fourteen inches of the hole, and was about to pick up his ball assuming the next putt had been conceded, when Lossit snarled at him to putt it out. Lossit of course was within his golfing rights, it was conceivable Killeyan could miss the putt, especially as he wasn't putting well so far, but even so these small concessions were customary. McLairg wondered if the bank manager was ill, or more likely if his wife was; but it wasn't his business, particularly on the golf course, and so he gave it no more thought.

Killeyan hated to be playing badly, especially when someone else was playing very well; and when that someone was a big, hen-pecked, thick-headed fellow who'd been lucky enough to fall heir to a thriving hotel, it was all the more disagreeable. Usually too, the hotel owner was solemn when playing, fatuously so sometimes, whereas this morning he kept grinning and chuckling. Once, when waiting for Killeyan to play – the ball was lying unfairly in a divot mark – McLairg went down on his hunkers nearby to pluck and hold to his nose a tiny flower. Killeyan knew golfers who would have regarded that squatting and sniffing as provocation, or at least distraction.

As for Lossit, Killeyan was becoming slowly aware that here was a man he could easily dislike. He remembered something Bessie had said about Mrs Lossit. 'She's a poor soul. I wouldn't be surprised if she had a bad pain somewhere. He never seems to notice.' Well, was a man who never noticed his wife was ill, might have cancer, was such a man fit to play golf, morally speaking?

That almost metaphysical question occurred to Killeyan as he stood on the seventh tee. Of all the tees on the course this was the one where he ought to have concentrated, eyes, heart and soul, on the ball. On the left were cliffs, in front was a deep gully. Elderly or nervous members bypassed that tee. But never once had Killeyan, in his previous dozens of games, sent the ball to disaster. This morning, though, his mind on moral matters, he swung too fast and hit the ball, not over the cliffs or into the gully, but into thick heather.

A bad shot always brings a feeling of shame. He slunk off, avoiding the gazes of his companions.

If he had told them why he had duffed that drive, that he had suddenly been seized by a sense of his own unworthiness, as golfer and man, they would not have sympathized, on the contrary they would have been offended by his bringing up on the golf course too important and personal a matter. If he had said a midge had got into his eye they would have nodded, in understanding and sympathy.

So humbled did he feel, and yet so well-disposed towards his fellow-men, whether they played golf or not, that when he came up to Lossit on the fairway he couldn't resist saying, 'Well, William, isn't it a glorious morning?'

'Aye,' grunted Lossit. He was concentrating.

As Killeyan waited he heard skylarks and seagulls, and saw the sun shining on the Arran peaks.

Lossit's ball came to rest on the green no more than ten feet from the pin. McLairg's was already there, even closer. Killeyan's own was in a bunker, but what did it matter?

'Donald's in great fettle today,' he said, as he and Lossit walked towards the green.

'Aye.'

Lossit had noticed Killeyan was preoccupied. Perhaps he had been having trouble with some truculent pupils. It was said in the town he tried to reason with louts, and failed sadly.

But Lossit did not want to think about Killeyan. Happy memories of Agnes had begun to occur to him. He could not say why. He had done nothing to evoke them. He remembered her in their son's garden in Inverness, playing with her three-year-old granddaughter. She had looked twenty years younger.

When it was his turn to putt and he had to clear everything out of his mind except line and distance, he found he did not want to stop remembering Agnes chasing wee Sheila among the roses. As a consequence his mind was divided. It was no surprise therefore when he did not strike the ball well and it stopped still two and a half feet from the hole. What was a surprise, though, was that he did not feel aggrieved or disappointed. It just seemed, for a visionary moment, unimportant, compared with that happy memory of Agnes.

As they were walking to the next tee, he wanted to go on remembering Agnes at Inverness. He was not pleased therefore when Killeyan, who seemed to be seeking reassurance of some sort, came alongside him, determined to speak.

'Would you say Walter Hagen was right? Remember what he said? "You should always take time off to smell the roses." When playing golf, he meant.'

'I know what he meant,' replied Lossit, crossly, though as before he did not feel cross. How could he, when he had been reminded of his own roses at home, so much admired by neighbours? Agnes used to make pot-pourri with the fallen petals.

'It hardly applies here,' he said, more amiably. 'There aren't any roses on the course.'

'Well, maybe not in September.'

'Not at any time, so far as I know.'

'In July there are. Wild roses.'

'Wild roses? On the course?'

Killeyan laughed. 'One bush. In the hollow to the right at the sixteenth tee. It's not much of a bush, and its leaves are rusted with the salt breezes, but it does have flowers. I've seen them.'

Yet he had never troubled to point them out. 'Even so,' said Lossit. 'Wild roses have no scent.'

Killeyan laughed again. 'Roses were just a symbol,' he said. 'Here, what would he have said?' He raised his head and gazed round. 'He could have said the sea, or the Arran hills, or the lighthouse yonder.'

They were on the tee now, standing judiciously apart from McLairg, who had his ball teed up ready to drive.

'Of course,' whispered Killeyan, 'he meant between shots.'

He winked, and Lossit found himself winking back. They were amused by the absurdity of any golfer thinking of roses or hills or lighthouses when about to play a shot.

They felt closer to each other than ever before, closer indeed than either of them wished.

Lossit thought that Killeyan, in spite of his typically school-masterish assumption of knowing everything, was well enough intentioned. He would never make a headmaster, though. He lacked authority. He hadn't enough confidence in himself. His wife told him what to do.

Killeyan thought that perhaps the reason why the bank manager found it hard to make friends wasn't because he had too high an opinion of himself, which was the town's view of him, but because, like McLairg, he lacked imagination. It was said Mrs Lossit was once a cheerful woman, as well as an enthusiastic golfer. She had wilted like a plant deprived of sunshine. A man without imagination was bound to have the same effect on his wife.

Killeyan felt encouraged. Even if all his subsequent applications and interviews were failures he would have the consolation of knowing that his wife was a happy, benevolent woman. While it would be arrogant for him to claim that it was his imaginativeness which had kept Bessie so fresh and bonny, he had a right to think it had played a part.

No man was given everything. There was McLairg, beaming after another splendid drive: he owned a big hotel, he was still a fine golfer, but his wife was plain and skinny, and he had no children.

As for Lossit, he might well be promoted to a larger bank in a larger town, and his son Ian was doing very well as a chartered accountant, but his wife was ailing and depressed, and he had no imagination.

From then on their play was often held up by slow-coaches in front. There were opportunities for conversations which Lossit was afraid Killeyan would seize. He was afraid only as a golfer anxious not to ruin his score; as a man he too wanted to talk. Indeed, it was he who spoke, as they stood waiting on the twelfth fairway.

Once again, McLairg kept aloof from them. They understood and approved. Heading for an excellent score, he did not want to be distracted by their chatter.

'I believe Mrs Killeyan helps out in the Oxfam shop these days,' said Lossit, pleasantly.

'Yes. Every Thursday afternoon.'

'Do you approve?'

He was puzzled by the astonishment on Killeyan's face.

'Why not?' said Killeyan, laughing. 'Anyway, I wasn't asked.'

Lossit was surprised by the man's levity and shallowness. 'One has to be very careful,' he said, 'how one helps people. Otherwise there is a danger one might take away from them their independence and initiative, with the result that for the rest of their lives they'll go on expecting to be helped.'

'You could be right, but I don't see how it can apply to starving children. Well, that's the green clear now.'

It was true the green was clear and the game could be resumed, but Lossit felt sure Killeyan had broken off the subject because he was shocked by Lossit's intelligent realism. Famine was ghastly, but it could be nature's way of drastically reducing populations that needed to be drastically reduced.

But it would not do to think of famine when hitting a golf ball. Therefore, with a smile, Lossit suspended thought on the subject, and concentrated on making sure he hit the ball neither to the right where the sea shore was out of bounds nor to the left where there was a bank with grass a foot tall. He swung smoothly. The ball flew straight. It came to rest on the green. It was a fine shot.

Killeyan's was not so good. His ball fell well short of the green. He had hit it half-heartedly. He must have been thinking of those starving children. Lossit smiled, and went on smiling when Killeyan, in too big a hurry, got the wheels of their caddy-cars entangled.

'Sorry,' muttered Killeyan, his eyes on the ground. 'By the way, Bessie was saying she wondered if Mrs Lossit would like to help. They need volunteers. She says being a banker's wife Mrs Lossit will be good at handling money. '

No doubt Mrs Killeyan had meant no sarcasm when making the remark, nor had Killeyan when repeating it. They had no way of knowing that Agnes was hopeless with money, so much so that it was he who calculated each week's budget. If she bought a new dress or coat he wrote out the cheque. It occurred to him, as he glanced down at his pale green cashmere pullover, bought last week for £12.50, that it had been a long time since Agnes had bought herself anything new to wear. He had been pleased with her thrift, but he realized now he should have insisted she buy herself some new clothes. As his wife she ought not to have let herself become dowdy. Perhaps it had been part of her campaign to make him pay attention to her. Poor Agnes.

For the next five holes they did not speak. Lossit was able to concentrate on his golf, but Killeyan evidently couldn't, judging from the number of bad shots he played. On the sixteenth tee Lossit had to look for the rosebush himself. Killeyan did not offer to point it out.

McLairg, sensible man, had taken no interest in their conversations. He was in sparkling form, hitting the ball better than they had seen him do in years. He would have been stupid to let anything divide his attention. His sniffs at the flower had really been sniffs at the course; it had been his way of stimulating his golfing instincts.

It seemed to Lossit that another advantage of having a wife to whom you could confidently leave all your business worries was that, on the golf course, you could put her completely out of your mind. Not that he would have exchanged Agnes for Martha McLairg. Agnes had once been a cheerful woman, Martha never. Agnes could be made cheerful again.

Killeyan had known at the back of his mind that McLairg was scoring well. He was marking McLairg's card and had been putting down many fours and more threes than fives; but he had only a vague idea that McLairg was heading for a really remarkable score.

As they were waiting on the eighteenth tee, he totted it up. He could not believe the total he arrived at, and tried again, with the same astounding result. If McLairg managed a four at the eighteenth, which was possible, he would have an overall score of 68. The par for the course was 72. The record, held by a Glasgow professional, was 66, though that of course was from the medal tees.

Killeyan was so impressed he showed the card to Lossit.

'Donald needs a four for a 68,' he whispered.

'I knew he must have a very good score,' whispered Lossit.

McLairg, as usual, was first to drive. He was practising his swing.

'Donald,' called Killeyan, 'do you know you need a four here for a sixty-eight?'

It was, as he and Lossit knew, a rhetorical question. Only golfers playing badly are vague about their scores. They expected McLairg to nod, with a golfer's curt modesty, and then to turn again and stare, with a golfer's impatience, at the plodders in front who were holding him up. They were astonished therefore when he smiled, shyly it seemed, and spoke.

'How's Ian getting on these days, Mr Lossit?' he asked. 'He's in Inverness, isn't he?'

Lossit was pleased as well as astonished. 'Yes. He's doing very well, thank you.'

'He would. Smart lad. Married, isn't he?'

'Yes.'

'Any family?'

'One wee girl.'

'He got married, didn't he, before he finished his training?'

'They all do these days, Donald.'

'A wee girl, eh? That's good. Mr Killeyan there knows all about wee girls. He's got two.'

'What's this Mr Killeyan nonsense?' said Killeyan. 'Name's Jack. Yes, I've got two. But they're not wee girls any longer, sorry to say. One's twenty and the other's twenty-three nearly.'

'I remember the younger one,' said McLairg. 'Plump little girl, with straight black hair?'

'That's Jeanie. She's not so plump now she's a nurse. She's to work too hard.'

'Donald,' murmured Lossit, 'they've moved on. You can hit off now.'

He had to mention it, because they too were being closely pursued by another threesome. He looked at Killeyan with apology for having interrupted the conversation, and Killeyan nodded, with a smile, expressing agreement that the game was the first consideration.

'Take it easy,' they advised McLairg, afraid lest the talk about their children should have upset him, who was childless. Besides, if he scored a 68 they too would share a little in the glory.

He drove. It was his best drive of the morning. Right down the middle of the fairway it flew. When it landed it ran on and on. From where it stopped was only an eight or nine iron shot to the green. His 68 looked almost a certainty now.

Their own drives were more than satisfactory. No matter how bad one's score, it was always gratifying to do well at the eighteenth, for members sitting in the clubhouse were sure to be watching critically.

They walked together up the fairway.

Killeyan thought that, if McLairg was lucky to have no promotion disappointments, he was also without malice or conceit. In fact, he was that combination that school-teachers often thanked God for in their pupils: slowness of mind compensated for by a happy and well-disposed nature.

Lossit thought that while McLairg was fortunate to have a sensible and business-like wife he deserved credit for the fact that she had remained sensible and business-like. Married to a less patient and more ambitious man, she might well have developed into a religious bigot.

Both of them felt sorry for McLairg. He had no children and yet he would have made a good father.

Their charitable moods were confirmed when they both had fine second shots and landed their balls safely on the green. They could not help exchanging congratulatory grins.

They stood still as stones as McLairg shaped up to play his shot. They prayed he would not strike the ball into the burn that ran alongside the fairway. To spoil his score now would be lamentable.

Suddenly, to their amazement, he stepped back and held up his club, a nine-iron, above his head, as if it was a spear, about to be hurled at the distant clubhouse, or the world beyond. Members watching must have thought he'd been attacked by a bee or even an adder.

Killeyan and Lossit knew there was no bee or snake. They could not understand what had come over him. Up till now he had behaved with exemplary golfing saneness. Why was he now acting more like a Zulu warrior than a golfer?

Except that the smile on his face was the very opposite of hostile or murderous. He looked inspiredly happy, as if, thought Killeyan, he had just discovered how to feed all the starving children without destroying their independence. It could hardly be a score of 68 that was causing such transcendental joy. Golf after all was only a game and had its limits.

When McLairg, moments later, strode up to the ball he was a golfer again. His swing was crisp. The ball glittered in the sunshine, and came to rest close to the flag on the green. Only one putt would be needed. He would have gone round in 67.

In awe Killeyan and Lossit wondered what marvellous thing could have been in their companion's mind to inspire him to hit so confident a shot.

When they arrived on the green they saw the critical faces at the clubhouse windows. Each of them therefore, as he studied his line and then as he crouched over his putter, was very remote as a man but intimately close as a golfer. Killeyan's putt stopped three inches from the hole, Lossit's six, and McLairg's went straight in. It was as masterly a conclusion to a game of golf as any threesome could have prayed for. Those watching from the clubhouse looked satisfied.

In spite of the sweetness of that last hole, Killeyan had taken 88 strokes and Lossit 82. Usually it was bitter not to be under 80, but somehow not today. Both of them felt dimly but strongly that they had achieved something more important than golfing success, though of course they could not say so openly, less the sincerity of their congratulations to McLairg be suspect.

They always went straight home. They were not drinking men, and even beer in the middle of the day seemed to them not quite proper. McLairg, though, often went into the bar for a whisky and a chat.

Today, as they shook hands and thanked one another for the game, McLairg, his big red face beaming, invited them in for a drink.

'To celebrate,' he said.

Somehow they got the impression he wasn't referring to his magnificent score.

Killeyan muttered he would like to but he'd promised his wife he'd be home by one-thirty; it was after that now; he really shouldn't keep her waiting any longer.

Lossit nodded, as if that was his reason too for having to hurry home.

Like the amiable chap he was, and like a magnanimous golfer who had just broken 70, McLairg accepted their excuses without fuss.

'Next Saturday then, gentlemen?' he asked.

Ever so briefly, they hesitated. Past his big ears they gazed at the sunlit course. They thought how stale life would seem without golf to look forward to. To give it up would be like giving up hope.

'Next Saturday, Donald,' they said, firmly and confidently.

The Golf

EMIL PACHOLEK

O N the Saturday morning before the start of the Open Championship in July, 1955, Robbie pedalled the three miles from Kincaple to the links at St Andrews to see the great golfers practise.

The wind was from the West and strong, sweeping him along, and the tyres of his bike fairly swished on the road still wet from the overnight rain.

As his legs pedalled, his heart hammered, and as his heart hammered, his head raced with his plan.

All the great golfers were there, all chasing the trophy and the fantastic cheque of one thousand pounds!

Robbie, in turn, was chasing them.

He watched them all day, following them round the Old Course, tagging along with the crowds, all the way out along the links to the Eden Estuary where he could just make out the shape of Kincaple Woods in the mirk, then round the loop and back towards the grey, cathedral city of St Andrews.

Even when the wind dropped and the rain came and the spectators thinned out and straggled for home, Robbie stayed on, waiting for the moment to be right.

Like when Peter Thomson put his tee-shot right in close at the short eighth. Or when Bobby Locke exploded the ball up and out of the wet, clinging sand in Hell Bunker. Or when the great Byron Nelson of America took his time to line up a long putt on the tricky green at the Road Hole, then sent the ball straight into the back of the cup. These were the moments Robbie chose.

With each golfer it was the same story.

'Excuse me, Mister,' he said. 'You're playing some grand-like golf – do you think you could sign one of your golf balls for me. It would be a fine thing having one wi' the winner's name on it . . .'

Put that way, it was a request none could refuse, particularly when it came from a drookit wee figure with his hair slicked down with the rain.

When Robbie cycled home at tea-time he was soaked through to the skin – but he had a dozen golf balls in his pockets, each and every one signed by a great player. It was raw cold on his bike and his trousers rubbed red on his legs, but he wobbled home into the wind triumphant. With a bit of luck one of the golf balls would have the winner's name on it . . .

On the Friday the Championship was over. To Robbie's delight, last year's winner, Peter Thomson, had done it again – and he was one of the players who'd signed.

On a newspaper in his room, Robbie painted an egg-cup silver, and when it was dry he placed the ball in it. It took pride of place, right in the middle of his mantelpiece.

The other golf balls were taken out into the wash-house and, in a pailful of hot, soapy Rinso, were scrubbed clean.

Robbie sold them to the grocer's van for tenpence each.

Acknowledgments

The Publisher has made every effort to contact the copyright holders of material reproduced in this book, and wishes to apologize to those he has been unable to trace. Grateful acknowledgment is made for permission to reprint the following:

'The Sweet Shot' by E.C. Bentley, copyright The Estate of the Late E.C. Bentley 1946.

'Scratch Man' from the The Golf Omnibus by P.G. Wodehouse, reproduced by permission of Hutchinson, London and A.P Watt Ltd on behalf of The Trustees of the Wodehouse Estate.

'An Unlucky Golfer' from By Way of Introduction copyright A.A. Milne, reproduced by permission of Curtis Brown, London and copyright 1929 by E.P. Dutton, copyright renewal 1957 by Daphne Milne.

'Is a Golfer a Gentleman?' by A.P. Herbert, by permission of A.P. Watt Ltd on behalf of Crystal Hale and Jocelyn Herbert.

'Farrell's Caddie' by John Updike, reprinted by permission; © 1992 John Updike. Originally in The New Yorker.

'Beautiful Husbands' from Trust Me by John Updike, copyright © 1987 by John Updike. Reprinted by permission of Alfred A. Knopf Inc.

'Miss Hogg and Miss Cairns' by Fred Urquhart, by permission of A.P. Watt on behalf of Fred Urquhart.